P9-EJZ-759

THE NEW FOLGER LIBRARY SHAKESPEARE

Designed to make Shakespeare's plays and poems available to all readers, the New Folger Library edition of Shakespeare provides accurate texts in modern spelling and punctuation, as well as scene-by-scene action summaries, full explanatory notes, many pictures clarifying Shakespeare's language, and notes recording all significant departures from the early printed versions. Each play is prefaced by a brief introduction, by a guide to reading Shakespeare's language, and by accounts of his life and theater. Each is followed by an annotated list of further readings and by a "Modern Perspective" written by an expert on that particular play.

Barbara A. Mowat is Director of Academic Programs at the Folger Shakespeare Library, Executive Editor of *Shakespeare Quarterly*, Chair of the Folger Institute, and author of *The Dramaturgy of Shakespeare's Romances* and of essays on Shakespeare's plays and on the editing of Shakespeare.

Paul Werstine is Professor of English at the Graduate School and at King's University College at the University of Western Ontario. He is general editor of the New Variorum Shakespeare and author of many papers and articles on the printing and editing of Shakespeare's plays.

The Folger Shakespeare Library

The Folger Shakespeare Library in Washington, D.C., a privately funded research library dedicated to Shakespeare and the civilization of early modern Europe, was founded in 1932 by Henry Clay and Emily Jordan Folger. In addition to its role as the world's preeminent Shakespeare collection and its emergence as a leading center for Renaissance studies, the Folger Library offers a wide array of cultural and educational programs and services for the general public.

EDITORS

BARBARA A. MOWAT
Director of Academic Programs
Folger Shakespeare Library

PAUL WERSTINE
Professor of English
King's University College at the
University of Western Ontario, Canada

FOLGER SHAKESPEARE LIBRARY

The Merry Wives of Windsor

By
WILLIAM SHAKESPEARE

WITHDRAWN

EDITED BY BARBARA A. MOWAT
AND PAUL WERSTINE

SIMON & SCHUSTER PAPERBACKS
NEW YORK LONDON TORONTO SYDNEY

The sale of this book without its cover is unauthorized. If you purchased this book without a cover, you should be aware that it was reported to the publisher as "unsold and destroyed." Neither the author nor the publisher has received payment for the sale of this "stripped book."

Simon & Schuster Paperbacks
A Division of Simon & Schuster, Inc.
1230 Avenue of the Americas
New York, NY 10020

Copyright © 2004 by The Folger Shakespeare Library

All rights reserved, including the right to reproduce this book
or portions thereof in any form whatsoever. For information, address
Simon & Schuster Paperbacks Subsidiary Rights Department,
1230 Avenue of the Americas, New York, NY 10020.

Washington Square Press New Folger Edition July 2004
This Simon & Schuster paperback edition June 2009

SIMON & SCHUSTER PAPERBACKS and colophon are
registered trademarks of Simon & Schuster, Inc.

For information regarding special discounts for bulk purchases,
please contact Simon & Schuster Special Sales at
1-866-506-1949 or business@simonandschuster.com.

The Simon & Schuster Speakers Bureau can bring authors to your
live event. For more information or to book an event, contact the
Simon & Schuster Speakers Bureau at 1-866-248-3049 or visit our
website at www.simonspeakers.com.

Manufactured in the United States of America

15   14   13   12   11   10   9   8   7   6   5

ISBN 978-0-671-72278-4

From the Director of the Library

Shakespeare has never been more alive as author and playwright than he is today, with productions being staged all over the world, new film versions appearing on screen every year, and millions of students in classrooms at all levels absorbed in the human drama and verbal richness of his works.

The New Folger Library Shakespeare editions welcome the interested reader with newly edited texts, commentary in a friendly facing-page format, and illustrations, drawn from the Folger archives, that wonderfully illuminate references and images in the plays. A synopsis of every scene makes the action clear.

In these editions, students, teachers, actors, and thousands of other readers will find the best of modern textual scholarship, along with up-to-date critical essays, written especially for these volumes, that offer original and often surprising interpretations of Shakespeare's characters, action, and language.

I thank editors Barbara Mowat and Paul Werstine for undertaking this ambitious project, which is nothing less than an entirely new look at the texts from the earliest printed versions. Lovers of Shakespeare everywhere must be grateful for the breadth of their learning, the liveliness of their imaginations, and the scholarly rigor that they bring to the challenge of re-editing the plays.

Gail Kern Paster, Director
The Folger Shakespeare Library

Contents

Contents

Editors' Preface

In recent years, ways of dealing with Shakespeare's texts and with the interpretation of his plays have been undergoing significant change. This edition, while retaining many of the features that have always made the Folger Shakespeare so attractive to the general reader, at the same time reflects these current ways of thinking about Shakespeare. For example, modern readers, actors, and teachers have become interested in the differences between, on the one hand, the early forms in which Shakespeare's plays were first published and, on the other hand, the forms in which editors through the centuries have presented them. In response to this interest, we have based our edition on what we consider the best early printed version of a particular play (explaining our rationale in a section called "An Introduction to This Text") and have marked our changes in the text—unobtrusively, we hope, but in such a way that the curious reader can be aware that a change has been made and can consult the "Textual Notes" to discover what appeared in the early printed version.

Current ways of looking at the plays are reflected in our brief prefaces, in many of the commentary notes, in the annotated lists of "Further Reading," and especially in each play's "Modern Perspective," an essay written by an outstanding scholar who brings to the reader his or her fresh assessment of the play in the light of today's interests and concerns.

As in the Folger Library General Reader's Shakespeare, which this edition replaces, we include explanatory notes designed to help make Shakespeare's language clearer to a modern reader, and we place the notes on the page facing the text that they explain. We also follow the earlier edition in including illustrations—of objects, of clothing, of mythological figures—from books and manuscripts in the Folger Library collection. We provide fresh accounts of the life of Shakespeare, of the publishing of his plays, and of the theaters in which his plays were performed, as well as an introduction to the text itself. We also include a section called "Reading Shakespeare's Language," in which we try to help readers learn to "break the code" of Elizabethan poetic language.

For each section of each volume, we are indebted to a host of generous experts and fellow scholars. The "Reading Shakespeare's Language" sections, for example, could not have been written had not Arthur King, of Brigham Young University, and Randall Robinson, author of *Unlocking Shakespeare's Language*, led the way in untangling Shakespearean language puzzles and shared their insights and methodologies generously with us. "Shakespeare's Life" profited by the careful reading given it by the late S. Schoenbaum; "Shakespeare's Theater" was read and strengthened by Andrew Gurr, John Astington, and William Ingram; and "The Publication of Shakespeare's Plays" is indebted to the comments of Peter W. M. Blayney. We, as editors, take sole responsibility for any errors in our editions.

We are grateful to the authors of the "Modern Perspectives"; to Leeds Barroll and David Bevington for their generous encouragement; to the Huntington and Newberry Libraries for fellowship support; to King's University College for the grants it has provided to Paul Werstine; to the Social Sciences and Humanities Research Council of Canada, which provided him with a Research Time Stipend for 1990–91; to R. J. Shroyer of the University of Western Ontario for essential computer support; to the Folger Institute's Center for Shakespeare Studies for its sponsorship of a workshop on "Shakespeare's Texts for Students and Teachers" (funded by the National Endowment for the Humanities and led by Richard Knowles of the University of Wisconsin), a workshop from which we learned an enormous amount about what is wanted by college and high-school teachers of Shakespeare today; to Alice Falk for her expert copyediting; and especially to Stephen Llano, our production editor at Washington Square Press.

Our biggest debt is to the Folger Shakespeare Library—to Gail Kern Paster, Director of the Library, whose interest and support are unfailing, and to Werner Gundersheimer, the Library's Director from 1984 to 2002, who made possible our edition; to Deborah Curren-Aquino, who provides extensive editorial and production support; to Jean Miller, the Library's former Art Curator, who combs the Library holdings for illustrations, and to Julie Ainsworth, Head of the Photography Department, who carefully photographs them; to Peggy O'Brien, former Director of Education at the Folger and now Director of Education Programs at the Corporation for Public Broadcasting, who gave us expert advice about the needs being expressed by Shakespeare teachers and students (and to Martha Christian and other "master teachers" who used our texts in manuscript in their classrooms); to Allan Shnerson and Mary Bloodworth for their expert computer support; to the staff of the Academic Programs Division, especially Solvei Robertson (whose help is crucial), Mary Tonkinson, Kathleen Lynch, Carol Brobeck, Liz Pohland, Owen Williams, and Dan Busey; and, finally, to the generously supportive staff of the Library's Reading Room.

Barbara A. Mowat and Paul Werstine

A prospect of Windsor Castle.

From Elias Ashmole, *The institution, laws & ceremonies of the . . . Order of the Garter . . .* (1672).

Shakespeare's
The Merry Wives of Windsor

Shakespeare's "merry wives" are Mistress Ford and Mistress Page, both married to well-to-do citizens of Windsor, a town near London best known for its royal castle and its parks. ("Mistress," in their case, means what "Mrs." later came to mean.) The two are fast friends who cooperate with and completely trust each other, and who join together to play elaborate practical jokes on Mistress Ford's jealous husband and on the knight Sir John Falstaff, a visitor staying at Windsor's Garter Inn. As a collection of characters in a play, merry wives, jealous husbands, and predatory knights would have been familiar to Shakespeare's audience. This is a group found over and over again in a particular kind of popular play of Shakespeare's time called "citizen comedy" or "city comedy." The staple of such comedy, found throughout the seventeenth century, is a kind of class warfare in which courtiers, gentlemen, or knights prey on married citizens by using social superiority to seduce the wives, thereby gaining access to the married couples' money and turning the citizen-husbands into figures of scorn called *cuckolds* (a name for men whose wives are unfaithful). In these plays, proper wives stand out against such seducers and maintain a posture of silence, chastity, and obedience, but merry wives—those who enjoy and are animated by feasting and entertainment—often give in to the pleasures offered by their male social superiors.

Shakespeare's merry wives, though, do not follow the usual pattern. Instead, Falstaff's offer of himself as lover to both Mistress Page and Mistress Ford becomes the occasion of their extended torment of him. No matter how much they enjoy having fun, these wives are individually and collectively offended by his offer. They immediately turn their attention to taking revenge for his presuming to approach them. And when one of the husbands, Ford, is overcome by jealousy and seeks to expose what he believes is his wife's infidelity, he too becomes the target of the wives' merry schemes.

But the combination of Mistress Page and Mistress Ford is not the only comic engine in this play. While Falstaff is the butt of their jokes, he nonetheless responds to his plight with comic speeches filled with the same linguistic facility that Shakespeare gives this character in the history plays in which he also appears. There is a long, if quite groundless, tradition that Queen Elizabeth so enjoyed Falstaff in Shakespeare's *Henry IV, Part 1* and *Part 2* that she commanded the dramatist to write a play about Falstaff in love, a command that Shakespeare purportedly fulfilled in just two weeks. While the tradition has nothing factual to support it, it reflects the fact that Falstaff through the centuries has been regarded by audiences as the "hero" of the play.

After finishing the play, we invite you to read the essay titled *"The Merry Wives of Windsor:* A Modern Perspective," by Professor Natasha Korda of Wesleyan University, which is printed at the back of this book.

Reading Shakespeare's Language: *The Merry Wives of Windsor*

For many people today, reading Shakespeare's language can be a problem—but it is a problem that can be solved. Four hundred years of "static" intervene between his speaking and our hearing. Most of his immense vocabulary is still in use, but a few of his words are not, and, worse, some of his words now have meanings quite different from those they had in the sixteenth and seventeenth centuries. In the theater, most of these difficulties are solved for us by actors who study the language and articulate it for us so that the essential meaning is heard—or, when combined with stage action, is at least *felt*. When reading on one's own, one must do what each actor does: go over the lines (often with a dictionary close at hand) until the puzzles are solved and the characters speak in words and phrases that are, suddenly, rewarding and wonderfully memorable.

Shakespeare's Words

As you begin to read the opening scenes of a play by Shakespeare, you may notice occasional unfamiliar words. Some are unfamiliar simply because we no longer use them. In the opening scenes of *The Merry Wives of Windsor,* for example, you will find the words *fallow* (i.e., light brown), *cony-catching* (i.e., cheating), *pickpurse* (i.e., pickpocket), and *fap* (i.e., drunk). Words of this kind are explained in notes to the text and will become familiar the more of Shakespeare's plays you read.

In *The Merry Wives of Windsor,* as in all of Shakespeare's writing, more problematic are the words that we still use but that we use with a different meaning. In the opening scenes, for example, the word *marry* has the meaning of "indeed," *demands* is used where we would say "requests," *fair* is used where we would say "beautiful," *conceited* where we would say "ingenious," and *shift* where we would say "improvise." Such words will be explained in the notes to the text, but they, too, will become familiar as you continue to read Shakespeare's language.

Some words are strange not because of the "static" introduced by changes in language over the past centuries but because these are words that Shakespeare is having characters misuse. While Falstaff, late in the play, describes Sir Hugh Evans as one who "makes fritters of English" (5.5.151), Sir Hugh is not alone in his comic misspeaking. Slender, for example, very early in the play, transposes "successors" and "ancestors": "All his *successors* gone before him hath done 't, and all his *ancestors* that come after him may" (1.1.14–16). By including in the line itself the correct meanings of the abused English words, Shakespeare establishes in the clearest possible way the severe limitations of Slender's command of his native language. In this respect Slender greatly resembles Doctor Caius's servant Mistress Quickly, who as often as not chooses the wrong word. When, for example, she promises Fenton to "tell [him] more . . . the next time [they] have confidence" (1.4.166–67), the word she needs is not *confidence* but *conference* (which at that time meant "conversation"). Mistress Quickly also makes up words that were no more current in Shakespeare's time than in ours; she says, for instance, that Anne Page "is given too much to allicholy and musing" (1.4.158–59). *Allicholy* has never been an English word, but its sound and its pairing here with "musing" suggest that Quickly is using it for the word *melancholy*.

Among other prominent misusers of words are the Welsh parson Sir Hugh and the French Doctor Caius, each of whom is given, among other language characteristics, a distinctive foreign accent. Sir Hugh's accent becomes apparent in the play's first scene as Shakespeare gradually introduces it with "py" for *by* in Sir Hugh's third speech and "Got" for *God* in his fourth, thickening it in his next speech with "petter" for *better*, "prain" for *brain*, and "prings" for *brings*. Beyond this Welsh accent, Sir Hugh's speeches are also characterized by erroneous word choices; for instance, he calls Anne Page a "pretty virginity." Unlike Sir Hugh's, Doctor Caius's accent and his foreign-seeming syntax are heavy from the very beginning: "Vat [i.e., what] is you sing? I do not like dese [i.e., these] toys" (1.4.44). Doctor Caius's speeches also challenge the reader with their occasional use of French words and of English words that carry not their English meanings but those of the French words from which they derive. When, for example, he asks Quickly "Do intend vat I speak?" (46), *intend* has the sense "hear." Though this seems by Shakespeare's time no longer to have been a meaning of the word in English, it is the meaning of the French word *entendre*, from which *intend* ultimately derives. Among other speakers in *The Merry Wives of Windsor* who frequently use words in highly unusual ways are Pistol, Nym, and the Host of the Garter Inn. Notes to the text will explain as many of the misused words as seems helpful (and as space allows).

Shakespeare's Sentences

In most of Shakespeare's plays, speeches are predominantly in blank verse; this is not true of *The Merry Wives of Windsor*, where blank verse is to be found mainly in a few speeches by Master Fenton and in the play's last scene with the fairies. Master Fenton's first extensive speech to Anne Page, in which he tells her of her father's objections to him as her future husband, can serve as an example of the kind of dramatic verse that Shakespeare typically writes:

FENTON   Why, thou must be thyself.
He doth object I am too great of birth,
And that, my state being galled with my expense,
I seek to heal it only by his wealth.
Besides these, other bars he lays before me—
My riots past, my wild societies—
And tells me 'tis a thing impossible
I should love thee but as a property.

                                        (3.4.4–11)

In the above speech, as is his practice, Shakespeare shifts his sentences away from "normal" English arrangements—often to create the rhythm he seeks, sometimes to use a line's meter to emphasize a particular word. The first short sentence in this speech follows normal English word order, as does the beginning of the second sentence. After the verb ("doth object"), however, the second sentence becomes elliptical (i.e., leaves something out). The word *that* is omitted at the beginning of the first object of the verb (i.e., the clause "I am too great of birth"), an omission that preserves the largely iambic rhythm of the line: "He doth | ob*ject'* | I am | too *great'* | of *birth'* |." The second object-clause ("that, my state being galled with my expense, / I seek to heal it only by his wealth") also departs from normal word order; we would expect "that" to be immediately followed by the subject of the clause ("I"), but Shakespeare holds back the subject in order to insert before it an absolute construction, "my state [estate] being galled [depleted; literally, chafed] with my expense [extravagance]." This insertion provides the grounds for the second objection of Master Page, the presentation of which completes the sentence: "I seek to heal it only by his wealth." In the third sentence, normal word order and sentence construction are again altered, with the object of the sentence "other bars" coming before the subject and verb ("he lays") and with *that* twice omitted, once before " 'tis a thing" and again before "I should love," the ellipses here giving Fenton's speech an informal, colloquial tone.

Most of the challenges and rewards of reading Shakespeare's sentences in *The Merry Wives* are quite unlike those just analyzed. The play is largely prose, and normal word order is usually observed. Yet Shakespeare introduces into his prose all kinds of comic distortions of sentence structure. We have already quoted Doctor Caius's sentence "Vat is you sing?"—an unidiomatic form of the sentence "What are you singing?" (or, "What do you sing?") that indicates how he has yet to master English as a second language. Mistress Quickly's utterances often refuse to conform to our expectations of sentence formation: "And the very yea and the no is, the French doctor, my master—I may call him my master, look you, for I keep his house, and I wash, wring, brew, bake, scour, dress meat and drink, make the beds, and do all myself" (1.4.98–102). This sentence begins in the usual way with a subject ("the very yea and the no") and verb ("is") and seems to be moving toward proper completion in a clause that has "the French doctor, my master" as its subject. But we will never know what this clause may have been because Mistress Quickly drops her first sentence to begin a second: "I may call him my master. . . ." Inconsequence, or lack of sequence, is the distinctive mark of Mistress Quickly's sentences. When her sentences do conform to grammatical sequence, they often escape logical sequence. For instance, when Falstaff calls her "good" maid" (i.e., "good virgin") she replies "I'll be sworn—as my mother was, the first hour I was born" (2.2.36–38), thus confusedly vowing that she is every bit the virgin that her mother was just after giving birth to her.

Falstaff's sentences provide a very different kind of comedy: the pleasure of reading or listening to his speeches is often that of following the elaborate patterning that Shakespeare has used to shape them. One prominent example comes near the end of the play when Falstaff excuses his disguising himself in pursuit of a woman by calling on Jove, who transformed himself into a bull to capture Europa and into a swan to seduce Leda:

[1] Remember, Jove, thou wast a bull for thy Europa; love set on thy horns. [2] O powerful love, that in some respects makes a beast a man, in some other a man a beast! [3] You were also, Jupiter, a swan for the love of Leda. [4] O omnipotent love, how near the god drew to the complexion of a goose! [5] A fault done first in the form of a beast; O Jove, a beastly fault! [6] And then another fault in the semblance of a fowl; think on't, Jove, a foul fault.

(5.5.3–11)

Here Shakespeare creates the illusion of Falstaff's great mastery of language by having him utter sentences that, to some extent, mirror each other in their form. We rearrange these sentences schematically to call attention to their patterns of repetition, and we print in bold the parallel elements. At the same time, we print in italic those words in each sentence that echo each other either through outright repetition or through their similar sounds.

[1] Remember,   *Jove,* thou wast *a* **bull** *for* thy
                                      Europa. . . .
[3] You were also, *Jupiter,*   *a* **swan** *for* **the love**
                                      of Leda.

[2] *O* powerful *love,* that   *in some* respects makes
                                                    a beast a man,
                                          in some other
                                                    a man a beast!

[4] *O* omnipotent *love,* how near the *god* drew to the
                                                    complexion of
                                                    a *goose!*

_____

[5] A   *fault* done *first* in the form
                                                    of a beast; O
                                                              Jove,
                                                    a beastly fault!

[6] And then another *fault*   *in the* semblance
                                                    of a fowl; think
                                                    on't,
                                                              Jove,
                                                    a foul fault.

As these examples show, Falstaff is capable not only of
choosing precisely the right words for their sense but
also of playing with the sounds of these words as a way
of mocking both Jove and himself.

Shakespearean Wordplay

Shakespeare plays with language so often and so variously that entire books are written on the topic. Here
we will mention only three kinds of wordplay: puns,
metaphors, and similes. A pun is a play on words that
sound somewhat the same but that have different
meanings (or a play on a single word that has more
than one meaning). The language-learning scene (4.1)
in *The Merry Wives of Windsor* exhibits sustained pun-
ning that turns on the similarity of sound between the

Latin words on which William Page is being tested and the English words that Mistress Quickly, in her ignorance of Latin, substitutes for them. When William is asked "What is 'fair'?" and responds correctly with the Latin adjective *pulcher,* Mistress Quickly substitutes the English noun *polecats,* meaning "weasels," and declares "There are fairer things than polecats" (25–29). When she hears the plural possessives or genitives of the Latin word meaning "this," which are *horum, harum, horum,* she substitutes the English *whore* and rails against the schoolmaster: "You do ill to teach the child such words" (64–65).

A metaphor is a play on words in which one object or idea is expressed as if it were something else, something with which it shares common features. For instance, in Fenton's speech quoted above, he speaks of his "state" (i.e., estate) as if it were a body that his extravagance has "galled" or chafed, but that can be healed through the medicine of Master Page's "wealth."

A simile is a play on words in which an object or idea is, through the use of "like" or "as," explicitly compared to something else. Just as Falstaff is made the master of the schematic sentence, so is he the master of the simile. When, for example, he describes "the pangs of three several deaths" he suffered in his dunking in the river, he is allowed to find a term of comparison for his every state:

> to be compassed, *like a good bilbo* [i.e., flexible sword], in the circumference of a peck, hilt to point, heel to head; and then, to be stopped in, *like a strong distillation,* with stinking clothes that fretted in their own grease. . . . And in the height of this bath, when I was more than half-stewed in grease, *like a Dutch*

dish, to be thrown into the Thames and cooled, glowing hot, in that surge, *like a horseshoe!*

(3.5.110, 112–23)

Implied Stage Action

Finally, in reading Shakespeare's plays we should always remember that what we are reading is a performance script. The dialogue is written to be spoken by actors who, at the same time, are moving, gesturing, picking up objects, shaking their fists. We should try to remain alert to signals for action as we stage the play in our imaginations. Some signals are provided in what are called "stage directions"; some are suggested within the dialogue itself.

For editors attempting to provide helpful and accurate stage directions, *The Merry Wives of Windsor* presents special challenges because the only complete text of the play, the First Folio text of 1623, is quite bare of such directions, except for some entrances and end-of-scene exits. Thus editors must reconstruct the action of the play entirely from what is suggested by the dialogue itself, supplemented by reference to the stage directions printed in the truncated and deficient Quarto text of 1602. (For more discussion of the Quarto, see "An Introduction to This Text," page xlviii.) As editors, we have introduced stage directions from the Quarto or of our own devising only when we felt confident that they are signaled by the dialogue, placing them in half-brackets to alert readers to the fact that they are not in the Folio text that is the basis for our edition.

Fortunately, the dialogue in this play is often clear about the action that should accompany the language.

When, in 3.3, for example, Falstaff says "I will ensconce me behind the arras" and Mistress Ford responds "Pray you, do so" (89–91), it is clear from these lines and from those that then follow that Falstaff does hide behind an arras (i.e., a wall hanging). A few lines later, the stage action suggested by the dialogue is again clear. Falstaff, frightened out of his hiding place by the threat of Master Ford's approach and desperate to get into a handy laundry basket in order to be carried secretly out of the house, says "Help me away. Let me creep in here" (139–40). The line that follows, Mistress Ford's "Help to cover your master, boy," makes it clear that Falstaff has indeed gotten into the basket and hidden himself under the dirty linen. We feel comfortable, then, adding the stage direction *"Falstaff goes into the basket; they cover him with dirty clothes."*

Sometimes, though, signals to the reader are not so clear. How, for example, should Mistress Page and Mistress Ford act toward Falstaff when they meet him in the play's first scene? Mistress Page reflects back on that meeting in 2.1, after she has received a love letter from Falstaff, and she expresses bewilderment about what she might have done when in his company that would have encouraged his forwardness; Mistress Ford, receiving her own such letter, joins her in her bewilderment: "What doth he think of us?" (83). While the Folio text gives us no help about stage action in the opening scene, the Quarto includes a stage direction for Falstaff to kiss Mistress Ford (1.1.189). We have incorporated this direction into our edition, but we have acknowledged in our commentary notes that in Shakespeare's time, in contrast to ours, the kiss could be merely a form of polite salutation. Thus readers, actors, and directors are free to imagine what, if anything, the women do in the first scene to attract Falstaff's predatory attention—including the likelihood that they behave with complete propriety and that his perception of their "leer of invitation" (1.3.43–44) arises from his own conceit and greed.

Another place where stage action is problematic is in the play's last scene. According to the play's dialogue, the scene includes rather complicated action in which the fairies punish a disguised Falstaff and in which three men each take away a "fairy" that each thinks is a disguised Anne Page. Here again the Quarto provides a stage direction, this one reading:

> *Here they pinch him* [i.e., Falstaff], *and sing about him, & the Doctor comes one way & steales away a boy in red. And Slender another way he takes a boy in greene: And Fenton steales misteris Anne, being in white.*

Unfortunately, this direction does not completely cohere with the Folio dialogue, which mentions nothing about a red costume, and which clothes Anne Page and her replicas in colors that do not match those in the Quarto stage direction. We have therefore adapted the Quarto stage direction to make it conform to the Folio dialogue:

> *Here they pinch him and sing about him, and Doctor Caius comes one way and steals away a boy in white. And Slender comes another way; he takes a boy in green. And Fenton steals Mistress Anne Page.* (5.5.98)

As with much of the action in this eventful scene, the moment thus described may actually be staged in any number of ways. Although we provide our best guess about the action, directors and actors—and read-

ers in their imaginations—are at the same liberty as
editors to imagine this moment on stage.

It is immensely rewarding to work carefully with
Shakespeare's language so that the words, the sentences, the wordplay, and the implied stage action all
become vivid—as readers for the past four centuries
have discovered. It may be more pleasurable to attend
a good performance of a play—though not everyone
has thought so. But the joy of being able to stage one of
Shakespeare's plays in one's imagination, to return to
passages that continue to yield further meanings (or
further questions) the more one reads them—these are
pleasures that, for many, rival (or at least augment)
those of the performed text, and certainly make it
worth considerable effort to "break the code" of Elizabethan drama and let free the remarkable language
that makes up a Shakespeare text.

Shakespeare's Life

Surviving documents that give us glimpses into the
life of William Shakespeare show us a playwright,
poet, and actor who grew up in the market town of
Stratford-upon-Avon, spent his professional life in
London, and returned to Stratford a wealthy landowner. He was born in April 1564, died in April 1616,
and is buried inside the chancel of Holy Trinity
Church in Stratford.

We wish we could know more about the life of the
world's greatest dramatist. His plays and poems are tes-
taments to his wide reading—especially to his knowl-

edge of Virgil, Ovid, Plutarch, Holinshed's *Chronicles*, and the Bible—and to his mastery of the English language, but we can only speculate about his education. We know that the King's New School in Stratford-upon-Avon was considered excellent. The school was one of the English "grammar schools" established to educate young men, primarily in Latin grammar and literature. As in other schools of the time, students began their studies at the age of four or five in the attached "petty school," and there learned to read and write in English, studying primarily the catechism from the Book of Common Prayer. After two years in the petty school, students entered the lower form (grade) of the grammar school, where they began the serious study of Latin grammar and Latin texts that would occupy most of the remainder of their school days. (Several Latin texts that Shakespeare used repeatedly in writing his plays and poems were texts that schoolboys memorized and recited.) Latin comedies were introduced early in the lower form; in the upper form, which the boys entered at age ten or eleven, students wrote their own Latin orations and declamations, studied Latin historians and rhetoricians, and began the study of Greek using the Greek New Testament.

Since the records of the Stratford "grammar school" do not survive, we cannot prove that William Shakespeare attended the school; however, every indication (his father's position as an alderman and bailiff of Stratford, the playwright's own knowledge of the Latin classics, scenes in the plays that recall grammar-school experiences—for example, *The Merry Wives of Windsor*, 4.1) suggests that he did. We also lack generally accepted documentation about Shakespeare's life after his schooling ended and his professional life in London began. His marriage in 1582 (at age eighteen) to

Anne Hathaway and the subsequent births of his daughter Susanna (1583) and the twins Judith and Hamnet (1585) are recorded, but how he supported himself and where he lived are not known. Nor do we know when and why he left Stratford for the London theatrical world, nor how he rose to be the important figure in that world that he had become by the early 1590s.

We do know that by 1592 he had achieved some prominence in London as both an actor and a playwright. In that year was published a book by the playwright Robert Greene attacking an actor who had the audacity to write blank-verse drama and who was "in his own conceit [i.e., opinion] the only Shake-scene in a country." Since Greene's attack includes a parody of a line from one of Shakespeare's early plays, there is little doubt that it is Shakespeare to whom he refers, a "Shake-scene" who had aroused Greene's fury by successfully competing with university-educated dramatists like Greene himself. It was in 1593 that Shakespeare became a published poet. In that year he published his long narrative poem *Venus and Adonis;* in 1594, he followed it with *The Rape of Lucrece.* Both poems were dedicated to the young earl of Southampton (Henry Wriothesley), who may have become Shakespeare's patron.

It seems no coincidence that Shakespeare wrote these narrative poems at a time when the theaters were closed because of the plague, a contagious epidemic disease that devastated the population of London. When the theaters reopened in 1594, Shakespeare apparently resumed his double career of actor and playwright and began his long (and seemingly profitable) service as an acting-company shareholder. Records for December of 1594 show him to be a leading member of the Lord Chamberlain's Men. It was this company of actors, later named the King's Men, for whom he would be a principal actor, dramatist, and shareholder for the rest of his career.

So far as we can tell, that career spanned about twenty years. In the 1590s, he wrote his plays on English history as well as several comedies and at least two tragedies (*Titus Andronicus* and *Romeo and Juliet*). These histories, comedies, and tragedies are the plays credited to him in 1598 in a work, *Palladis Tamia*, that in one chapter compares English writers with "Greek, Latin, and Italian Poets." There the author, Francis Meres, claims that Shakespeare is comparable to the Latin dramatists Seneca for tragedy and Plautus for comedy, and calls him "the most excellent in both kinds for the stage." He also names him "Mellifluous and honey-tongued Shakespeare": "I say," writes Meres, "that the Muses would speak with Shakespeare's fine filed phrase, if they would speak English." Since Meres also mentions Shakespeare's "sugared sonnets among his private friends," it is assumed that many of Shakespeare's sonnets (not published until 1609) were also written in the 1590s.

In 1599, Shakespeare's company built a theater for themselves across the river from London, naming it the Globe. The plays that are considered by many to be Shakespeare's major tragedies (*Hamlet*, *Othello*, *King Lear*, and *Macbeth*) were written while the company was resident in this theater, as were such comedies as *Twelfth Night* and *Measure for Measure*. Many of Shakespeare's plays were performed at court (both for Queen Elizabeth I and, after her death in 1603, for King James I), some were presented at the Inns of Court (the residences of London's legal societies), and some were doubtless performed in other towns, at the universities, and at great houses when the King's Men went on

A stylized representation of the Globe theater.
From Claes Jansz Visscher, *Londinum florentissima
Britanniae urbs* . . . [c. 1625].

tour; otherwise, his plays from 1599 to 1608 were, so far as we know, performed only at the Globe. Between 1608 and 1612, Shakespeare wrote several plays—among them *The Winter's Tale* and *The Tempest*—presumably for the company's new indoor Blackfriars theater, though the plays seem to have been performed also at the Globe and at court. Surviving documents describe a performance of *The Winter's Tale* in 1611 at the Globe, for example, and performances of *The Tempest* in 1611 and 1613 at the royal palace of Whitehall.

Shakespeare wrote very little after 1612, the year in which he probably wrote *King Henry VIII*. (It was at a performance of *Henry VIII* in 1613 that the Globe caught fire and burned to the ground.) Sometime between 1610 and 1613 he seems to have returned to live in Stratford-upon-Avon, where he owned a large house and considerable property, and where his wife and his two daughters and their husbands lived. (His son Hamnet had died in 1596.) During his professional years in London, Shakespeare had presumably derived income from the acting company's profits as well as from his own career as an actor, from the sale of his play manuscripts to the acting company, and, after 1599, from his shares as an owner of the Globe. It was presumably that income, carefully invested in land and other property, which made him the wealthy man that surviving documents show him to have become. It is also assumed that William Shakespeare's growing wealth and reputation played some part in inclining the crown, in 1596, to grant John Shakespeare, William's father, the coat of arms that he had so long sought. William Shakespeare died in Stratford on April 23, 1616 (according to the epitaph carved under his bust in Holy Trinity Church) and was buried on April 25. Seven years after his death, his collected plays were published as *Mr. William Shakespeares Comedies, Histories, & Tragedies* (the work now known as the First Folio).

The years in which Shakespeare wrote were among the most exciting in English history. Intellectually, the discovery, translation, and printing of Greek and Roman classics were making available a set of works and worldviews that interacted complexly with Christian texts and beliefs. The result was a questioning, a vital intellectual ferment, that provided energy for the period's amazing dramatic and literary output and that fed directly into Shakespeare's plays. The Ghost in *Hamlet*, for example, is wonderfully complicated in part because he is a figure from Roman tragedy—the spirit of the dead returning to seek revenge—who at the same time inhabits a Christian hell (or purgatory); Hamlet's description of humankind reflects at one moment the Neoplatonic wonderment at mankind ("What a piece of work is a man!") and, at the next, the Christian disparagement of human sinners ("And yet, to me, what is this quintessence of dust?").

As intellectual horizons expanded, so also did geographical and cosmological horizons. New worlds—both North and South America—were explored, and in them were found human beings who lived and worshiped in ways radically different from those of Renaissance Europeans and Englishmen. The universe during these years also seemed to shift and expand. Copernicus had earlier theorized that the earth was not the center of the cosmos but revolved as a planet around the sun. Galileo's telescope, created in 1609, allowed scientists to see that Copernicus had been correct; the universe was not organized with the earth at the center, nor was it so nicely circumscribed as people had, until that time, thought. In terms of expanding horizons, the impact of these discoveries on people's beliefs—religious, scientific, and philosophical—cannot be overstated.

London, too, rapidly expanded and changed during the years (from the early 1590s to around 1610) that Shakespeare lived there. London—the center of England's government, its economy, its royal court, its overseas trade—was, during these years, becoming an exciting metropolis, drawing to it thousands of new citizens every year. Troubled by overcrowding, by poverty, by recurring epidemics of the plague, London was also a mecca for the wealthy and the aristocratic, and for those who sought advancement at court, or power in government or finance or trade. One hears in Shakespeare's plays the voices of London—the struggles for power, the fear of venereal disease, the language of buying and selling. One hears as well the voices of Stratford-upon-Avon—references to the nearby Forest of Arden, to sheepherding, to small-town gossip, to village fairs and markets. Part of the richness of Shakespeare's work is the influence felt there of the various worlds in which he lived: the world of metropolitan London, the world of small-town and rural England, the world of the theater, and the worlds of craftsmen and shepherds.

That Shakespeare inhabited such worlds we know from surviving London and Stratford documents, as well as from the evidence of the plays and poems themselves. From such records we can sketch the dramatist's life. We know from his works that he was a voracious reader. We know from legal and business documents that he was a multifaceted theater man who became a wealthy landowner. We know a bit about his family life and a fair amount about his legal and financial dealings. Most scholars today depend upon such evidence as they draw their picture of the world's greatest playwright. Such, however, has not always been the case. Until the late eighteenth century, the William Shakespeare who lived in most biographies was the creation of legend and tradition. This was the Shakespeare who was supposedly caught poaching deer at Charlecote, the estate of Sir Thomas Lucy close by Stratford; this was the Shakespeare who fled from Sir Thomas's vengeance and made his way in London by taking care of horses outside a playhouse; this was the Shakespeare who reportedly could barely read but whose natural gifts were extraordinary, whose father was a butcher who allowed his gifted son sometimes to help in the butcher shop, where William supposedly killed calves "in a high style," making a speech for the occasion. It was this legendary William Shakespeare whose Falstaff (in *1* and *2 Henry IV*) so pleased Queen Elizabeth that she demanded a play about Falstaff in love, and demanded that it be written in fourteen days (hence the existence of *The Merry Wives of Windsor*). It was this legendary Shakespeare who reached the top of his acting career in the roles of the Ghost in *Hamlet* and old Adam in *As You Like It*—and who died of a fever contracted by drinking too hard at "a merry meeting" with the poets Michael Drayton and Ben Jonson. This legendary Shakespeare is a rambunctious, undisciplined man, as attractively "wild" as his plays were seen by earlier generations to be. Unfortunately, there is no trace of evidence to support these wonderful stories.

Perhaps in response to the disreputable Shakespeare of legend—or perhaps in response to the fragmentary and, for some, all-too-ordinary Shakespeare documented by surviving records—some people since the mid–nineteenth century have argued that William Shakespeare could not have written the plays that bear his name. These persons have put forward some dozen names as more likely authors, among them Queen Elizabeth, Sir Francis Bacon, Edward de Vere (earl of Oxford), and Christopher Marlowe. Such attempts to find what for these people is a more believable author of the plays is a tribute to the regard in which the plays are held. Unfortunately for their claims, the documents that exist that provide evidence for the facts of Shakespeare's life tie him inextricably to the body of plays and poems that bear his name. Unlikely as it seems to those who want the works to have been written by an aristocrat, a university graduate, or an "important" person, the plays and poems seem clearly to have been produced by a man from Stratford-upon-Avon with a very good "grammar-school" education and a life of experience in London and in the world of the London theater. How this particular man produced the works that dominate the cultures of much of the world almost four hundred years after his death is one of life's mysteries—and one that will continue to tease our imaginations as we continue to delight in his plays and poems.

Shakespeare's Theater

The actors of Shakespeare's time performed plays in a great variety of locations. They played at court (that is, in the great halls of such royal residences as Whitehall, Hampton Court, and Greenwich); they played in halls at the universities of Oxford and Cambridge, and at the Inns of Court (the residences in London of the legal societies); and they also played in the private houses of great lords and civic officials. Sometimes acting companies went on tour from London into the provinces, often (but not only) when outbreaks of bubonic plague in the capital forced the closing of theaters to reduce the possibility of contagion in crowded audiences. In the provinces the actors usually staged their plays in churches (until around 1600) or in guildhalls. While surviving records show only a handful of occasions when actors played at inns while on tour, London inns were important playing places up until the 1590s.

The building of theaters in London had begun only shortly before Shakespeare wrote his first plays in the 1590s. These theaters were of two kinds: outdoor or public playhouses that could accommodate large numbers of playgoers, and indoor or private theaters for much smaller audiences. What is usually regarded as the first London outdoor public playhouse was called simply the Theatre. James Burbage—the father of Richard Burbage, who was perhaps the most famous actor in Shakespeare's company—built it in 1576 in an area north of the city of London called Shoreditch. Among the more famous of the other public playhouses that capitalized on the new fashion were the Curtain and the Fortune (both also built north of the city), the Rose, the Swan, the Globe, and the Hope (all located on the Bankside, a region just across the Thames south of the city of London). All these playhouses had to be built outside the jurisdiction of the city of London because many civic officials were hostile to the performance of drama and repeatedly petitioned the royal council to abolish it.

The theaters erected on the Bankside (a region under the authority of the Church of England, whose head was the monarch) shared the neighborhood with houses of prostitution and with the Paris Garden, where the blood sports of bearbaiting and bullbaiting were carried on. There may have been no clear distinction between playhouses and buildings for such sports, for the Hope was used for both plays and baiting, and Philip Henslowe, owner of the Rose and, later, partner in the ownership of the Fortune, was also a partner in a monopoly on baiting. All these forms of entertainment were easily accessible to Londoners by boat across the Thames or over London Bridge.

Evidently Shakespeare's company prospered on the Bankside. They moved there in 1599. Threatened by difficulties in renewing the lease on the land where their first playhouse (the Theatre) had been built, Shakespeare's company took advantage of the Christmas holiday in 1598 to dismantle the Theatre and transport its timbers across the Thames to the Bankside, where, in 1599, these timbers were used in the building of the Globe. The weather in late December 1598 is recorded as having been especially harsh. It was so cold that the Thames was "nigh [nearly] frozen," and there was heavy snow. Perhaps the weather aided Shakespeare's company in eluding their landlord, the snow hiding their activity and the freezing of the Thames allowing them to slide the timbers across to the Bankside without paying tolls for repeated trips over London Bridge. Attractive as this narrative is, it remains just as likely that the heavy snow hampered transport of the timbers in wagons through the London streets to the river. It also must be remembered that the Thames was, according to report, only "nigh frozen" and therefore as impassable as it ever was. Whatever the precise circumstances of this fascinating event in English theater history, Shakespeare's company was able to begin playing at their new Globe theater on the Bankside in 1599. After the first Globe burned down in 1613 during the staging of Shakespeare's *Henry VIII* (its thatch roof was set alight by cannon fire called for by the performance), Shakespeare's company immediately rebuilt on the same location. The second Globe seems to have been a grander structure than its predecessor. It remained in use until the beginning of the English Civil War in 1642, when Parliament officially closed the theaters. Soon thereafter it was pulled down.

The public theaters of Shakespeare's time were very different buildings from our theaters today. First of all, they were open-air playhouses. As recent excavations of the Rose and the Globe confirm, some were polygonal or roughly circular in shape; the Fortune, however, was square. The most recent estimates of their size put the diameter of these buildings at 72 feet (the Rose) to 100 feet (the Globe), but they were said to hold vast audiences of two or three thousand, who must have been squeezed together quite tightly. Some of these spectators paid extra to sit or stand in the two or three levels of roofed galleries that extended, on the upper levels, all the way around the theater and surrounded an open space. In this space were the stage and, perhaps, the tiring house (what we would call dressing rooms), as well as the so-called yard. In the yard stood the spectators who chose to pay less, the ones whom Hamlet contemptuously called "groundlings." For a roof they had only the sky, and so they were exposed to all kinds of weather. They stood on a floor that was sometimes made of mortar and sometimes of ash mixed with the shells of hazelnuts. The latter provided a porous and therefore dry footing for the crowd, and the shells may have been more comfortable to stand on because they were not as hard as mortar. Availability of shells may not have been a problem if hazelnuts were a favorite food for Shakespeare's audiences to munch on as they watched his plays. Archaeologists who are today unearthing the remains of theaters from this period have discovered quantities of these nutshells on theater sites.

Unlike the yard, the stage itself was covered by a roof. Its ceiling, called "the heavens," is thought to have been elaborately painted to depict the sun, moon, stars, and planets. Just how big the stage was remains hard to determine. We have a single sketch of part of the interior of the Swan. A Dutchman named Johannes de Witt visited this theater around 1596 and sent a sketch of it back to his friend, Arend van Buchel. Because van Buchel found de Witt's letter and sketch of interest, he copied both into a book. It is van Buchel's copy, adapted, it seems, to the shape and size of the page in his book, that survives. In this sketch, the stage appears to be a large rectangular platform that thrusts far out into the yard, perhaps even as far as the center of the circle formed by the surrounding galleries. This drawing, combined with the specifications for the size of the stage in the building contract for the Fortune, has led scholars to conjecture that the stage on which Shakespeare's plays were performed must have measured approximately 43 feet in width and 27 feet in depth, a vast acting area. But the digging up of a large part of the Rose by archaeologists has provided evidence of a quite different stage design. The Rose stage was a platform tapered at the corners and much shallower than what seems to be depicted in the van Buchel sketch. Indeed, its measurements seem to be about 37.5 feet across at its widest point and only 15.5 feet deep. Because the surviving indications of stage size and design differ from each other so much, it is possible that the stages in other playhouses, like the Theatre, the Curtain, and the Globe (the outdoor playhouses where Shakespeare's plays were performed), were different from those at both the Swan and the Rose.

After about 1608 Shakespeare's plays were staged not only at the Globe but also at an indoor or private playhouse in Blackfriars. This theater had been constructed in 1596 by James Burbage in an upper hall of a former Dominican priory or monastic house. Although Henry VIII had dissolved all English monasteries in the 1530s (shortly after he had founded the Church of England), the area remained under church, rather than hostile civic, control. The hall that Burbage had purchased and renovated was a large one in which Parliament had once met. In the private theater that he constructed, the stage, lit by candles, was built across the narrow end of the hall, with boxes flanking it. The rest of the hall offered seating room only. Because there was no provision for standing room, the largest audience it could hold was less than a thousand, or about a quarter of what the Globe could accommodate. Admission to Blackfriars was correspondingly more expensive. Instead of a penny to stand in the yard at the Globe, it cost a minimum of sixpence to get into Blackfriars. The best seats at the Globe (in the Lords' Room in the gallery above and behind the stage) cost sixpence; but the boxes flanking the stage at Blackfriars were half a crown, or five times sixpence. Some spectators who were particularly interested in displaying themselves paid even more to sit on stools on the Blackfriars stage.

Whether in the outdoor or indoor playhouses, the stages of Shakespeare's time were different from ours. They were not separated from the audience by the dropping of a curtain between acts and scenes. Therefore the playwrights of the time had to find other ways of signaling to the audience that one scene (to be imagined as occurring in one location at a given time) had ended and the next (to be imagined at perhaps a different location at a later time) had begun. The customary way used by Shakespeare and many of his contemporaries was to have everyone onstage exit at the end of one scene and have one or more different characters enter to begin the next. In a few cases, where characters remain onstage from one scene to another, the dialogue or stage action makes the change of location clear, and the characters are generally to be imagined as having moved from one place to another. For example, in *Romeo and Juliet*, Romeo and his friends remain onstage in Act 1 from scene 4 to scene 5, but they are represented as having moved between scenes from the street that leads to Capulet's house into Capulet's house itself. The new location is signaled in part by the appearance onstage of Capulet's servingmen carrying napkins, something they would not take into the streets. Playwrights had to be quite resourceful in the use of hand properties, like the napkin, or in the use of dialogue to specify where the action was taking place in their plays because, in contrast to most of today's theaters, the playhouses of Shakespeare's time did not use movable scenery to dress the stage and make the setting precise. As another consequence of this difference, however, the playwrights of Shakespeare's time did not have to specify exactly where the action of their plays was set when they did not choose to do so, and much of the action of their plays is tied to no specific place.

Usually Shakespeare's stage is referred to as a "bare stage," to distinguish it from the stages of the last two or three centuries with their elaborate sets. But the stage in Shakespeare's time was not completely bare. Philip Henslowe, owner of the Rose, lists in his inventory of stage properties a rock, three tombs, and two mossy banks. Stage directions in plays of the time also call for such things as thrones (or "states"), banquets (presumably tables with plaster replicas of food on them), and beds and tombs to be pushed onto the stage. Thus the stage often held more than the actors.

The actors did not limit their performing to the stage alone. Occasionally they went beneath the stage, as the Ghost appears to do in the first act of *Hamlet*. From there they could emerge onto the stage through a trapdoor. They could retire behind the hangings across the back of the stage (or the front of the tiring house), as, for example, the actor playing Polonius does when he hides behind the arras. Sometimes the hangings could be drawn back during a performance to "discover" one or more actors behind them. When performance required that an actor appear "above," as when Juliet is imagined to stand at the window of her chamber in the famous and misnamed "balcony scene," then the actor probably climbed the stairs to the gallery over the back of the stage and temporarily shared it with some of the spectators. The stage was also provided with ropes and winches so that actors could descend from, and reascend to, the "heavens."

Perhaps the greatest difference between dramatic performances in Shakespeare's time and ours was that in Shakespeare's England the roles of women were played by boys. (Some of these boys grew up to take male roles in their maturity.) There were no women in the acting companies, only in the audience. It had not always been so in the history of the English stage. There are records of women on English stages in the thirteenth and fourteenth centuries, two hundred years before Shakespeare's plays were performed. After the accession of James I in 1603, the queen of England and her ladies took part in entertainments at court called masques, and with the reopening of the theaters in 1660 at the restoration of Charles II, women again took their place on the public stage.

The chief competitors for the companies of adult actors such as the one to which Shakespeare belonged and for which he wrote were companies of exclusively boy actors. The competition was most intense in the early 1600s. There were then two principal children's companies: the Children of Paul's (the choirboys from St. Paul's Cathedral, whose private playhouse was near the cathedral); and the Children of the Chapel Royal (the choirboys from the monarch's private chapel, who performed at the Blackfriars theater built by Burbage in 1596, which Shakespeare's company had been stopped from using by local residents who objected to crowds). In *Hamlet* Shakespeare writes of "an aerie [nest] of children, little eyases [hawks], that cry out on the top of question and are most tyrannically clapped for 't. These are now the fashion and . . . berattle the common stages [attack the public theaters]." In the long run, the adult actors prevailed. The Children of Paul's dissolved around 1606. By about 1608 the Children of the Chapel Royal had been forced to stop playing at the Blackfriars theater, which was then taken over by the King's company of players, Shakespeare's own troupe.

Acting companies and theaters of Shakespeare's time were organized in different ways. For example, Philip Henslowe owned the Rose and leased it to companies of actors, who paid him from their takings. Henslowe would act as manager of these companies, initially paying playwrights for their plays and buying properties, recovering his outlay from the actors. With the building of the Globe, Shakespeare's company, however, managed itself, with the principal actors, Shakespeare among them, having the status of "sharers" and the right to a share in the takings, as well as the responsibility for a part of the expenses. Five of the sharers, including Shakespeare, owned the Globe. As actor, as

sharer in an acting company and in ownership of theaters, and as playwright, Shakespeare was about as
involved in the theatrical industry as one could imagine. Although Shakespeare and his fellows prospered,
their status under the law was conditional upon the
protection of powerful patrons. "Common players"—
those who did not have patrons or masters—were
classed in the language of the law with "vagabonds and
sturdy beggars." So the actors had to secure for themselves the official rank of servants of patrons. Among
the patrons under whose protection Shakespeare's
company worked were the lord chamberlain and, after
the accession of King James in 1603, the king himself.

   We are now perhaps on the verge of learning a great
deal more about the theaters in which Shakespeare
and his contemporaries performed—or at least of
opening up new questions about them. Already about
70 percent of the Rose has been excavated, as has
about 10 percent of the second Globe, the one built in
1614. It is to be hoped that soon more will be available
for study. These are exciting times for students of
Shakespeare's stage.

The Publication of
Shakespeare's Plays

Eighteen of Shakespeare's plays found their way into
print during the playwright's lifetime, but there is nothing to suggest that he took any interest in their publication. These eighteen appeared separately in editions
called quartos. Their pages were not much larger than
the one you are now reading, and these little books

were sold unbound for a few pence. The earliest of the quartos that still survive were printed in 1594, the year that both *Titus Andronicus* and a version of the play now called *2 King Henry VI* became available. While almost every one of these early quartos displays on its title page the name of the acting company that performed the play, only about half provide the name of the playwright, Shakespeare. The first quarto edition to bear the name Shakespeare on its title page is *Love's Labor's Lost* of 1598. A few of these quartos were popular with the book-buying public of Shakespeare's lifetime; for example, quarto *Richard II* went through five editions between 1597 and 1615. But most of the quartos were far from best-sellers; *Love's Labor's Lost* (1598), for instance, was not reprinted in quarto until 1631. After Shakespeare's death, two more of his plays appeared in quarto format: *Othello* in 1622 and *The Two Noble Kinsmen,* coauthored with John Fletcher, in 1634.

In 1623, seven years after Shakespeare's death, *Mr. William Shakespeares Comedies, Histories, & Tragedies* was published. This printing offered readers in a single book thirty-six of the thirty-eight plays now thought to have been written by Shakespeare, including eighteen that had never been printed before. And it offered them in a style that was then reserved for serious literature and scholarship. The plays were arranged in double columns on pages nearly a foot high. This large page size is called "folio," as opposed to the smaller "quarto," and the 1623 volume is usually called the Shakespeare First Folio. It is reputed to have sold for the lordly price of a pound. (One copy at the Folger Library is marked fifteen shillings—that is, three-quarters of a pound.)

In a preface to the First Folio entitled "To the great

Variety of Readers," two of Shakespeare's former fellow actors in the King's Men, John Heminge and Henry Condell, wrote that they themselves had collected their dead companion's plays. They suggested that they had seen his own papers: "we have scarce received from him a blot in his papers." The title page of the Folio declared that the plays within it had been printed "according to the True Original Copies." Comparing the Folio to the quartos, Heminge and Condell disparaged the quartos, advising their readers that "before you were abused with divers stolen and surreptitious copies, maimed, and deformed by the frauds and stealths of injurious impostors." Many Shakespeareans of the eighteenth and nineteenth centuries believed Heminge and Condell and regarded the Folio plays as superior to anything in the quartos.

Once we begin to examine the Folio plays in detail, it becomes less easy to take at face value the word of Heminge and Condell about the superiority of the Folio texts. For example, of the first nine plays in the Folio (one-quarter of the entire collection), four were essentially reprinted from earlier quarto printings that Heminge and Condell had disparaged; and four have now been identified as printed from copies written in the hand of a professional scribe of the 1620s named Ralph Crane; the ninth, *The Comedy of Errors*, was apparently also printed from a manuscript, but one whose origin cannot be readily identified. Evidently then, eight of the first nine plays in the First Folio were not printed, in spite of what the Folio title page announces, "according to the True Original Copies," or Shakespeare's own papers, and the source of the ninth is unknown. Since today's editors have been forced to treat Heminge and Condell's pronouncements with skepticism, they must choose whether to base their own editions upon quartos or the Folio on grounds other than Heminge and Condell's story of where the quarto and Folio versions originated.

Editors have often fashioned their own narratives to explain what lies behind the quartos and Folio. They have said that Heminge and Condell meant to criticize only a few of the early quartos, the ones that offer much shorter and sometimes quite different, often garbled, versions of plays. Among the examples of these are the 1600 quarto of *Henry V* (the Folio offers a much fuller version) or the 1603 *Hamlet* quarto (in 1604 a different, much longer form of the play got into print as a quarto). Early-twentieth-century editors speculated that these questionable texts were produced when someone in the audience took notes from the plays' dialogue during performances and then employed "hack poets" to fill out the notes. The poor results were then sold to a publisher and presented in print as Shakespeare's plays. More recently this story has given way to another in which the shorter versions are said to be re-creations from memory of Shakespeare's plays by actors who wanted to stage them in the provinces but lacked manuscript copies. Most of the quartos offer much better texts than these so-called bad quartos. Indeed, in most of the quartos we find texts that are at least equal to or better than what is printed in the Folio. Many Shakespeare enthusiasts persuaded themselves that most of the quartos were set into type directly from Shakespeare's own papers, although there is nothing on which to base this conclusion except the desire for it to be true. Thus speculation continues about how the Shakespeare plays got to be printed. All that we have are the printed texts.

The book collector who was most successful in bringing together copies of the quartos and the First

Folio was Henry Clay Folger, founder of the Folger
Shakespeare Library in Washington, D.C. While it is
estimated that there survive around the world only
about 230 copies of the First Folio, Mr. Folger was
able to acquire more than seventy-five copies, as well
as a large number of fragments, for the library that
bears his name. He also amassed a substantial number
of quartos. For example, only fourteen copies of the
First Quarto of *Love's Labor's Lost* are known to exist,
and three are at the Folger Shakespeare Library. As a
consequence of Mr. Folger's labors, scholars visiting
the Folger Library have been able to learn a great deal
about sixteenth- and seventeenth-century printing
and, particularly, about the printing of Shakespeare's
plays. And Mr. Folger did not stop at the First Folio,
but collected many copies of later editions of Shakespeare, beginning with the Second Folio (1632), the
Third (1663–64), and the Fourth (1685). Each of these
later folios was based on its immediate predecessor
and was edited anonymously. The first editor of Shakespeare whose name we know was Nicholas Rowe,
whose first edition came out in 1709. Mr. Folger collected this edition and many, many more by Rowe's
successors.

An Introduction to This Text

A version of *The Merry Wives of Windsor* was first published in a quarto of 1602; this text is a little more than
half the length of the second version subsequently published in the 1623 collection of Shakespeare's plays
now known as the First Folio. Despite the variation in

length, the two published texts present substantially the same dramatic action. They also provide dialogue that is sometimes almost identical and that sometimes diverges widely.

The convergence and divergence of dialogue do not finally assume an intelligible pattern, even though the possibility of such a pattern may seem initially to emerge in connection with the entrances and exits of the character known as the Host of the Garter Inn (suggesting to some that the actor playing the Host was responsible for the Quarto text). Sometimes when the Host enters, the Quarto's dialogue, which has been quite divergent from the Folio's, suddenly snaps into nearly perfect alignment with the Folio's. This change occurs with the Host's entrances in 1.3, 2.1, 2.3, and 4.5. In some scenes as well, when the dialogue of both texts has been very nearly the same, it suddenly becomes very different with the Host's exit; a good example is to be found in 2.1. But striking as this pattern seems at first to be, it is not sustained. The Host's entrances in 3.1, 3.2, 4.3, and 4.6 do not make nearly the difference that his other four entrances do, and occasionally the convergence of the two texts' dialogue is much more impressive when the Host is offstage than when he is onstage. For example, immediately following the entrance of Falstaff, Pistol, Bardolph, and Nym in 1.1, the dialogue of the two texts suddenly converges, even though the two texts had just previously borne virtually no verbal resemblance to each other. (For further discussion of this topic and examples of Quarto dialogue, see Paul Werstine's "A Century of 'Bad' Shakespeare Quartos," *Shakespeare Quarterly* 50 [1999]: 310–33.)

From this evidence, many have argued that the Quarto is to some extent a memorial reconstruction

A

Moſt pleaſaunt and

excellent conceited Co-
medie, of Syr *Iohn Falſtaffe*, and the
merrie Wiues of *Windſor*.

Entermixed with ſundrie

variable and pleaſing humors, of Syr *Hugh*
the Welch Knight, Iuſtice *Shallow*, and his
wiſe Couſin M. *Slender*.

With the ſwaggering vaine of Auncient
Piſtoll, and Corporall *Nym*.

By *William Shakeſpeare*.

As it hath bene diuers times Acted by the right Honorable
my Lord Chamberlaines ſeruants. Both before her
Maieſtie, and elſe-where.

LONDON

Printed by T. C. for Arthur Iohnſon, and are to be ſold at
his ſhop in Powles Church-yard, at the ſigne of the
Flower de Leuſe and the Crowne.
1602.

Title page of the 1602 Quarto of
The Merry Wives of Windsor.
(From the Folger Library collection.)

THE
Merry Wiues of Windsor.

Actus primus, Scena prima.

Enter Iustice Shallow, Slender, Sir Hugh Euans, Master Page, Falstaffe, Bardolph, Nym, Pistoll, Anne Page, Mistresse Ford, Mistresse Page, Simple.

Shallow.

SIr *Hugh*, perswade me not: I will make a Star-Chamber matter of it, if hee were twenty Sir *Iohn Falstaffe*, he shall not abuse *Robert Shallow* Esquire. (*Coram*.

Slen. In the County of *Glocester*, Iustice of Peace and *Cust-alorum*.

Shal. I (Cosen *Slender*) and *Cust-alorum*.

Slen. I, and *Rato lorum* too : and a Gentleman borne (Master *Parson*) who writes himselfe *Armigero*, in any Bill, Warrant, Quittance, or Obligation, *Armigero*.

Shal. I that I doe, and haue done any time these three hundred yeeres.

Slen. All his successors (gone before him) hath don't: and all his Ancestors (that come after him) may : they may giue the dozen white Luces in their Coate.

Shal. It is an olde Coate.

Euans. The dozen white Lowses doe become an old Coat well : it agrees well passant : It is a familiar beast to man, and signifies Loue.

Shal. The Luse is the fresh-fish, the salt-fish, is an old Coate.

Slen. I may quarter (Coz.)

Shal. You may, by marrying.

Euans. It is marring indeed, if he quarter it.

Shal. Not a whit.

Euan. Yes per-lady : if he ha's a quarter of your coat, there is but three Skirts for your selfe, in my simple coniectures ; but that is all one : if Sir *Iohn Falstaffe* haue committed disparagements vnto you, I am of the Church and will be glad to do my beneuolence, to make attonements and compremifes betweene you.

Shal. The Councell shall heare it, it is a Riot.

Euan. It is not meet the Councell heare a Riot : there is no feare of Got in a Riot : The Councell (looke you) shall desire to heare the feare of Got, and not to heare a Riot : take your viza-ments in that.

Shal. Ha ; o'my life, if I were yong againe, the sword should end it.

Euans. It is petter that friends is the sword, and end it : and there is also another deuice in my praine, which peraduenture prings goot discretions with it; There is *Anne Page*, which is daughter to Master *Thomas Page*, which is pretty virginity.

Slen. Mistris *Anne Page?* she has browne haire, and speakes small like a woman.

Euans. It is that ferry person for all the orld, as iust as you will desire, and seuen hundred pounds of Moneyes, and Gold, and Siluer, is her Grand-sire vpon his deaths-bed, (Got deliuer to a ioyfull resurrection) giue, when she is able to ouertake scuenteene yeeres old. It were a goot motion, if we leaue our pribbles and prabbles, and desire a marriage betweene Master *Abraham*, and Mistris *Anne Page*.

Slen. Did her Grand-sire leaue her seauen hundred pound?

Euan. I, and her father is make her a petter penny.

Slen. I know the young Gentlewoman, she has good gifts.

Euan. Seuen hundred pounds, and possibilities, is goot gifts.

Shal. Wel, let vs see honest Mr *Page* is *Falstaffe* there?

Euan. Shall I tell you a lye? I doe despise a lyer, as I doe despise one that is false, or as I despise one that is not true : the Knight Sir *Iohn* is there, and I beseech you be ruled by your well-willers : I will peat the doore for Mr. *Page.* What hoa? Got-plesse your house heere.

Mr. Page. Who's there?

Euan. Here is gu't's plessing and your friend, and Iustice *Shallow*, and heere yong Master *Slender* : that peraduentures shall tell you another tale, if matters grow to your likings.

Mr. Page. I am glad to see your Worships well : I thanke you for my Venison Master *Shalow*.

Shal. Master *Page*, I am glad to see you : much good doe it your good heart : I wish'd your Venison better, it was ill kill'd : how doth good Mistresse *Page?* and I thank you alwaies with my heart, la : with my heart.

Mr. Page. Sir, I thanke you.

Shal. Sir, I thanke you : by yea, and no I doe.

M. Pa. I am glad to see you, good Master *Slender*.

Slen. How do's your fallow Greyhound, Sir, I heard say he was out-run on *Cotsall*.

M. Pa. It could not be iudg'd, Sir.

Slen. You'll not confesse : you'll not confesse.

Shal. That he will not, 'tis your fault, 'tis your fault : 'tis a good dogge.

M. Pa. A Cur, Sir.

Shal. Sir : hee's a good dog, and a faire dog, can there be more said? he is good, and faire. Is Sir *Iohn Falstaffe* heere?

M. Pa. Sir, hee is within : and I would I could doe a good office betweene you.

Euan. It is spoke as a Christians ought to speake.

Shal. He hath wrong'd mee (Master *Page*.)

M. Pa. Sir, he doth in some sort confesse it.

From the 1623 First Folio.
(Copy 3 in the Folger Library collection.)

of what was later published in the Folio—in other words, that Quarto and Folio constitute two versions of the same text of the play, the Folio simply being much more successful than the Quarto in reproducing this single text. However, if the Quarto indeed represents an effort to re-create the Folio text, that effort was carried out quite sporadically. It is therefore equally possible that the Quarto represents, however imperfectly, another version of the play—a version not wholly but nonetheless still widely divergent from the Folio. We as editors have therefore felt that we could draw on the Quarto for a reading to correct an evident error in the Folio only if there is, at that point in the dialogue, a very high level of convergence between the two texts.

But the Quarto is useful to editors for its many stage directions. These are valuable because the Folio, in contrast, contains almost no stage directions; it includes only lists of the characters that are to appear in each scene. These lists are printed at the head of each scene, even though in many cases a number of the named characters do not enter until late in the scene. (The single exception to this pattern is the mid-scene stage direction *"Enter Fairies."* at 5.5.39.) Scholars have convincingly argued that such mass entries derive from the scribe Ralph Crane, who used this style of stage direction in some of his surviving transcripts of non-Shakespearean plays and who is thought, on good grounds, to have prepared printer's copy for some of the plays in the Folio. Whatever the origin of the Folio's stage directions, they need to be supplemented in the editing of a modern edition. We have drawn liberally from the Quarto's stage directions in this edition, sometimes emending them to make them conform to modern idiom or to bring them into agreement with the Folio's dialogue.

In spite of our occasional reference to the Quarto

for readings and, more often, for stage directions, this present edition remains an edition of the Folio printing of the play.* For the convenience of the reader, we have modernized the punctuation and the spelling of the Folio. Sometimes we go so far as to modernize certain old forms of words; for example, usually when *a* means *he*, we change it to *he;* we change *mo* to *more*, and *ye* to *you*. But it is not our practice in editing any of the plays to modernize words that sound distinctly different from modern forms. For example, when the early printed texts read *sith* or *apricocks* or *porpentine*, we have not modernized to *since, apricots, porcupine*. When the forms *an, and,* or *and if* appear instead of the modern form *if*, we have reduced *and* to *an* but have not changed any of these forms to their modern equivalent, *if*. We also modernize and, where necessary, correct passages in foreign languages, unless an error in the early printed text can be reasonably explained as a joke. (For our treatment of Dr. Caius's French, see the longer note to 1.4.64, page 208.)

Whenever we change the wording of the First Folio or add anything to its stage directions, we mark the change by enclosing it in superior half-brackets (⌈ ⌉). We want our readers to be immediately aware when we have intervened. (Only when we correct an obvious typographical error in the First Folio does the change not get marked.) Whenever we change either the First Folio's wording or its punctuation so that meaning changes, we list the change in the textual notes at the back of the book, even if all we have done is fix an obvious error.

We regularize spellings of a number of the proper

---

*We have also consulted the computerized text of the First Folio provided by the Text Archive of the Oxford University Computing Centre, to which we are grateful.

names, as is the usual practice in modern editions of the play. For example, the Folio sometimes calls Falstaff by the names "Falstaffe," "Falstaff," "Falstaf," "Falstoffe," and "Falstoff," and once calls Fenton by the name "Fenten," but we use the spellings "Falstaff" and "Fenton" throughout the text.

This edition differs from many earlier ones in its efforts to aid the reader in imagining the play as a performance rather than as a series of actual events. For example, when the fiction of the play calls for one character to give another a letter or letters, the onstage action will show one actor giving another a paper or papers. Thus our stage directions usually indicate an exchange of papers, not of fictional letters, unless such a direction might cause confusion. When, for example, the play presents Mistress Page reading a letter at the beginning of Act 2, we do not say that she is reading "a paper," because such a stage direction might well lead readers to imagine her reading something besides a letter, say, a newspaper. Whenever it is reasonably certain, in our view, that a speech is accompanied by a particular action, we provide a stage direction describing the action, setting the added direction in brackets to signal that it is not found in the Folio. (Occasional exceptions to this rule occur when the action is so obvious that to add a stage direction would insult the reader.) Stage directions for the entrance of a character in mid-scene are, with rare exceptions, silently placed so that they immediately precede the character's participation in the scene, even though these entrances appear at the beginning of the scene in the Folio text. The textual notes include the full text of the Folio stage directions and record their positions in the text. Latin stage directions (e.g., *Exeunt*) are translated into English (e.g., *They exit*).

We expand the often severely abbreviated forms of names used as speech headings in early printed texts into the full names of the characters. We also regularize the speakers' names in speech headings, using only a single designation for each character, even though the early printed texts sometimes use a variety of designations. Variations in the speech headings of the early printed texts are recorded in the textual notes.

In the present edition, as well, we mark with a dash any change of address within a speech, unless a stage direction intervenes. When the -ed ending of a word is to be pronounced, we mark it with an accent. Like editors for the past two centuries, we print metrically linked lines in the following way:

ANNE
  Alas, how then?
FENTON   Why, thou must be thyself.
                            (3.4.3—4)

However, when there are a number of short verse-lines that can be linked in more than one way, we do not, with rare exceptions, indent any of them.

The Explanatory Notes

The notes that appear on the pages facing the text are designed to provide readers with the help that they may need to enjoy the play. Whenever the meaning of a word in the text is not readily accessible in a good contemporary dictionary, we offer the meaning in a note. Sometimes we provide a note even when the relevant meaning is to be found in the dictionary but when the word has acquired since Shakespeare's time other potentially confusing meanings. In our notes, we try to offer modern synonyms for Shakespeare's words. We also try to indicate to the reader the connection between the word in the play and the modern synonym. For example, Shakespeare sometimes uses the word *head* to mean *source*, but, for modern readers, there may be no connection evident between these two words. We provide the connection by explaining Shakespeare's usage as follows: **"head:** fountainhead, source." On some occasions, a whole phrase or clause needs explanation. Then we rephrase in our own words the difficult passage, and add at the end synonyms for individual words in the passage. When scholars have been unable to determine the meaning of a word or phrase, we acknowledge the uncertainty. Whenever we provide a passage from the Bible to illuminate the text of the play, we use the Geneva Bible of 1560, with the spelling modernized.

THE
MERRY WIVES
OF WINDSOR

Characters in the Play

MISTRESS FORD
FORD, her husband
JOHN
ROBERT } their servants

MISTRESS PAGE
PAGE, her husband
ANNE, their daughter
WILLIAM, their son

DOCTOR CAIUS, a French doctor, suitor to Anne Page
MISTRESS QUICKLY, the doctor's housekeeper
JOHN RUGBY, the doctor's manservant

SIR HUGH Evans, a Welsh parson

HOST of the Garter Inn

Windsor Children, disguised as fairies

Sir John FALSTAFF, an impoverished knight
ROBIN, his page
BARDOLPH
PISTOL } Falstaff's servants
NYM

FENTON, a gentleman, suitor to Anne Page

Robert SHALLOW, a visiting justice of the peace
Abraham SLENDER, his nephew, a young gentleman suitor
    to Anne Page
SIMPLE, Slender's servant

THE
MERRY WIVES
OF WINDSOR

ACT 1

1.1 Justice Shallow and his nephew Slender accompany Sir Hugh the parson to the Pages' home. There they meet Sir John Falstaff, whom Shallow accuses of killing his deer, while Slender accuses Falstaff's men of robbing him. Falstaff meets Mistress Ford and Mistress Page, and Slender clumsily attempts to court Anne Page.

———

0 SD. **Sir:** a title of courtesy for a clergyman

1. **persuade me not:** do not try to convince me

2. **Star-Chamber:** the highest court in England (See longer note, page 205.)

4. **Esquire:** title one degree below knighthood

5. **Gloucester:** i.e., Gloucestershire

6. **Coram:** used in confusion for the Latin *quorum* (a title for select judges)

7. **Cousin:** kinsman; **Custalorum:** a corruption of **custos rotulorum,** Latin for "keeper of the rolls," a title for the chief justice of peace in a county

8. **Ratolorum:** Slender's corruption of **rotulorum,** which he adds in ignorance of the repetition

9. **writes himself:** designates himself by the title; **Armigero:** *Armiger* is Latin for "Esquire."

10. **bill:** i.e., deed; **quittance:** receipt; **obligation:** contract

12–13. **Ay . . . years:** Shallow confuses himself with his lineage.

14–16. **All . . . may:** Slender transposes **successors** and **ancestors**—one of his many errors.

16–17. **give . . . coat:** i.e., display a **dozen white luces** (freshwater pike) **in their coat** of arms (See picture, page 144.)

(continued)

6

ACT 1

Scene 1

Enter Justice Shallow, Slender, ⌈and⌉ Sir Hugh Evans.

SHALLOW   Sir Hugh, persuade me not. I will make a
    Star-Chamber matter of it. If he were twenty Sir
    John Falstaffs, he shall not abuse Robert Shallow,
    Esquire.

SLENDER   In the county of Gloucester, Justice of Peace   5
    and Coram.

SHALLOW   Ay, Cousin Slender, and Custalorum.

SLENDER   Ay, and Ratolorum too; and a gentleman born,
    Master Parson, who writes himself "Armigero"
    in any bill, warrant, quittance, or obligation—   10
    "Armigero!"

SHALLOW   Ay, that I do, and have done any time these
    three hundred years.

SLENDER   All his successors gone before him hath
    done 't, and all his ancestors that come after him   15
    may. They may give the dozen white luces in their
    coat.

SHALLOW   It is an old coat.

SIR HUGH   The dozen white louses do become an old
    coat well. It agrees well, passant. It is a familiar   20
    beast to man and signifies love.

SHALLOW   The luce is the fresh fish. The salt fish is an
    old coat.

SLENDER   I may quarter, coz.

7

18. **old coat:** ancient **coat** of arms

20. **well, passant:** i.e., passing (surpassingly) **well** (with wordplay on **passant** as a heraldic term)

20–21. **It . . . man:** Proverbial: "A louse is a man's companion."

22. **fresh:** freshwater; **salt:** saltwater

23. **coat:** perhaps a joke about Sir Hugh's pronunciation of **coat** as "cod"

24. **quarter:** add to one's coat of arms that of the family into which one marries so that each coat appears twice (See picture, page 176.) **coz:** cousin

26. **marring:** Proverbial: "Marrying is **marring**." **quarter it:** i.e., cut the **coat** into quarters

28. **py'r Lady:** i.e., by Our Lady (an oath on the name of the Virgin Mary) Shakespeare gives Sir Hugh language that parodies a Welsh-accented English. Thus Sir Hugh regularly substitutes *p* for *b* at the beginning of words; he also confuses *d* with *t* and *f* with *v*, and omits *w* at the beginning of such words as "world" and "woman."

29. **is:** i.e., are (Sir Hugh also confuses singular and plural forms.) **three skirts:** i.e., **three** of the four panels (or tails) on a long **coat**

32–33. **do my benevolence:** i.e., lend my friendly offices

33. **atonements:** reconciliation, concord

35. **Council:** i.e., Court of Star Chamber (See longer note on 1.1.2, page 205.) Sir Hugh uses **Council** to mean "**Council** of the Church" (line 36).

36. **meet:** i.e., appropriate that

37. **Got:** i.e., God

39. **Take your visaments:** i.e., **take** advisement, consider

(continued)

SHALLOW	You may, by marrying.	25
SIR HUGH	It is marring indeed, if he quarter it.	
SHALLOW	Not a whit.	

SIR HUGH   Yes, py'r Lady. If he has a quarter of your coat, there is but three skirts for yourself, in my simple conjectures. But that is all one. If Sir John 30 Falstaff have committed disparagements unto you, I am of the Church, and will be glad to do my benevolence to make atonements and compromises between you.

SHALLOW   The Council shall hear it; it is a riot. 35

SIR HUGH   It is not meet the Council hear a riot. There is no fear of Got in a riot. The Council, look you, shall desire to hear the fear of Got, and not to hear a riot. Take your visaments in that.

SHALLOW   Ha! O' my life, if I were young again, the 40 sword should end it.

SIR HUGH   It is petter that friends is the sword, and end it. And there is also another device in my prain, which peradventure prings goot discretions with it. There is Anne Page, which is daughter to Master 45 Thomas Page, which is pretty virginity.

SLENDER   Mistress Anne Page? She has brown hair and speaks small like a woman?

SIR HUGH   It is that fery person for all the 'orld, as just as you will desire. And seven hundred pounds of 50 moneys, and gold, and silver, is her grandsire upon his death's-bed (Got deliver to a joyful resurrections!) give, when she is able to overtake seventeen years old. It were a goot motion if we leave our pribbles and prabbles, and desire a marriage be- 55 tween Master Abraham and Mistress Anne Page.

SLENDER   Did her grandsire leave her seven hundred pound?

SIR HUGH   Ay, and her father is make her a petter penny. 60

42. **It . . . sword:** perhaps, "**It is** better to employ **friends** than **the sword.**"

44. **peradventure:** perhaps; **discretions:** i.e., judgment, decision

45. **Master:** used for modern "Mr."

46. **Thomas:** Elsewhere Page's first name is given as George. **which . . . virginity:** i.e., (and) who is a pretty virgin

47. **Mistress:** used for modern "Miss," "Mrs.," and "Ms."

48. **small:** i.e., quietly, gently

49. **as just:** i.e., exactly

51–53. **is her grandsire . . . give:** i.e., has her grandfather . . . given her

54. **motion:** suggestion

55. **pribbles and prabbles:** perhaps, brabbles (i.e., quibbles; paltry altercations; frivolous lawsuits)

56. **Master Abraham:** i.e., Slender

59–60. **is . . . penny:** i.e., will provide her with more money (proverbial: "**a** better **penny**")

61. **gentlewoman:** woman of good birth

62. **gifts:** natural endowments

63. **possibilities:** prospects of coming into money

65. **honest:** worthy

70. **well-willers:** those who wish you well

76. **another tale:** i.e., something more

78. **your Worships:** a title of honor

82. **ill:** unskillfully; wrongfully

86. **by yea and no:** a Puritan oath (See Matthew 5.34–37: "Swear not at all, . . . but let your communication be yea, yea; nay, nay.")

88. **fallow:** light brown

(continued)

10

SLENDER I know the young gentlewoman. She has
   good gifts.

SIR HUGH Seven hundred pounds and possibilities is
   goot gifts.

SHALLOW Well, let us see honest Master Page. Is Fal-   65
   staff there?

SIR HUGH Shall I tell you a lie? I do despise a liar as I
   do despise one that is false, or as I despise one that
   is not true. The knight Sir John is there, and I beseech you be ruled by your well-willers. I will peat   70
   the door for Master Page. ⌐*He knocks.*⌐ What ho?
   Got pless your house here.

PAGE, ⌐*within*⌐ Who's there?

SIR HUGH Here is Got's plessing, and your friend, and
   Justice Shallow, and here young Master Slender,   75
   that peradventures shall tell you another tale, if
   matters grow to your likings.

Enter Master Page.

PAGE I am glad to see your Worships well. I thank you
   for my venison, Master Shallow.

SHALLOW Master Page, I am glad to see you. Much   80
   good do it your good heart! I wished your venison
   better; it was ill killed. How doth good Mistress
   Page? And I thank you always with my heart, la,
   with my heart.

PAGE Sir, I thank you.   85

SHALLOW Sir, I thank you; by yea and no, I do.

PAGE I am glad to see you, good Master Slender.

SLENDER How does your fallow greyhound, sir? I
   heard say he was outrun on Cotsall.

PAGE It could not be judged, sir.   90

SLENDER You'll not confess, you'll not confess.

SHALLOW That he will not. 'Tis your fault, 'tis your
   fault. 'Tis a good dog.

PAGE A cur, sir.

89. **on Cotsall:** i.e., in the Cotswold hills (presumably in coursing matches)

92. **'Tis your fault:** perhaps, you (Slender) are to blame (for teasing Page about his dog); or, perhaps, it is your mistake

94. **A cur:** an ordinary dog

96. **good . . . fair:** racing jargon

98. **would:** wish

99. **office:** service, kindness

102. **in some sort:** to some extent

103. **If . . . redressed:** Proverbial: "Confession of a fault is half amends."

105. **at a word:** i.e., without more ado, in short

109. **King:** The overlap of this play's characters with Shakespeare's history plays places it in the reign of Henry IV or Henry V.

111. **lodge:** house in a forest that serves as a temporary residence during hunting season

112. **keeper's:** i.e., gamekeeper's

113. **pin:** trifle; **answered:** satisfied, recompensed

114. **answer:** reply to; **straight:** straightway

117–18. **in counsel:** in private, in confidence

119. **Pauca verba:** few words (Latin); **worts:** Sir Hugh's pronunciation of *words* (but used by Falstaff with its meaning "coleworts, cabbages")

121. **broke your head:** cut your scalp with a blow; **matter:** allegation

123. **Marry:** i.e., indeed; **matter:** (1) allegations; (2) pus

124. **cony-catching:** cheating

126. **You Banbury cheese:** An appropriate attack on Slender's name and (presumably) appear-

(continued)

SHALLOW   Sir, he's a good dog and a fair dog. Can there   95
   be more said? He is good and fair. Is Sir John Falstaff here?

PAGE   Sir, he is within, and I would I could do a good
   office between you.

SIR HUGH   It is spoke as a Christians ought to speak.   100

SHALLOW   He hath wronged me, Master Page.

PAGE   Sir, he doth in some sort confess it.

SHALLOW   If it be confessed, it is not redressed. Is not
   that so, Master Page? He hath wronged me, indeed
   he hath; at a word, he hath. Believe me. Robert   105
   Shallow, Esquire, saith he is wronged.

Enter ⌜Sir John⌝ Falstaff, Bardolph, Nym, ⌜and⌝ Pistol.

PAGE   Here comes Sir John.

FALSTAFF   Now, Master Shallow, you'll complain of me
   to the King?

SHALLOW   Knight, you have beaten my men, killed my   110
   deer, and broke open my lodge.

FALSTAFF   But not kissed your keeper's daughter.

SHALLOW   Tut, a pin. This shall be answered.

FALSTAFF   I will answer it straight: I have done all this.
   That is now answered.   115

SHALLOW   The Council shall know this.

FALSTAFF   'Twere better for you if it were known in
   counsel. You'll be laughed at.

SIR HUGH   *Pauca verba*, Sir John, good worts.

FALSTAFF   Good worts? Good cabbage!—Slender, I   120
   broke your head. What matter have you against
   me?

SLENDER   Marry, sir, I have matter in my head against
   you and against your cony-catching rascals, Bardolph, Nym, and Pistol.   125

BARDOLPH   You Banbury cheese!

SLENDER   Ay, it is no matter.

PISTOL   How now, Mephostophilus?

ance, since Banbury cheeses were proverbial for their thinness (being only an inch or so thick).

127. **it . . . matter:** i.e., never mind

128. **Mephostophilus:** i.e., Mephistopheles (Pistol's speech is characterized by mangled lines of poetry, archaic language, and scraps of verse from other plays.)

130. **Slice:** perhaps a threat of swordplay; **Pauca:** i.e., *Pauca verba*, as in line 119; **humór:** mood (but see longer note to 1.1.161, page 205)

131. **man:** i.e., manservant

135. **fidelicet:** i.e., *videlicet* (Latin for "namely")

137. **mine . . . Garter:** the landlord of the **Garter** Inn (For the connection between Windsor and the Order of the Garter, see longer note, page 205.)

139. **prief:** i.e., brief, summary, short account

143. **He . . . ears:** Perhaps an allusion to Psalm 44.1: "We have heard with our ears."

144. **tam:** i.e., dam, or mother (Proverbial: "The devil and his dam.")

149. **seven groats:** i.e., 28 pence worth; **mill-sixpences:** silver sixpences stamped in a mill (Slender's arithmetic is inaccurate.)

150. **Edward shovel-boards:** shillings minted during the reign of Edward VI (1547–53) (These coins, once they were worn smooth, were used in playing the game shovel-board, the antecedent to present-day shuffleboard. Slender paid more than twice their face value for them.)

151. **Yed:** Ed, or Ned

154. **it:** i.e., he; **pickpurse:** i.e., pickpocket

(continued)

14

SLENDER   Ay, it is no matter.

NYM   Slice, I say! *Pauca, pauca.* Slice, that's my humor.   130

SLENDER, ⌜(*to Shallow*)⌝ Where's Simple, my man?
   Can you tell, cousin?

SIR HUGH   Peace, I pray you. Now let us understand;
   there is three umpires in this matter, as I understand: that is, Master Page (*fidelicet* Master Page);   135
   and there is myself (*fidelicet* myself); and the three
   party is, lastly and finally, mine Host of the Garter.

PAGE   We three to hear it and end it between them.

SIR HUGH   Fery goot. I will make a prief of it in my
   notebook, and we will afterwards 'ork upon the   140
   cause with as great discreetly as we can.

FALSTAFF   Pistol.

PISTOL   He hears with ears.

SIR HUGH   The tevil and his tam! What phrase is this,
   "He hears with ear"? Why, it is affectations.   145

FALSTAFF   Pistol, did you pick Master Slender's purse?

SLENDER   Ay, by these gloves, did he—or I would I
   might never come in mine own great chamber
   again else—of seven groats in mill-sixpences,
   and two Edward shovel-boards that cost me two   150
   shilling and twopence apiece of Yed Miller, by
   these gloves.

FALSTAFF   Is this true, Pistol?

SIR HUGH   No, it is false, if it is a pickpurse.

PISTOL   Ha, thou mountain foreigner!—Sir John and   155
   master mine, I combat challenge of this latten
   bilbo.—Word of denial in thy *labras* here! Word of
   denial! Froth and scum, thou liest.

SLENDER, ⌜*indicating Nym*⌝ By these gloves, then 'twas
   he.   160

NYM   Be avised, sir, and pass good humors. I will say
   "marry trap with you" if you run the nuthook's
   humor on me. That is the very note of it.

155. **mountain foreigner:** i.e., Welshman (alluding to the mountains of Wales)

156. **combat challenge of:** i.e., **challenge** to a duel or to a trial by combat; **latten:** yellow brasslike metal alloy (greatly inferior to steel)

157. **bilbo:** sword (from the Spanish town Bilbao, where fine swords were made); **labras:** lips (a corruption of the Latin *labra*)

161. **Be advised:** (1) act only after consideration; (2) seek counsel; **humors:** See longer note, page 205.

162. **marry . . . you:** an unexplained insult

162–63. **run . . . me:** i.e., threaten me with a constable

168. **Scarlet and John:** the names of two of Robin Hood's companions (Will **Scarlet** and Little **John**)—both names apparently used to address Bardolph, whose **red face** (line 164) suggests the name **Scarlet**

173. **fap:** drunk

174. **cashiered:** dismissed

174–75. **passed the careers:** took short gallops at full speed (a term from horsemanship)

178. **for:** because of

181. **mind:** intention

SD 189. **He kisses her:** a polite salutation in this time period

191. **pasty to:** pie for

194. **Songs and Sonnets:** the title of a collection of poems published first in 1557 and regularly thereafter for most of the rest of the sixteenth century

SLENDER   By this hat, then, he in the red face had it.
For, though I cannot remember what I did when   165
you made me drunk, yet I am not altogether an
ass.

FALSTAFF   What say you, Scarlet and John?

BARDOLPH   Why, sir, for my part, I say the gentleman
had drunk himself out of his five sentences.   170

SIR HUGH   It is "his five senses." Fie, what the ignorance is!

BARDOLPH, ⌈*to Falstaff*⌉ And being fap, sir, was, as
they say, cashiered. And so conclusions passed the
careers.   175

SLENDER   Ay, you spake in Latin then too. But 'tis no
matter. I'll ne'er be drunk whilst I live again but in
honest, civil, godly company, for this trick. If I be
drunk, I'll be drunk with those that have the fear of
God, and not with drunken knaves.   180

SIR HUGH   So Got 'udge me, that is a virtuous mind.

FALSTAFF   You hear all these matters denied, gentlemen. You hear it.

Enter Anne Page ⌈*with wine.*⌉

PAGE   Nay, daughter, carry the wine in. We'll drink
within.   ⌈*Anne Page exits.*⌉   185

SLENDER   O heaven, this is Mistress Anne Page.

Enter Mistress Ford ⌈*and*⌉ *Mistress Page.*

PAGE   How now, Mistress Ford?

FALSTAFF   Mistress Ford, by my troth, you are very well
met. By your leave, good mistress. ⌈*He kisses her.*⌉

PAGE   Wife, bid these gentlemen welcome.—Come, we   190
have a hot venison pasty to dinner. Come, gentlemen, I hope we shall drink down all unkindness.
            ⌈*All but Slender, Shallow, and Sir Hugh exit.*⌉

SLENDER   I had rather than forty shillings I had my
book of *Songs and Sonnets* here!

196–97. **Book of Riddles:** often used as a conversational aid (See longer note, page 206, and picture, page 118.)

199. **Allhallowmas:** November 1

200. **Michaelmas:** September 29 (perhaps Simple's error for **Martlemas**, November 11)

201. **stay:** wait

203. **tender:** offer

204. **afar off:** indirectly (literally, at a distance)

209. **motions:** proposal

214. **country:** district; **simple . . . here:** an apologetic or modest phrase   **simple:** undistinguished

221. **demands:** requests

224. **parcel of:** i.e., part of

Enter Simple.

How now, Simple? Where have you been? I must   195
wait on myself, must I? You have not the *Book of
Riddles* about you, have you?

SIMPLE   *Book of Riddles?* Why, did you not lend it to
Alice Shortcake upon Allhallowmas last, a fort-
night afore Michaelmas?   200

SHALLOW, ⌈*to Slender*⌉ Come, coz; come, coz. We stay
for you. A word with you, coz. Marry, this, coz:
there is, as 'twere, a tender, a kind of tender, made
afar off by Sir Hugh here. Do you understand me?

SLENDER   Ay, sir, you shall find me reasonable. If it be   205
so, I shall do that that is reason.

SHALLOW   Nay, but understand me.

SLENDER   So I do, sir.

SIR HUGH   Give ear to his motions, Master Slender. I
will description the matter to you, if you be capac-   210
ity of it.

SLENDER   Nay, I will do as my cousin Shallow says. I
pray you, pardon me. He's a Justice of Peace in his
country, simple though I stand here.

SIR HUGH   But that is not the question. The question is   215
concerning your marriage.

SHALLOW   Ay, there's the point, sir.

SIR HUGH   Marry, is it, the very point of it—to Mistress
Anne Page.

SLENDER   Why, if it be so, I will marry her upon any   220
reasonable demands.

SIR HUGH   But can you affection the 'oman? Let us command to know that of your mouth, or of your lips;
for divers philosophers hold that the lips is parcel of
the mouth. Therefore, precisely, can you carry your   225
good will to the maid?

SHALLOW   Cousin Abraham Slender, can you love her?

231. **positable:** perhaps Sir Hugh's corruption of "positively"

233. **upon:** i.e., conditionally upon

237. **conceive:** understand

240–44. **But if . . . another:** Slender's nonsensical version of the proverb "Marry first and love will come after."

245. **content:** The proverb "Familiarity breeds contempt" leads some editors to change **content** to "contempt."

248. **fall:** perhaps for "fault"

253. **fair:** beautiful (but also, probably, light-skinned and light-haired, for these features then constituted beauty)

257. **wait on:** i.e., join (literally, visit)

SLENDER   I hope, sir, I will do as it shall become one
that would do reason.

SIR HUGH   Nay, Got's lords and His ladies! You must   230
speak positable, if you can carry her your desires
towards her.

SHALLOW   That you must. Will you, upon good dowry,
marry her?

SLENDER   I will do a greater thing than that, upon your   235
request, cousin, in any reason.

SHALLOW   Nay, conceive me, conceive me, sweet coz.
What I do is to pleasure you, coz. Can you love the
maid?

SLENDER   I will marry her, sir, at your request. But if   240
there be no great love in the beginning, yet heaven
may decrease it upon better acquaintance, when
we are married and have more occasion to know
one another. I hope upon familiarity will grow
more content. But if you say "Marry her," I will   245
marry her. That I am freely dissolved, and dissolutely.

SIR HUGH   It is a fery discretion answer, save the fall is
in the 'ord "dissolutely." The 'ort is, according to
our meaning, "resolutely." His meaning is good.   250

SHALLOW   Ay, I think my cousin meant well.

SLENDER   Ay, or else I would I might be hanged, la!

⌜*Enter Anne Page.*⌝

SHALLOW   Here comes fair Mistress Anne.—Would I
were young for your sake, Mistress Anne.

ANNE   The dinner is on the table. My father desires   255
your Worships' company.

SHALLOW   I will wait on him, fair Mistress Anne.

SIR HUGH   'Od's plessèd will, I will not be absence at
the grace.   ⌜*Sir Hugh and Shallow exit.*⌝

ANNE, ⌜*to Slender*⌝   Will 't please your Worship to come   260
in, sir?

262. **forsooth:** in truth, indeed

264. **attends:** awaits

266. **sirrah:** term of address to a male social inferior; **for all:** even though

267. **wait upon:** attend

268. **beholding:** i.e., beholden, obliged

269. **friend:** kinsman, relative; **man:** male servant

270. **what though:** i.e., **what** of that

277–81. **I bruised . . . since:** Slender attributes his lack of appetite for hot food to his association of his **bruised shin** with eating hot **stewed prunes.** (Since **stewed prunes** were associated with brothels and **hot meat** was a term applied to prostitutes, Slender's explanation is filled with double meanings.) **fence:** fencing **veneys:** bouts of fencing

284. **sport:** i.e., bearbaiting (in which a bear chained by the neck to a post was attacked by mastiffs) See picture, page 152.

284–85. **quarrel at it:** i.e., **quarrel** with other spectators during **it**

289. **Sackerson:** a famous bear kept in Southwark Bear Garden, near the Globe playhouse

291. **passed:** surpassed description

292–93. **ill-favored:** ugly

294. **stay:** wait

SLENDER   No, I thank you, forsooth, heartily. I am very
well.

ANNE   The dinner attends you, sir.

SLENDER   I am not ahungry, I thank you, forsooth. ⌜(*To*   265
Simple.)⌝ Go, sirrah, for all you are my man, go
wait upon my cousin Shallow. ⌜(*Simple exits.*)⌝ A
Justice of Peace sometime may be beholding to his
friend for a man. I keep but three men and a boy
yet, till my mother be dead. But what though? Yet   270
I live like a poor gentleman born.

ANNE   I may not go in without your Worship. They will
not sit till you come.

SLENDER   I' faith, I'll eat nothing. I thank you as much
as though I did.   275

ANNE   I pray you, sir, walk in.

SLENDER   I had rather walk here, I thank you. I bruised
my shin th' other day with playing at sword and
dagger with a master of fence—three veneys for a
dish of stewed prunes—and, by my troth, I cannot   280
abide the smell of hot meat since. Why do your
dogs bark so? Be there bears i' th' town?

ANNE   I think there are, sir. I heard them talked of.

SLENDER   I love the sport well, but I shall as soon quarrel at it as any man in England. You are afraid if   285
you see the bear loose, are you not?

ANNE   Ay, indeed, sir.

SLENDER   That's meat and drink to me, now. I have
seen Sackerson loose twenty times, and have taken
him by the chain. But, I warrant you, the women   290
have so cried and shrieked at it that it passed. But
women, indeed, cannot abide 'em; they are very ill-
favored rough things.

⌜*Enter Page.*⌝

PAGE   Come, gentle Master Slender, come. We stay for
you.   295

297. **By cock and pie:** a mild oath (**Cock** is a perversion of the word *God* used in oaths; **pie** is a name given the book setting forth the Roman Catholic order of service, but in this oath may refer only to a **pie** made from a **cock,** or rooster.)

299–307. **Nay . . . indeed, la:** Slender clumsily refuses to go through the door first and thus take precedence over Anne and Page, but he is finally persuaded to do so.

1.2 Sir Hugh sends Slender's servant Simple with a letter to Mistress Quickly asking her to intercede with Anne Page on Slender's behalf.

———————

1. **Go your ways:** i.e., **go**

1–2. **ask . . . way:** i.e., **ask the way** to **Doctor Caius' house** (**Caius** was probably pronounced to rhyme with "play us," though other pronunciations—e.g., "Ki-us" and "Keys"—are possible.)

4. **dry nurse:** literally, a **nurse** who has charge of a young child or children (but who does not suckle them, as a "wet **nurse**" does with an infant)—another of Sir Hugh's incorrect word choices, as are **laundry** (for "laundress," line 4) and **acquaintance** (for "acquainted," line 9)

10–11. **solicit . . . desires:** i.e., urge Slender's wishes (though **solicit,** in the context of courtship, often implied immoral intentions)

13. **pippins:** apples

SLENDER   I'll eat nothing, I thank you, sir.
PAGE   By cock and pie, you shall not choose, sir! Come,
    come.
SLENDER   Nay, pray you, lead the way.
PAGE   Come on, sir.   300
SLENDER   Mistress Anne, yourself shall go first.
ANNE   Not I, sir. Pray you, keep on.
SLENDER   Truly, I will not go first, truly, la! I will not do
    you that wrong.
ANNE   I pray you, sir.   305
SLENDER   I'll rather be unmannerly than troublesome.
    You do yourself wrong, indeed, la!
                                              They exit.

Scene 2

Enter ⌈Sir Hugh⌉ Evans and Simple.

SIR HUGH   Go your ways, and ask of Doctor Caius'
    house which is the way. And there dwells one Mis-
    tress Quickly, which is in the manner of his nurse,
    or his dry nurse, or his cook, or his laundry—his
    washer and his wringer.   5
SIMPLE   Well, sir.
SIR HUGH   Nay, it is petter yet. Give her this letter
    ⌈*(handing him a paper)*,⌉ for it is a 'oman that alto-
    gether's acquaintance with Mistress Anne Page;
    and the letter is to desire and require her to solicit   10
    your master's desires to Mistress Anne Page. I pray
    you, be gone. I will make an end of my dinner;
    there's pippins and cheese to come.
                                              They exit.

1.3 Falstaff, in desperate need of funds, dismisses his servant Bardolph, who enters the employ of the Host of the Garter. Falstaff plans to seduce Mistress Ford and Mistress Page to gain access to their husbands' wealth. When Pistol and Nym refuse to act as his go-betweens, he dismisses them from his service. They plot revenge against him.

---

2. **bullyrook:** jolly comrade (*Bully* is a term of endearment or familiarity; *rook* is recorded only as a term of abuse, and can mean "dupe" or "simpleton," but Falstaff and, later, others do not respond to **bullyrook** as if the Host were abusing them.)

6. **Discard, cashier:** dismiss; **Hercules:** in classical mythology, a hero of extraordinary strength and courage; **wag:** depart

8. **sit at:** i.e., reside here at the cost of

9. **Caesar:** Roman **emperor; Keiser:** i.e., Kaiser (See longer note, page 206.)

10. **Pheazar:** (1) a Turkish vizier; (2) one who feezes, i.e., beats, flogs; (3) one who fixes or does for others; **entertain:** employ

10–11. **draw, tap:** i.e., **draw** liquor from a cask, serve as a tapster (See picture, page 68.)

11. **Hector:** eldest son of King Priam of Troy and leader of the Trojan army against the Greeks (See picture, page 168.)

14. **froth:** i.e., pour beer so that it froths, and thus less of it fills the container; **lime:** i.e., add lime (calcium carbonate) to wine to improve its sour taste; **am at a word:** i.e., speak briefly

(continued)

Scene 3

Enter ⌜Sir John⌝ Falstaff, Host, Bardolph, Nym, Pistol,
⌜and Robin, Falstaff's⌝ Page.

FALSTAFF Mine Host of the Garter!

HOST What says my bullyrook? Speak scholarly and
wisely.

FALSTAFF Truly, mine Host, I must turn away some of
my followers.   5

HOST Discard, bully Hercules, cashier. Let them wag;
trot, trot.

FALSTAFF I sit at ten pounds a week.

HOST Thou'rt an emperor—Caesar, Keiser, and
Pheazar. I will entertain Bardolph. He shall draw,   10
he shall tap. Said I well, bully Hector?

FALSTAFF Do so, good mine Host.

HOST I have spoke. Let him follow.—Let me see thee
froth and ⌜lime.⌝ I am at a word. Follow.
                                              ⌜*Host exits.*⌝

FALSTAFF Bardolph, follow him. A tapster is a good   15
trade. An old cloak makes a new jerkin, a withered
servingman a fresh tapster. Go. Adieu.

BARDOLPH It is a life that I have desired. I will thrive.

PISTOL O base Hungarian wight, wilt thou the spigot
wield?   ⌜*Bardolph exits.*⌝ 20

NYM He was gotten in drink. Is not the humor conceited?

FALSTAFF I am glad I am so acquit of this tinderbox.
His thefts were too open. His filching was like an
unskillful singer; he kept not time.   25

NYM The good humor is to steal at a minute's rest.

PISTOL "Convey," the wise it call. "Steal"? Foh, a *fico*
for the phrase!

FALSTAFF Well, sirs, I am almost out at heels.

PISTOL Why, then, let kibes ensue.   30

FALSTAFF There is no remedy. I must cony-catch, I
must shift.

16–17. **An old . . . tapster:** Variations of the proverbs "His old brass will make you a new pan" and "An old servingman, a young beggar." **jerkin:** short, tight-fitting jacket

19. **Hungarian:** a slang term for "thievish" or "needy"; **spigot:** tap on a cask of liquor

21. **gotten in drink:** i.e., conceived when one or both of his parents were drunk (The proverb "Who goes drunk to bed begets but a girl" may suggest that Nym is disparaging Bardolph's manhood.) **humor:** See longer note to 1.1.161, page 205.

21–22. **conceited:** ingenious

23. **acquit:** set free, rid; **tinderbox:** inflammable person (with possible reference to Bardolph's inflamed face)

25. **kept not time:** i.e., stole at bad times

26. **at a minute's rest:** i.e., in a minute, with possible wordplay on *minim rest*, a minim being, in ancient music, the shortest note

27. **Convey:** i.e., remove, carry away; **fico:** fig (an insulting term often accompanied by an obscene gesture)

29. **out at heels:** i.e., broke, impoverished (literally, with stockings or shoes worn through **at** the **heels**)

30. **kibes:** chilblains on the **heels**

31. **cony-catch:** steal

32. **shift:** improvise

33. **Young . . . food:** A variant of the proverb "Young birds must have meat [i.e., food]."

35. **ken:** know; **wight:** person; **of substance good:** wealthy

(continued)

PISTOL   Young ravens must have food.

FALSTAFF   Which of you know Ford of this town?

PISTOL   I ken the wight. He is of substance good.   35

FALSTAFF   My honest lads, I will tell you what I am
   about.

PISTOL   Two yards and more.

FALSTAFF   No quips now, Pistol. Indeed, I am in the
   waist two yards about, but I am now about no   40
   waste; I am about thrift. Briefly, I do mean to make
   love to Ford's wife. I spy entertainment in her. She
   discourses; she carves; she gives the leer of invitation. I can construe the action of her familiar style;
   and the hardest voice of her behavior, to be En-   45
   glished rightly, is "I am Sir John Falstaff's."

PISTOL, ⌐*aside to Nym*¬   He hath studied her will and
   translated her will—out of honesty into English.

NYM, ⌐*aside to Pistol*¬   The anchor is deep. Will that
   humor pass?   50

FALSTAFF   Now, the report goes, she has all the rule of
   her husband's purse. He hath a ⌐legion¬ of angels.

PISTOL, ⌐*aside to Nym*¬   As many devils entertain, and
   "To her, boy," say I.

NYM, ⌐*aside to Pistol*¬   The humor rises; it is good.   55
   Humor me the angels.

FALSTAFF, ⌐*showing two papers*¬   I have writ me here a
   letter to her; and here another to Page's wife, who
   even now gave me good eyes too, examined my
   parts with most judicious ⌐oeillades.¬ Sometimes   60
   the beam of her view gilded my foot, sometimes
   my portly belly.

PISTOL, ⌐*aside to Nym*¬   Then did the sun on dunghill
   shine.

NYM, ⌐*aside to Pistol*¬   I thank thee for that humor.   65

FALSTAFF   O, she did so course o'er my exteriors with
   such a greedy intention that the appetite of her
   eye did seem to scorch me up like a burning-glass.

37. **about:** intending, scheming (Pistol uses **about** in the sense of "around the outside.")

41. **thrift:** thriving, prospering

41–42. **make love:** i.e., pay amorous attention

42. **entertainment:** i.e., a welcome

43. **carves:** possibly a term for sexual availability (In the play *Misogonus,* from around 1570, a womanizer is called a carver.) **leer:** look

44. **construe:** (1) interpret; (2) translate (introducing wordplay in which [in lines 45–48] Mistress Ford is figured as a text with a **style** and **voice** that can be **Englished rightly,** or correctly **translated into** plain **English,** and **studied.**) **familiar:** (1) plain, easy to understand; (2) affable; (3) intimate

45. **hardest:** (1) **hardest** to understand; (2) harshest; **voice:** (1) grammatical **voice**—i.e., active, passive, or middle; (2) utterance or expression

47. **will:** desire, especially sexual desire; sexual parts; last **will** and testament

48. **honesty:** chastity

49. **The anchor is deep:** an expression of uncertain meaning

50. **pass:** be acceptable

52. **a legion of angels:** i.e., an abundance of money (literally, a great number of gold coins stamped with the figure of Michael the archangel and valued at ten shillings [with an allusion to Matthew 26.53: "twelve legions of angels"])

53. **As many devils entertain:** i.e., employ **a legion of devils**

57. **writ me:** i.e., written

59. **even now:** just **now**

(continued)

Here's another letter to her. She bears the purse
too; she is a region in Guiana, all gold and bounty.   70
I will be cheaters to them both, and they shall be
exchequers to me; they shall be my East and West
Indies, and I will trade to them both. Go bear thou
this letter to Mistress Page—and thou this to Mistress Ford. We will thrive, lads, we will thrive.   75

PISTOL
Shall I Sir Pandarus of Troy become,
And by my side wear steel? Then Lucifer take all!

NYM, ⌈*to Falstaff*⌉ I will run no base humor. Here, take
the humor-letter. I will keep the havior of reputation.   80

FALSTAFF, ⌈*giving papers to Robin*⌉
Hold, sirrah, bear you these letters tightly;
Sail like my pinnace to these golden shores.—
Rogues, hence, avaunt, vanish like hailstones, go,
Trudge, plod away i' th' hoof, seek shelter, pack!
Falstaff will learn the ⌈humor⌉ of the age: 85
French thrift, you rogues—myself and skirted page.
                    ⌈*Falstaff and Robin exit.*⌉

PISTOL
Let vultures gripe thy guts! For gourd and fullam
    holds,
And high and low beguiles the rich and poor.
Tester I'll have in pouch when thou shalt lack,   90
Base Phrygian Turk!

NYM I have operations which be humors of revenge.

PISTOL Wilt thou revenge?

NYM By welkin and her star!

PISTOL With wit or steel?   95

NYM With both the humors, I. I will discuss the
humor of this love to Ford.

PISTOL
And I to Page shall eke unfold
    How Falstaff, varlet vile,

60. **parts:** attributes; **oeillades:** amorous glances

61. **beam:** i.e., sunbeam

63–64. **Then . . . shine:** Proverbial: "The sun is never the worse for shining on a dunghill."

66. **course o'er:** i.e., run over the particulars of

67. **intention:** intense observation; **appetite:** desire; hunger

68. **burning-glass:** lens used to focus and intensify the sun's rays

70. **Guiana:** like **East and West Indies** (lines 72–73), considered a source of fabulous wealth (See longer note, page 206.)

71. **cheaters:** escheators or assessors informing the king's exchequer of lands that were forfeit to the monarch because there were no qualified heirs to inherit them (with possible wordplay on "one who cheats")

72. **exchequers:** treasuries

76. **Sir Pandarus of Troy:** i.e., a pander, a pimp

79–80. **keep . . . reputation:** i.e., act so as to maintain my **reputation   havior:** deportment, behavior

81. **Hold:** here; **tightly:** properly

82. **pinnace:** light (and therefore fast) ship

83–84. **avaunt, plod . . . hoof, pack:** go away

85. **humor:** fashion

86. **French   thrift . . . page:** i.e., imitate the French in economizing by retaining only a **page,** rather than a large retinue (See longer note, page 206.)   **skirted:** wearing a coat with skirts or tails

87. **gripe:** grasp tightly with claws; **gourd, fullam:** two different kinds of loaded dice

(continued)

His dove will prove, his gold will hold,   100
    And his soft couch defile.
NYM   My humor shall not cool. I will incense Ford to
    deal with poison. I will possess him with yellow-
    ness, for the revolt of mine is dangerous. That is
    my true humor.   105
PISTOL   Thou art the Mars of malcontents. I second
    thee. Troop on.

                                            They exit.

                        Scene 4

            Enter Mistress Quickly ⌜and⌝ Simple.

MISTRESS QUICKLY   What, John Rugby! (*Enter John
    Rugby.*) I pray thee, go to the casement and see if
    you can see my master, Master Doctor Caius, com-
    ing. If he do, i' faith, and find anybody in the
    house, here will be an old abusing of God's pa-   5
    tience and the King's English.
RUGBY   I'll go watch.
MISTRESS QUICKLY   Go, and we'll have a posset for 't
    soon at night, in faith, at the latter end of a seacoal
    fire. ⌜(*Rugby exits.*)⌝ An honest, willing, kind fellow   10
    as ever servant shall come in house withal; and, I
    warrant you, no telltale nor no breed-bate. His
    worst fault is that he is given to prayer. He is some-
    thing peevish that way, but nobody but has his
    fault. But let that pass. Peter Simple you say your   15
    name is?
SIMPLE   Ay, for fault of a better.
MISTRESS QUICKLY   And Master Slender's your master?
SIMPLE   Ay, forsooth.
MISTRESS QUICKLY   Does he not wear a great round   20
    beard like a glover's paring knife?
SIMPLE   No, forsooth. He hath but a little wee face,
    with a little yellow beard, a Cain-colored beard.

88. **holds:** i.e., hold, last, endure
89. **high and low:** dice loaded so as to turn up either **high** or **low** numbers
90. **Tester:** sixpenny coin
91. **Phrygian:** i.e., Trojan
92. **operations:** workings (i.e., plans)
94. **welkin:** sky
95. **wit:** ingenious plan or device; **steel:** the sword (i.e., violence)
96. **discuss:** make known
98. **eke:** also; **unfold:** disclose
100. **prove:** put to the test
102–4. **Ford . . . yellowness:** See longer note, page 207. **yellowness:** jealousy
104. **the revolt of mine:** i.e., my **revolt**
106. **Mars:** i.e., most warlike, most valiant (literally, Roman god of war)

1.4 Delivering Sir Hugh's letter to Mistress Quickly, Simple is discovered by her employer Dr. Caius (another of Anne's suitors). Furious with Sir Hugh for interfering on behalf of Slender, Dr. Caius writes Sir Hugh challenging him to a duel.

---

1. **What:** an exclamation of impatience
5. **old:** plentiful, excessive
8. **posset:** a hot spiced drink of milk curdled with ale or other liquor; **for 't:** i.e., as a reward
9. **soon at night:** early tonight; **seacoal:** mined coal, as opposed to charcoal
10. **honest:** worthy

(continued)

MISTRESS QUICKLY   A softly-sprited man, is he not?
SIMPLE   Ay, forsooth. But he is as tall a man of his   25
    hands as any is between this and his head. He hath
    fought with a warrener.
MISTRESS QUICKLY   How say you? O, I should remem-
    ber him. Does he not hold up his head, as it were,
    and strut in his gait?   30
SIMPLE   Yes, indeed, does he.
MISTRESS QUICKLY   Well, heaven send Anne Page no
    worse fortune! Tell Master Parson Evans I will do
    what I can for your master. Anne is a good girl, and
    I wish—   35

⌜*Enter Rugby.*⌝

RUGBY   Out, alas! Here comes my master.
MISTRESS QUICKLY   We shall all be shent.—Run in here,
    good young man. Go into this closet. He will not
    stay long. ⌜(*Simple exits.*)⌝ What, John Rugby!
    John! What, John, I say! Go, John, go enquire for   40
    my master. I doubt he be not well, that he comes
    not home.   ⌜*Rugby exits.*⌝
    ⌜(*She sings.*)⌝ And down, down, adown 'a, etc.

Enter Doctor Caius.

DOCTOR CAIUS   Vat is you sing? I do not like dese toys.
    Pray you, go and vetch me in my closet *un boîtier*   45
    vert, a box, a green-a box. Do intend vat I speak?
    A green-a box.
MISTRESS QUICKLY   Ay, forsooth. I'll fetch it you.
    ⌜(*Aside.*)⌝ I am glad he went not in himself. If he
    had found the young man, he would have been   50
    horn-mad.   ⌜*She exits.*⌝
DOCTOR CAIUS   *Fe, fe, fe, fe! Ma foi, il fait fort chaud. Je*
    m'en vais à la cour—la grande affaire.

⌜*Enter Mistress Quickly with a small box.*⌝

MISTRESS QUICKLY   Is it this, sir?
DOCTOR CAIUS   *Oui, mets-le à mon* pocket. *Dépêche,*   55
    quickly. Vere is dat knave Rugby?

11. **withal:** with

12. **breed-bate:** mischief maker

13–14. **something peevish:** somewhat silly; somewhat perverse (See longer note, page 208.)

14–15. **but . . . fault:** i.e., is free of fault

17. **for fault:** i.e., for lack

23. **Cain-colored:** i.e., the color of Cain's beard as pictured in tapestries

24. **softly-sprited:** i.e., soft-spirited, quiet

25–26. **as tall . . . hands:** as valiant a fighter

26. **between . . . head:** i.e., in these parts (a cliché)

27. **warrener:** a gamekeeper; a servant in charge of a rabbit warren

28–29. **I should remember:** This apparently means "I remember."

36. **Out, alas:** an exclamation of alarm

37. **shent:** disgraced, ruined

38. **closet:** private room

39–43. **What . . . etc.:** Mistress Quickly's ruse to deceive Doctor Caius into believing she is unaware of his approach **enquire:** i.e., seek **doubt:** fear **And . . . etc.:** a typical refrain for a song

44. **Vat, dese:** Doctor Caius is given a parody of French-accented English, often pronouncing *w, wh,* and *f* as *v,* and *th* as *d.* **toys:** trifles

46. **intend:** i.e., you hear (French *entendre*)

51. **horn-mad:** mad as a horned beast in mating season

52–53. **Ma foi . . . affaire:** i.e., "My faith, it is very hot. I am going to court—the great affair."

55. **Oui . . . mon:** Yes, put it in my; **Dépêche:** act quickly

(continued)

MISTRESS QUICKLY   What, John Rugby, John!

⌐*Enter Rugby.*¬

RUGBY   Here, sir.

DOCTOR CAIUS   You are John Rugby, and you are Jack
Rugby. Come, take-a your rapier, and come after   60
my heel to the court.

RUGBY   'Tis ready, sir, here in the porch.

DOCTOR CAIUS   By my trot, I tarry too long. Od's
me! *Qu'ai-j'oublié?* Dere is some simples in my
closet dat I vill not for the varld I shall leave   65
behind.   ⌐*He exits.*¬

MISTRESS QUICKLY   Ay me! He'll find the young man
there, and be mad!

⌐*Enter Doctor Caius.*¬

DOCTOR CAIUS   *O diable, diable!* Vat is in my closet? Villainy! *Larron!* ⌐*(Pulling out Simple.)*¬ Rugby, my   70
rapier!

MISTRESS QUICKLY   Good master, be content.

DOCTOR CAIUS   Wherefore shall I be content-a?

MISTRESS QUICKLY   The young man is an honest man.

DOCTOR CAIUS   What shall de honest man do in my   75
closet? Dere is no honest man dat shall come in
my closet.

MISTRESS QUICKLY   I beseech you, be not so phlegmatic.
Hear the truth of it. He came of an errand to me
from Parson Hugh.   80

DOCTOR CAIUS   Vell?

SIMPLE   Ay, forsooth. To desire her to—

MISTRESS QUICKLY   Peace, I pray you.

DOCTOR CAIUS   Peace-a your tongue.—Speak-a your
tale.   85

SIMPLE   To desire this honest gentlewoman, your
maid, to speak a good word to Mistress Anne Page
for my master in the way of marriage.

59. **Jack:** with possible wordplay on the word's meaning as a common noun, "knave" or "villain"

63. **trot:** i.e., troth, truth, faith

63–64. **Od's me:** probably, "God save me"

64. **Qu'ai-j'oublié:** What have I forgotten? (See longer note, page 208.) **simples:** medicinal herbs

68. **mad:** insane (with rage)

69. **diable:** devil

70. **Larron:** thief

72. **content:** calm

73. **Wherefore shall:** why should

78. **phlegmatic:** Quickly's confusion for "choleric," angry (See longer note, page 208.)

79. **came of:** i.e., **came** on

89–90. **I'll ne'er . . . not:** Proverbial for "I'll not meddle where I need not." **and need:** i.e., if it **need**

92. **baille:** bring; give

95. **throughly moved:** thoroughly angry

97. **do you:** i.e., **do**

100. **look you:** i.e., you see

101. **dress meat:** prepare food

103. **charge:** load of trouble; responsibility

105. **advised o':** i.e., aware of (literally, informed of, apprised of)

108. **I . . . of it:** i.e., keep this in confidence

112–13. **jack'nape:** jackanapes, monkey

113. **By gar:** i.e., by God

115. **scurvy:** worthless

115–16. **meddle or make:** interfere

117. **stones:** testicles

118. **stone . . . dog:** proverbial

120. **ver:** i.e., for

122. **jack:** knave, villain

MISTRESS QUICKLY   This is all, indeed, la! But I'll ne'er
put my finger in the fire, and need not.   90

DOCTOR CAIUS, ⌐*to Simple*¬   Sir Hugh send-a you?—
Rugby, *baille* me some paper.—Tarry you a little-a
while.

⌐*Rugby brings paper, and Doctor Caius writes.*¬

MISTRESS QUICKLY, ⌐*aside to Simple*¬   I am glad he is so
quiet. If he had been throughly moved, you should   95
have heard him so loud and so melancholy. But
notwithstanding, man, I'll do you your master
what good I can. And the very yea and the no is,
the French doctor, my master—I may call him my
master, look you, for I keep his house, and I wash,   100
wring, brew, bake, scour, dress meat and drink,
make the beds, and do all myself—

SIMPLE, ⌐*aside to Quickly*¬   'Tis a great charge to come
under one body's hand.

MISTRESS QUICKLY, ⌐*aside to Simple*¬   Are you advised o'   105
that? You shall find it a great charge. And to be up
early and down late. But notwithstanding—to tell
you in your ear; I would have no words of it—my
master himself is in love with Mistress Anne Page.
But notwithstanding that, I know Anne's mind.   110
That's neither here nor there.

DOCTOR CAIUS, ⌐*handing paper to Simple*¬   You, jack'-
nape, give-a this letter to Sir Hugh. By gar, it is a
shallenge. I will cut his troat in de park, and I will
teach a scurvy jackanape priest to meddle or   115
make. You may be gone. It is not good you tarry
here.—By gar, I will cut all his two stones. By gar,
he shall not have a stone to throw at his dog.

⌐*Simple exits.*¬

MISTRESS QUICKLY   Alas, he speaks but for his friend.

DOCTOR CAIUS   It is no matter-a ver dat. Do not you tell-a   120
me dat I shall have Anne Page for myself? By gar, I
vill kill de jack priest; and I have appointed mine

123. **Jarteer:** i.e., Garter; **to measure our weapon:** i.e., to serve as umpire of our duel (literally, **to measure our** swords to ensure that both are the same length and there is thus a fair fight)

126. **We . . . prate:** Proverbial: "Give losers leave to speak."

126–27. **What the goodyear:** i.e., "what the devil"

132–33. **Anne—fool's head:** As Doctor Caius departs, Mistress Quickly turns her promise (that he will have **Anne**) into a proverbial insult.

138. **trow:** wonder; **near:** i.e., in, into

145. **honest:** chaste; **gentle:** wellborn, courteous, mild; **one . . . friend: one** who favors you

147. **do any good:** make any progress, thrive

148. **suit:** i.e., attempt to win Anne

155. **such another Nan: such** an extraordinary Anne; **detest:** confusion for "protest"

Host of de Jarteer to measure our weapon. By gar,
I will myself have Anne Page.

MISTRESS QUICKLY   Sir, the maid loves you, and all shall   125
be well. We must give folks leave to prate. What
the goodyear!

DOCTOR CAIUS   Rugby, come to the court with me. ⌐(*To*
Mistress Quickly.)⌐ By gar, if I have not Anne Page,
I shall turn your head out of my door.—Follow my   130
heels, Rugby.

MISTRESS QUICKLY   You shall have Anne—

                      ⌐*Caius and Rugby exit.*⌐

fool's head of your own. No, I know Anne's mind
for that. Never a woman in Windsor knows more
of Anne's mind than I do, nor can do more than I   135
do with her, I thank heaven.

FENTON, ⌐*within*⌐   Who's within there, ho?

MISTRESS QUICKLY   Who's there, I trow? Come near the
house, I pray you.

Enter Fenton.

FENTON   How now, good woman? How dost thou?   140

MISTRESS QUICKLY   The better that it pleases your good
Worship to ask.

FENTON   What news? How does pretty Mistress Anne?

MISTRESS QUICKLY   In truth, sir, and she is pretty, and
honest, and gentle; and one that is your friend, I   145
can tell you that by the way, I praise heaven for it.

FENTON   Shall I do any good, think'st thou? Shall I not
lose my suit?

MISTRESS QUICKLY   Troth, sir, all is in His hands above.
But notwithstanding, Master Fenton, I'll be sworn   150
on a book she loves you. Have not your Worship a
wart above your eye?

FENTON   Yes, marry, have I. What of that?

MISTRESS QUICKLY   Well, thereby hangs a tale. Good
faith, it is such another Nan! But, I detest, an hon-   155

156. **maid:** young, unmarried woman

159. **allicholy:** confusion for "melancholy"

160. **go to:** an expression of protest

161. **Hold:** wait

163. **voice:** support

163–64. **before me:** i.e., **before** I do

164. **commend me:** (1) convey my regards; (2) say good things about me

167. **confidence:** confusion for "conference," or conversation

172. **Out upon 't:** an expression of indignation

THE
MERRY WIVES
OF WINDSOR

est maid as ever broke bread. We had an hour's
talk of that wart. I shall never laugh but in that
maid's company. But, indeed, she is given too
much to allicholy and musing. But, for you,—well,
go to.   160

FENTON Well, I shall see her today. Hold, there's
money for thee. ⌜(*He hands her money.*)⌝ Let me
have thy voice in my behalf. If thou see'st her before me, commend me.

MISTRESS QUICKLY Will I? I' faith, that we will. And I   165
will tell your Worship more of the wart the next
time we have confidence, and of other wooers.

FENTON Well, farewell. I am in great haste now.

MISTRESS QUICKLY Farewell to your Worship.
                              ⌜(*Fenton exits.*)⌝
Truly an honest gentleman—but Anne loves him   170
not, for I know Anne's mind as well as another
does. Out upon 't! What have I forgot?
                              She exits.

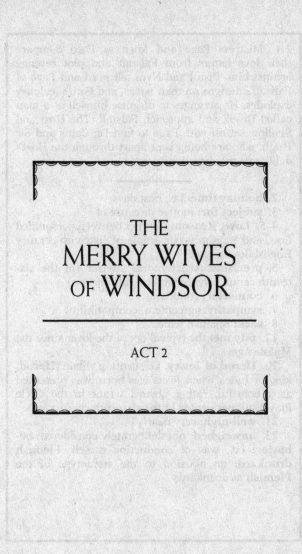

THE
MERRY WIVES
OF WINDSOR

ACT 2

2.1 Mistress Page and Mistress Ford compare their love letters from Falstaff and plot revenge against him. Pistol and Nym tell Ford and Page of Falstaff's designs on their wives, and Ford's jealousy explodes. He arranges to disguise himself as a man called Brook and approach Falstaff. The Host and Shallow set off with Page to find Dr. Caius and Sir Hugh, who are being kept apart through the Host's deliberate misdirections.

———

2. **holiday time:** i.e., best days

3. **subject for:** motive or cause of

4–5. **Love, Reason:** Conflict between personified Love and Reason was a staple of sixteenth-century English love poetry.

5. **precisian:** strict moral advisor (in the sixteenth century, synonymous with Puritan)

6. **counselor:** confidant

7. **sympathy:** agreement, compatibility

8. **sack:** Spanish wine

12. **pity me:** the typical cry of the lover since the Middle Ages

20. **Herod of Jewry:** i.e., ranting villain (**Herod,** king of Judea when Jesus was born, was presented as a boastful, rather absurd tyrant in the Cycle Plays, still performed in the sixteenth century.)

21. **well-nigh:** very nearly

23. **unweighed:** not deliberately considered; **behavior:** i.e., way of conducting myself; **Flemish drunkard:** an allusion to the stereotype of the **Flemish** as drunkards

ACT 2

Scene 1

Enter Mistress Page ⌜reading a letter.⌝

MISTRESS PAGE What, have ⌜I⌝ 'scaped love letters in
the holiday time of my beauty, and am I now a
subject for them? Let me see.
⌜*She reads.*⌝
*Ask me no reason why I love you, for though Love
use Reason for his precisian, he admits him not for* 5
*his counselor. You are not young; no more am I. Go
to, then, there's sympathy. You are merry; so am I.
Ha, ha, then, there's more sympathy. You love sack,
and so do I. Would you desire better sympathy? Let
it suffice thee, Mistress Page—at the least, if the love* 10
*of soldier can suffice—that I love thee. I will not say
pity me—'tis not a soldier-like phrase—but I say love
me. By me,*

> *Thine own true knight,*
> *By day or night,* 15
> *Or any kind of light,*
> *With all his might*
> *For thee to fight,*

> *John Falstaff.*

What a Herod of Jewry is this! O wicked, wicked 20
world! One that is well-nigh worn to pieces with
age, to show himself a young gallant! What an
unweighed behavior hath this Flemish drunkard

47

24. **with:** often emended to "in" or "i' "—the reading of the Third Folio of 1664

24–25. **conversation:** conduct

25. **assay:** make trial of, test

27. **should I say:** i.e., could I have said

28. **exhibit:** introduce; **bill:** draft of legislation

29. **putting down:** extermination (with bawdy wordplay)

31. **puddings:** a kind of sausage made of stuffed entrails of animals (with wordplay on **puddings** as also another word for human **guts**)

36–37. **have . . . contrary:** i.e., **have** something here that proves **the contrary**

44. **respect:** point, detail

45. **Hang the trifle:** i.e., let **the trifle** go to the devil

47–48. **would . . . or so:** i.e., **would** consent merely to be punished for eternity

50. **hack:** of uncertain meaning (perhaps, "be promiscuous")

51. **article of thy gentry:** i.e., matter of your inherited social rank

52. **burn daylight:** proverbial for "waste time"

55–56. **make difference of:** i.e., discriminate among

56. **liking:** physical condition

picked—with the devil's name!—out of my conversation, that he dares in this manner assay me?   25
Why, he hath not been thrice in my company!
What should I say to him? I was then frugal of my
mirth. Heaven forgive me! Why, I'll exhibit a bill
in the Parliament for the putting down of men.
How shall I be revenged on him? For revenged I   30
will be, as sure as his guts are made of puddings.

Enter Mistress Ford.

MISTRESS FORD   Mistress Page! Trust me, I was going to
your house.
MISTRESS PAGE   And, trust me, I was coming to you.
You look very ill.   35
MISTRESS FORD   Nay, I'll ne'er believe that. I have to
show to the contrary.
MISTRESS PAGE   Faith, but you do, in my mind.
MISTRESS FORD   Well, I do, then. Yet I say I could show
you to the contrary. O Mistress Page, give me some   40
counsel.
MISTRESS PAGE   What's the matter, woman?
MISTRESS FORD   O woman, if it were not for one trifling
respect, I could come to such honor!
MISTRESS PAGE   Hang the trifle, woman; take the honor.   45
What is it? Dispense with trifles. What is it?
MISTRESS FORD   If I would but go to hell for an eternal
moment or so, I could be knighted.
MISTRESS PAGE   What, thou liest! Sir Alice Ford? These
knights will hack, and so thou shouldst not alter   50
the article of thy gentry.
MISTRESS FORD   We burn daylight. Here, read, read. Perceive how I might be knighted. ⌈(*She gives a paper
to Mistress Page, who reads it.*)⌉ I shall think the
worse of fat men as long as I have an eye to make   55
difference of men's liking. And yet he would not
swear; ⌈praised⌉ women's modesty; and gave such

58–59. **uncomeliness:** indecency

60. **gone to the truth of:** i.e., been guided by

61. **adhere:** agree

62. **Hundredth Psalm:** a well-known psalm of praise ("Make a joyful noise unto the Lord.")

63. **Greensleeves:** a popular love song; **trow:** wonder

64. **tuns:** barrels, casks

66. **were . . . hope:** i.e., would be to lead him on

69. **but that:** except that

71. **mystery of ill opinions:** i.e., (Falstaff's) inexplicable mistaken and poor **opinions** (of us)

73. **inherit first:** i.e., **first,** as the elder of the twins, take possession of Falstaff's favors

76–77. **of the second edition:** i.e., from the **second** batch of copies (The legal limit of printed copies of an ordinary book was 1,250 to 1,500.)

78. **into the press:** (1) **into the** process of being printed; (2) **into** an instrument of torture in which great weight (in this case, Falstaff's body) was brought to bear on a victim

80. **Mount Pelion:** In attempting to ascend to the heavens and defeat the gods, the giants of classical mythology piled **Mount Pelion** atop Mount Ossa. The gods punished the giants by confining them beneath the mountains. (With **giantess** [line 79], Mistress Page adapts the myth to her situation.)

81. **turtles:** i.e., turtledoves, proverbial for their fidelity to their mates (See picture, page 94.)

83. **hand:** handwriting

85. **wrangle:** dispute; **honesty:** chastity (called into question by Falstaff's propositions)

85–86. **entertain:** treat, deal with

(continued)

orderly and well-behaved reproof to all uncomeliness that I would have sworn his disposition
would have gone to the truth of his words. But 60
they do no more adhere and keep place together
than the ⌐Hundredth Psalm⌐ to the tune of
"Greensleeves." What tempest, I trow, threw this
whale, with so many tuns of oil in his belly, ashore
at Windsor? How shall I be revenged on him? I 65
think the best way were to entertain him with hope
till the wicked fire of lust have melted him in his
own grease. Did you ever hear the like?

MISTRESS PAGE Letter for letter, but that the name of
Page and Ford differs! To thy great comfort in this 70
mystery of ill opinions, here's the twin brother of
thy letter. ⌐(*She gives a paper to Mistress Ford, who
reads it.*)⌐ But let thine inherit first, for I protest
mine never shall. I warrant he hath a thousand of
these letters writ with blank space for different 75
names—sure, more—and these are of the second
edition. He will print them, out of doubt; for he
cares not what he puts into the press, when he
would put us two. I had rather be a giantess and lie
under Mount Pelion. Well, I will find you twenty 80
lascivious turtles ere one chaste man.

MISTRESS FORD Why, this is the very same—the very
hand, the very words. What doth he think of us?

MISTRESS PAGE Nay, I know not. It makes me almost
ready to wrangle with mine own honesty. I'll enter- 85
tain myself like one that I am not acquainted
withal; for, sure, unless he know some strain in
me that I know not myself, he would never have
boarded me in this fury.

MISTRESS FORD "Boarding" call you it? I'll be sure to 90
keep him above deck.

MISTRESS PAGE So will I. If he come under my hatches,
I'll never to sea again. Let's be revenged on him.
Let's appoint him a meeting, give him a show of

87. **withal:** i.e., with

89. **boarded:** assailed (with wordplay on attacking a ship, wordplay that continues with bawdy references to **above deck** and **under my hatches** [lines 91, 92]); **fury:** fierce passion

95. **comfort:** encouragement; **suit:** courtship

95–96. **fine-baited:** i.e., finely (expertly) enticing

99. **chariness:** carefully preserved state

100. **that:** i.e., if only

103. **good man:** i.e., goodman, husband (though with possible emphasis on Page's goodness as a **man**)

107. **greasy:** filthy

110. **curtal dog:** literally, a dock-tailed **dog**

111. **affects:** (1) seeks to obtain; (2) loves

115. **gallimaufry:** mixture (literally, a hash made of scraps); **perpend:** consider

117. **liver:** regarded as the seat of both love and lust; **Prevent:** forestall by taking precautions

118. **Sir Acteon:** In mythology, **Acteon** was transformed into a stag by Diana, chaste goddess of hunting, and killed by his own hounds. (See note to line 122, and picture, page 180.)

119. **Ringwood:** the name of one of Acteon's hounds in Arthur Golding's translation of the Acteon story for his *P. Ouidius Naso, entytuled Metamorphosis* of 1567.

122. **horn:** i.e., the **name** of cuckold (Cuckolds are often pictured wearing horns. [See picture, page 134.] Acteon's being turned into a horned beast seems to have made him a figure of the cuckold, as he is at 3.2.41. See longer note, page 209.)

123. **foot:** walk

(continued)

52

comfort in his suit, and lead him on with a fine-   95
baited delay till he hath pawned his horses to mine
Host of the Garter.

MISTRESS FORD   Nay, I will consent to act any villainy
against him that may not sully the chariness of our
honesty. O, that my husband saw this letter! It   100
would give eternal food to his jealousy.

MISTRESS PAGE   Why, look where he comes, and my
good man too. He's as far from jealousy as I am
from giving him cause, and that, I hope, is an
unmeasurable distance.   105

MISTRESS FORD   You are the happier woman.

MISTRESS PAGE   Let's consult together against this greasy
knight. Come hither.   ⌈*They talk aside.*⌉

Enter Ford ⌈with⌉ Pistol, and Page ⌈with⌉ Nym.

FORD   Well, I hope it be not so.

PISTOL
  Hope is a curtal dog in some affairs.   110
  Sir John affects thy wife.

FORD   Why, sir, my wife is not young.

PISTOL
  He woos both high and low, both rich and poor,
  Both young and old, one with another, Ford.
  He loves the gallimaufry. Ford, perpend.   115

FORD   Love my wife?

PISTOL
  With liver burning hot. Prevent,
  Or go thou like Sir Acteon, he,
  With Ringwood at thy heels.
  O, odious is the name!   120

FORD   What name, sir?

PISTOL   The horn, I say. Farewell.
  Take heed, have open eye, for thieves do foot by
    night.
  Take heed, ere summer comes or cuckoo birds do   125
    sing.—

125–26. cuckoo birds do sing: Because the **cuckoo** leaves its eggs for other birds to hatch and feed, its song of "cuckoo" is linked to the "cuckold," who well might unknowingly raise other men's children. The cuckoo's song was considered a mocking cry directed to married men. (See picture, page 76.)

127–28. He speaks: i.e., Nym **speaks**

129. patient: calm; **find out this:** i.e., discover the validity of Pistol's accusation

133. upon my necessity: i.e., when I need it

134. the short and the long: the then-proverbial form of the modern proverbial saying "**the long and the short** of it" (i.e., the whole thing)

137–38. bread and cheese: i.e., a poor diet (such as Nym must consume as Falstaff's follower or as a masterless man)

140. his: i.e., its

142. affecting: affected

145. Cataian: untrustworthy boaster (alluding to explorers who mistakenly claimed to have discovered riches in places they believed to be Cathay)

155. crotchets: whims, fancies

157. Have with you: i.e., I'm coming

Away, Sir Corporal Nym.—Believe it, Page. He
speaks sense.   ⌜*He exits.*⌝
FORD, ⌜*aside*⌝ I will be patient. I will find out this.
NYM, ⌜*to Page*⌝ And this is true. I like not the humor of   130
    lying. He hath wronged me in some humors. I
    should have borne the humored letter to her; but I
    have a sword, and it shall bite upon my necessity.
    He loves your wife; there's the short and the long.
    My name is Corporal Nym. I speak and I avouch.   135
    'Tis true. My name is Nym, and Falstaff loves your
    wife. Adieu. I love not the humor of bread and
    cheese. Adieu.   ⌜*He exits.*⌝
PAGE, ⌜*aside*⌝ "The humor of it," quoth he? Here's a fel-
    low frights English out of his wits.   140
FORD, ⌜*aside*⌝ I will seek out Falstaff.
PAGE, ⌜*aside*⌝ I never heard such a drawling, affecting
    rogue.
FORD, ⌜*aside*⌝ If I do find it—well.
PAGE, ⌜*aside*⌝ I will not believe such a Cataian, though   145
    the priest o' th' town commended him for a true
    man.
FORD, ⌜*aside*⌝ 'Twas a good sensible fellow—well.

⌜*Mistress Page and Mistress Ford come forward.*⌝

PAGE, ⌜*to Mistress Page*⌝ How now, Meg?
MISTRESS PAGE Whither go you, George? Hark you.   150
                      ⌜*They talk aside.*⌝
MISTRESS FORD, ⌜*to Ford*⌝ How now, sweet Frank? Why
    art thou melancholy?
FORD I melancholy? I am not melancholy. Get you
    home. Go.
MISTRESS FORD Faith, thou hast some crochets in thy   155
    head now.—Will you go, Mistress Page?
MISTRESS PAGE Have with you.—You'll come to dinner,
    George? ⌜*(Aside to Mistress Ford.)*⌝ Look who
    comes yonder.

160. **paltry:** despicable

161. **on:** i.e., of; **fit:** be suitable for

166. **We:** i.e., we'll

173. **offer:** try

174. **yoke:** pair

175. **very rogues:** true **rogues** (in the strict legal sense of the term) See longer note, page 209. **be out of service:** i.e., no longer have a master

177. **Marry:** a mild oath (originally on the name of the Virgin Mary)

178. **lie:** reside

181. **turn her loose to him:** language usually applied to bringing animals together for mating

182. **of her:** i.e., from her

183. **lie on my head:** rest on me as my responsibility (In line 186, Ford's use of the expression has reference to the cuckold's horns.)

184. **misdoubt:** mistrust

185. **turn them together:** See note to line 181.

188. **ranting:** bombastic (i.e., talking in an extravagant, high-flown manner)

Enter ⌈Mistress⌉ Quickly.

She shall be our messenger to this paltry knight.   160

MISTRESS FORD Trust me, I thought on her. She'll fit it.

MISTRESS PAGE, ⌈*to Mistress Quickly*⌉ You are come to
see my daughter Anne?

MISTRESS QUICKLY Ay, forsooth. And, I pray, how does
good Mistress Anne?   165

MISTRESS PAGE Go in with us and see. We have an
hour's talk with you.

> ⌈*Mistress Page, Mistress Ford, and*
> *Mistress Quickly exit.*⌉

PAGE How now, Master Ford?

FORD You heard what this knave told me, did you not?

PAGE Yes, and you heard what the other told me?   170

FORD Do you think there is truth in them?

PAGE Hang 'em, slaves! I do not think the knight
would offer it. But these that accuse him in his in-
tent towards our wives are a yoke of his discarded
men, very rogues, now they be out of service.   175

FORD Were they his men?

PAGE Marry, were they.

FORD I like it never the better for that. Does he lie at
the Garter?

PAGE Ay, marry, does he. If he should intend this voy-   180
age toward my wife, I would turn her loose to him;
and what he gets more of her than sharp words, let
it lie on my head.

FORD I do not misdoubt my wife, but I would be loath
to turn them together. A man may be too confi-   185
dent. I would have nothing lie on my head. I cannot be thus satisfied.

Enter Host.

PAGE Look where my ranting Host of the Garter
comes. There is either liquor in his pate or money
in his purse when he looks so merrily.—How now,   190
mine Host?

193. **Cavaleiro:** i.e., courtly gentleman, gallant (originally, Spanish for "horseman"; here used by the ranting Host as a title for Justice Shallow)

194–95. **Good even and twenty:** i.e., good afternoon, many times over

196. **have . . . hand:** i.e., are going to have some fun **sport:** jest, practical joke

204–5. **hath . . . weapons:** i.e., is the umpire (See note to 1.4.123.)

206. **places:** i.e., meeting **places**

208. **suit:** lawsuit

209. **guest cavalier:** i.e., Falstaff (a resident **guest** at the Garter Inn)

210. **pottle:** half-gallon

211. **burnt sack:** heated or mulled wine

212. **Brook:** See longer note, page 209.

213–14. **shalt . . . regress:** i.e., may go and come (the legal phrase "**egress** [or, ingress] and **regress**")

216. **ameers:** i.e., emirs, Arabian chieftains (The Folio's reading "An-heires" is quite unintelligible and is variously emended.)

217. **Have with you:** i.e., I'm coming (as also at line 227)

221. **you stand on distance:** i.e., people insist on the **distance** separating combatants in a duel

221–22. **your passes, stoccados:** fencing jargon for forward thrusts (**Your** implies loosely "that you know" and often expresses contempt.)

222. **heart:** considered the seat of courage

224. **long sword:** heavy, old-fashioned weapon, in contrast to the rapier; **made you:** i.e., **made**; **tall:** brave, strong in combat

HOST   How now, bullyrook? Thou'rt a gentleman.—
    Cavaleiro Justice, I say!

Enter Shallow.

SHALLOW   I follow, mine Host, I follow.—Good even
    and twenty, good Master Page. Master Page, will   195
    you go with us? We have sport in hand.
HOST   Tell him, Cavaleiro Justice; tell him, bullyrook.
SHALLOW   Sir, there is a fray to be fought between
    Sir Hugh the Welsh priest and Caius the French
    doctor.   200
FORD   Good mine Host o' th' Garter, a word with you.
HOST   What say'st thou, my bullyrook?
                    ⌜*The Host and Ford talk aside.*⌝
SHALLOW, ⌜*to Page*⌝   Will you go with us to behold it?
    My merry Host hath had the measuring of their
    weapons and, I think, hath appointed them con-   205
    trary places; for, believe me, I hear the parson is no
    jester. Hark, I will tell you what our sport shall be.
                    ⌜*Shallow and Page talk aside.*⌝
HOST, ⌜*to Ford*⌝   Hast thou no suit against my knight,
    my guest cavalier?
⌜FORD⌝   None, I protest. But I'll give you a pottle of   210
    burnt sack to give me recourse to him, and tell him
    my name is ⌜Brook⌝—only for a jest.
HOST   My hand, bully. Thou shalt have egress and
    regress—said I well?—and thy name shall be
    ⌜Brook.⌝ It is a merry knight. ⌜(*To Shallow and*   215
    Page.)⌝ Will you go, ⌜ameers?⌝
SHALLOW   Have with you, mine Host.
PAGE   I have heard the Frenchman hath good skill
    in his rapier.
SHALLOW   Tut, sir, I could have told you more. In these   220
    times you stand on distance—your passes, stocca-
    dos, and I know not what. 'Tis the heart, Master
    Page; 'tis here, 'tis here. I have seen the time, with
    my long sword I would have made you four tall
    fellows skip like rats.   225

226. **wag:** go

229. **secure:** overconfident, careless

229–30. **stands . . . frailty:** i.e., puts such reliance on (that which in reality is) **his wife's** moral
weakness

232. **made:** i.e., did

234. **sound:** question; **honest:** chaste

2.2 Falstaff receives Mistress Ford's invitation to
visit; he then accepts "Brook's" money in exchange
for his promise to compromise Mistress Ford's reputation. Ford plans to trap Falstaff with Mistress
Ford.

----

5. **lay my countenance to pawn:** i.e., borrow
against the value of my reputation as your patron

5–6. **grated upon:** oppressed with burdensome
demands

7. **coach-fellow:** companion (literally, one of a
pair of horses harnessed to draw a coach)

8. **the grate:** i.e., prison bars; **gemini:** pair (literally, Latin for "twins")

10. **tall:** brave

11–12. **handle of her fan:** Fan handles were
sometimes made of precious metals, like silver.

12. **took 't:** i.e., swore

13. **share:** i.e., take your share (of the plunder)

16. **gratis:** for nothing; **At a word:** i.e., to be
brief

16–17. **hang . . . about me:** i.e., no longer be a
hanger-on of mine (with wordplay on "do not **hang**
(continued)

HOST   Here, boys, here, here! Shall we wag?
PAGE   Have with you. I had rather hear them scold
    than fight.   ⌜*Page, Host, and Shallow exit.*⌝
FORD   Though Page be a secure fool and stands so
    firmly on his wife's frailty, yet I cannot put off my   230
    opinion so easily. She was in his company at Page's
    house, and what they made there I know not. Well,
    I will look further into 't, and I have a disguise to
    sound Falstaff. If I find her honest, I lose not my
    labor. If she be otherwise, 'tis labor well bestowed.   235
                                       ⌜*He*⌝ *exits.*

Scene 2

Enter ⌜*Sir John*⌝ *Falstaff* ⌜*and*⌝ *Pistol.*

FALSTAFF   I will not lend thee a penny.
PISTOL   Why then, the world's mine oyster, which I
    with sword will open.
FALSTAFF   Not a penny. I have been content, sir, you
    should lay my countenance to pawn. I have grated   5
    upon my good friends for three reprieves for you
    and your coach-fellow Nym, or else you had
    looked through the grate like a gemini of baboons.
    I am damned in hell for swearing to gentlemen my
    friends you were good soldiers and tall fellows.   10
    And when Mistress Bridget lost the handle of her
    fan, I took 't upon mine honor thou hadst it not.
PISTOL   Didst not thou share? Hadst thou not fifteen
    pence?
FALSTAFF   Reason, you rogue, reason. Think'st thou I'll   15
    endanger my soul gratis? At a word, hang no more
    about me. I am no gibbet for you. Go—a short
    knife and a throng—to your manor of Pickt-hatch,
    go. You'll not bear a letter for me, you rogue? You
    stand upon your honor? Why, thou unconfinable   20

on me," wordplay that continues in line 17 with **"I am no gibbet"**) See picture, page 126.

17–18. **a short knife:** the instrument of the cut-purse

18. **manor:** lordly mansion or property; **Pickthatch:** perhaps, the name of a brothel or disreputable part of London (literally, a hatch half-door, with a row of pikes or spikes atop it)

20. **unconfinable:** limitless

22. **precise:** strictly observed

24. **fain:** required, obliged

25. **shuffle:** be evasive or deceitful; **hedge:** avoid committing myself; **lurch:** (1) lurk; (2) steal, cheat

26. **ensconce:** hide (as if in a fortification); **cat-a-mountain:** i.e., wild (literally, a leopard or panther) See picture, page 128.

27. **red-lattice:** tavernlike (Red-painted lattices signaled taverns and inns.)

30. **relent:** give up (my earlier decision); **What . . . of:** i.e., **what more** could you wish from

33. **morrow:** morning

34. **goodwife:** mistress of a house or other establishment; married woman

35. **an 't . . . Worship:** a deferential phrase of address to a person of note   **an 't:** i.e., if it

36. **maid:** virgin

37. **sworn:** i.e., **sworn** that I am (a **maid**)

37–38. **as . . . born:** Mistress Quickly mingles the proverbs "as good a **maid** as her **mother**" and "as innocent as a newborn babe."

40. **vouchsafe:** literally, deign to grant (perhaps a confusion for "beseech")

baseness, it is as much as I can do to keep the
terms of my honor precise. Ay, ay, I myself sometimes, leaving the fear of ⌜God⌝ on the left hand
and hiding mine honor in my necessity, am fain to
shuffle, to hedge, and to lurch; and yet you, rogue,   25
will ensconce your rags, your cat-a-mountain
looks, your red-lattice phrases, and your bold beating oaths under the shelter of your honor! You will
not do it? You?

PISTOL   I do relent. What would thou more of man?   30

Enter Robin.

ROBIN   Sir, here's a woman would speak with you.
FALSTAFF   Let her approach.

Enter ⌜Mistress⌝ Quickly.

MISTRESS QUICKLY   Give your Worship good morrow.
FALSTAFF   Good morrow, goodwife.
MISTRESS QUICKLY   Not so, an 't please your Worship.   35
FALSTAFF   Good maid, then.
MISTRESS QUICKLY   I'll be sworn—as my mother was,
the first hour I was born.
FALSTAFF   I do believe the swearer. What with me?
MISTRESS QUICKLY   Shall I vouchsafe your Worship a   40
word or two?
FALSTAFF   Two thousand, fair woman, and I'll vouch-
safe thee the hearing.
MISTRESS QUICKLY   There is one Mistress Ford, sir—I
pray, come a little nearer this ways. I myself dwell   45
with Master Doctor Caius.
FALSTAFF   Well, on. "Mistress Ford," you say—
MISTRESS QUICKLY   Your Worship says very true. I pray
your Worship, come a little nearer this ways.
FALSTAFF   I warrant thee, nobody hears. Mine own   50
people, mine own people.
MISTRESS QUICKLY   Are they so? ⌜God⌝ bless them and
make them His servants!

60. **canaries:** perhaps confusion for "quandary" (Literally, a *canary* is either a lively Spanish dance or a sweet wine from the Canary Islands.)

62. **lay at Windsor:** i.e., was resident **at Windsor** Castle (See longer note, page 210, and picture, page xii.)

63. **has:** i.e., have

67. **rushling:** possible mispronunciation of "rustling"

68. **alligant:** confusion for "elegant" or "eloquent"

71. **eye-wink of:** i.e., inviting glance from

72. **angels:** gold coins (presumably as a bribe); **defy:** reject, disdain

73. **sort:** manner

77. **pensioners:** gentlemen forming a bodyguard to the monarch within the palace (famous for their splendid uniforms)

77–78. **all is one with:** i.e., it **is one** and the same to

80. **she-Mercury:** In mythology, **Mercury** is the messenger of the gods.

83. **gives you to notify:** i.e., bids you take note

87. **wot:** know

FALSTAFF   Well, "Mistress Ford"—what of her?

MISTRESS QUICKLY   Why, sir, she's a good creature.   55
Lord, Lord, your Worship's a wanton! Well, heaven
forgive you and all of us, I pray!

FALSTAFF   "Mistress Ford"—come, "Mistress Ford"—

MISTRESS QUICKLY   Marry, this is the short and the long
of it: you have brought her into such a canaries as   60
'tis wonderful. The best courtier of them all, when
the court lay at Windsor, could never have brought
her to such a canary. Yet there has been knights,
and lords, and gentlemen, with their coaches, I
warrant you, coach after coach, letter after letter,   65
gift after gift, smelling so sweetly—all musk—and
so rushling, I warrant you, in silk and gold, and in
such alligant terms, and in such wine and sugar of
the best and the fairest, that would have won any
woman's heart; and, I warrant you, they could   70
never get an eye-wink of her. I had myself twenty
angels given me this morning, but I defy all angels
in any such sort, as they say, but in the way of
honesty. And, I warrant you, they could never get
her so much as sip on a cup with the proudest of   75
them all. And yet there has been earls—nay, which
is more, pensioners—but, I warrant you, all is one
with her.

FALSTAFF   But what says she to me? Be brief, my good
she-Mercury.   80

MISTRESS QUICKLY   Marry, she hath received your letter,
for the which she thanks you a thousand times,
and she gives you to notify that her husband will
be absence from his house between ten and eleven.

FALSTAFF   Ten and eleven?   85

MISTRESS QUICKLY   Ay, forsooth; and then you may come
and see the picture, she says, that you wot of. Master Ford, her husband, will be from home. Alas, the
sweet woman leads an ill life with him. He's a very

90. **frampold:** sour-tempered, peevish (This word usually described a person rather than, as here, a person's life.)

97. **fartuous:** confusion for "virtuous"

97–98. **civil, modest:** decent

98–99. **miss you:** i.e., miss (the ethic dative)

104. **charms:** magic spells

106. **parts:** qualities, including physical attributes

108. **has:** i.e., have

114. **of all loves:** a phrase of strong entreaty

115. **infection to:** Quickly's confusion for "affection for"

116. **honest:** worthy

122. **no remedy:** i.e., there is no alternative

A seventeenth-century view of Falstaff.
From *The wits, or, Sport upon sport . . .* (1662).

jealousy man. She leads a very frampold life with   90
him, good heart.

FALSTAFF   Ten and eleven. Woman, commend me to
her. I will not fail her.

MISTRESS QUICKLY   Why, you say well. But I have another messenger to your Worship. Mistress Page   95
hath her hearty commendations to you too; and,
let me tell you in your ear, she's as fartuous a civil
modest wife, and one, I tell you, that will not miss
you morning nor evening prayer, as any is in Windsor, whoe'er be the other. And she bade me tell   100
your Worship that her husband is seldom from
home, but she hopes there will come a time. I
never knew a woman so dote upon a man. Surely, I
think you have charms, la! Yes, in truth.

FALSTAFF   Not I, I assure thee. Setting the attraction of   105
my good parts aside, I have no other charms.

MISTRESS QUICKLY   Blessing on your heart for 't!

FALSTAFF   But I pray thee, tell me this: has Ford's wife
and Page's wife acquainted each other how they
love me?   110

MISTRESS QUICKLY   That were a jest indeed! They have
not so little grace, I hope. That were a trick indeed!
But Mistress Page would desire you to send her
your little page, of all loves. Her husband has a
marvelous infection to the little page; and, truly,   115
Master Page is an honest man. Never a wife in
Windsor leads a better life than she does. Do what
she will, say what she will, take all, pay all, go to
bed when she list, rise when she list—all is as she
will. And, truly, she deserves it, for if there be a   120
kind woman in Windsor, she is one. You must send
her your page, no remedy.

FALSTAFF   Why, I will.

MISTRESS QUICKLY   Nay, but do so then, and, look you,
he may come and go between you both. And in any   125

126. **nayword:** i.e., code word (literally, password, watchword)

130. **discretion:** judgment, wisdom

132. **yet:** still

134. **distracts:** bewilders

136. **punk:** prostitute; **carriers:** messengers

137. **Clap:** put; **fights:** screens raised to protect sailors in a sea battle

138. **prize:** booty, plunder; **whelm:** sink

141. **after thee:** i.e., at you

143. **grossly:** awkwardly

144. **so:** i.e., if; **fairly:** actually, fully (with wordplay on both **grossly** [corpulently] and **fairly** [handsomely] as descriptions of his body)

146. **fain:** gladly

148. **draught:** drink

154. **Go to:** an expression usually of impatience; **Via:** onward (a cry of encouragement)

A tapster. (1.3.10–11, 15; 2.2.160)
From Guillaume de la Perrière, *La morosophie* . . . (1553).

case have a nayword, that you may know one another's mind, and the boy never need to understand anything; for 'tis not good that children
should know any wickedness. Old folks, you know,
have discretion, as they say, and know the world.   130

FALSTAFF   Fare thee well. Commend me to them both.
There's my purse. ⌜(*He gives her money.*)⌝ I am yet
thy debtor.—Boy, go along with this woman. ⌜(*Mistress Quickly and Robin exit.*)⌝ This news distracts
me.   135

PISTOL, ⌜*aside*⌝
This punk is one of Cupid's carriers.
Clap on more sails, pursue; up with your fights;
Give fire! She is my prize, or ocean whelm them all!
⌜*He exits.*⌝

FALSTAFF   Sayst thou so, old Jack? Go thy ways. I'll
make more of thy old body than I have done. Will   140
they yet look after thee? Wilt thou, after the expense of so much money, be now a gainer? Good
body, I thank thee. Let them say 'tis grossly done;
so it be fairly done, no matter.

⌜*Enter Bardolph with wine.*⌝

BARDOLPH   Sir John, there's one Master ⌜Brook⌝ below   145
would fain speak with you and be acquainted with
you, and hath sent your Worship a morning's
draught of sack.   ⌜(*He hands Falstaff the wine.*)⌝

FALSTAFF   ⌜Brook⌝ is his name?

BARDOLPH   Ay, sir.   150

FALSTAFF   Call him in. Such ⌜Brooks⌝ are welcome to
me that o'erflows such liquor. ⌜(*Bardolph exits.*)⌝
Ah ha, Mistress Ford and Mistress Page, have I en-
compassed you? Go to. *Via!*

Enter ⌜*Bardolph with*⌝ *Ford* ⌜*disguised as Brook.*⌝

FORD, ⌜*as Brook*⌝   ⌜God⌝ bless you, sir.   155

FALSTAFF   And you, sir. Would you speak with me?

157. **make bold:** venture, take the liberty

159. **What's your will:** i.e., what may I do for you

159–60. **Give us leave:** i.e., go

160. **drawer:** tapster, bartender (addressed to Bardolph)

161. **that have:** i.e., who has

165. **sue for:** seek

166. **charge you:** burden you (with expense)

167. **plight:** state, condition

168. **the which:** i.e., **which** fact; **something:** somewhat

169. **unseasoned:** unseasonable, untimely

171. **on:** go forward

175. **carriage:** i.e., carrying of it, burden

181. **your servant:** i.e., of service to you (with possible wordplay on **servant** as **porter** [line 177])

184. **means:** i.e., opportunities

186. **discover:** reveal

189. **unfolded:** disclosed

189–90. **register:** record, list

190–91. **pass with a reproof the easier:** i.e., get off with **a lighter reproof**

191. **sith:** since

FORD, ⌜*as Brook*⌝ I make bold to press with so little
preparation upon you.

FALSTAFF You're welcome. What's your will?—Give us
leave, drawer.   ⌜*Bardolph exits.*⌝ 160

FORD, ⌜*as Brook*⌝ Sir, I am a gentleman that have spent
much. My name is ⌜Brook.⌝

FALSTAFF Good Master ⌜Brook,⌝ I desire more acquaintance of you.

FORD, ⌜*as Brook*⌝ Good Sir John, I sue for yours—not 165
to charge you, for I must let you understand I
think myself in better plight for a lender than you
are, the which hath something emboldened me to
this unseasoned intrusion; for they say, if money
go before, all ways do lie open.   170

FALSTAFF Money is a good soldier, sir, and will on.

FORD, ⌜*as Brook*⌝ Troth, and I have a bag of money
here troubles me. ⌜*He sets it down.*⌝ If you will help
to bear it, Sir John, take all, or half, for easing me
of the carriage.   175

FALSTAFF Sir, I know not how I may deserve to be your
porter.

FORD, ⌜*as Brook*⌝ I will tell you, sir, if you will give me
the hearing.

FALSTAFF Speak, good Master ⌜Brook.⌝ I shall be glad 180
to be your servant.

FORD, ⌜*as Brook*⌝ Sir, I hear you are a scholar—I will
be brief with you—and you have been a man long
known to me, though I had never so good means
as desire to make myself acquainted with you. I 185
shall discover a thing to you wherein I must very
much lay open mine own imperfection. But, good
Sir John, as you have one eye upon my follies, as
you hear them unfolded, turn another into the register of your own, that I may pass with a reproof 190
the easier, sith you yourself know how easy it is to
be such an offender.

199. **doting observance:** foolish (or perhaps extravagantly loving) observant care; **engrossed:** i.e., collected all possible

200. **fee'd:** employed (as if **every occasion** were a hired or paid servant)

200–201. **but niggardly:** i.e., even grudgingly or sparingly

203. **would have given:** i.e., wished to have **given** her

207. **meed:** reward

211–12. **substance love pursues:** i.e., wealth **pursues** the beloved (The couplet [lines 211–13] recalls in part the proverbial "**Love, like a shadow, flies** one following and **pursues** one fleeing." Note also the wordplay on **substance** as the antithesis of **shadow.**) See picture, page 84.

217. **importuned:** urged

220. **quality:** nature

221–23. **Like . . . erected it:** Proverbial: "Who builds upon another's ground loses both mortar and stones." **fair:** beautiful

227–28. **honest:** chaste

228. **enlargeth:** extends the scope of

229. **mirth:** gratification, pleasure, enjoyment; **shrewd construction:** harsh interpretation

FALSTAFF Very well, sir. Proceed.

FORD, ⌐*as Brook*¬ There is a gentlewoman in this
town—her husband's name is Ford.   195

FALSTAFF Well, sir.

FORD, ⌐*as Brook*¬ I have long loved her and, I protest
to you, bestowed much on her, followed her with
a doting observance, engrossed opportunities to
meet her, fee'd every slight occasion that could but   200
niggardly give me sight of her, not only bought
many presents to give her, but have given largely to
many to know what she would have given. Briefly,
I have pursued her as love hath pursued me, which
hath been on the wing of all occasions. But what-   205
soever I have merited, either in my mind or in my
means, meed I am sure I have received none, unless experience be a jewel. That I have purchased
at an infinite rate, and that hath taught me to say
this: 210
"Love like a shadow flies when substance love
    pursues,
Pursuing that that flies, and flying what pursues."

FALSTAFF Have you received no promise of satisfaction
at her hands?   215

FORD, ⌐*as Brook*¬ Never.

FALSTAFF Have you importuned her to such a purpose?

FORD, ⌐*as Brook*¬ Never.

FALSTAFF Of what quality was your love, then?   220

FORD, ⌐*as Brook*¬ Like a fair house built on another
man's ground, so that I have lost my edifice by
mistaking the place where I erected it.

FALSTAFF To what purpose have you unfolded this to
me?   225

FORD, ⌐*as Brook*¬ When I have told you that, I have
told you all. Some say that though she appear honest to me, yet in other places she enlargeth her
mirth so far that there is shrewd construction

232. **of great admittance:** i.e., widely received in society   **admittance:** admissibility

233. **authentic:** entitled to respect; **place:** high social rank

233–34. **generally allowed:** universally approved

235. **preparations:** accomplishments

240. **of it:** i.e., for it

244. **apply well to:** i.e., suit **well** with; **vehemency:** vehemence

245. **would:** wish to

246. **Methinks:** it seems to me that

250. **folly:** lewdness, wantonness

251. **against:** directly at

252. **detection:** accusation, criminal information

253. **instance:** example, evidence

254. **ward:** defensive posture; protection

256. **other her defenses: other defenses** of hers

257. **embattled:** fortified

260. **make bold with:** i.e., help myself to, **make free with**

262. **will:** wish

265. **Want:** lack

made of her. Now, Sir John, here is the heart of my   230
purpose: you are a gentleman of excellent breed-
ing, admirable discourse, of great admittance,
authentic in your place and person, generally
allowed for your many warlike, courtlike, and
learned preparations.   235

FALSTAFF   O, sir!

FORD, ⌜*as Brook*⌝   Believe it, for you know it. There is
money. ⌜(*He points to the bag.*)⌝ Spend it, spend
it, spend more; spend all I have. Only give me so
much of your time in exchange of it as to lay an   240
amiable siege to the honesty of this Ford's wife.
Use your art of wooing; win her to consent to you.
If any man may, you may as soon as any.

FALSTAFF   Would it apply well to the vehemency of
your affection that I should win what you would   245
enjoy? Methinks you prescribe to yourself very
preposterously.

FORD, ⌜*as Brook*⌝   O, understand my drift. She dwells
so securely on the excellency of her honor that the
folly of my soul dares not present itself; she is too   250
bright to be looked against. Now, could I come to
her with any detection in my hand, my desires had
instance and argument to commend themselves. I
could drive her then from the ward of her purity,
her reputation, her marriage vow, and a thousand   255
other her defenses, which now are too too strongly
embattled against me. What say you to 't, Sir
John?

FALSTAFF, ⌜*taking the bag*⌝   Master ⌜Brook,⌝ I will first
make bold with your money; next, give me your   260
hand; and, last, as I am a gentleman, you shall, if
you will, enjoy Ford's wife.

FORD, ⌜*as Brook*⌝   O, good sir!

FALSTAFF   I say you shall.

FORD, ⌜*as Brook*⌝   Want no money, Sir John; you shall   265
want none.

269. **Even:** just

274. **speed:** succeed, fare

279. **wittolly:** complaisantly cuckolded (resigned to his wife's infidelity)

280. **for the which:** i.e., because of **which**

280–81. **well-favored:** attractive

282. **my harvest home:** i.e., the bringing in of **my harvest**

283. **would:** wish

285. **mechanical:** vulgar (literally, engaged in manual labor); **salt-butter:** miserly (buying only inferior imported, rather than fresh, butter)

287. **meteor:** i.e., portent

290. **soon at night:** early tonight

291. **aggravate his style:** i.e., add to his title of **knave** the additional title of **cuckold   aggravate:** increase; worsen   **style:** honorific title

302. **stand under:** be exposed to; **the adoption of abominable terms:** i.e., being called loathsome, detestable names (**Adoption** here means, literally, the act of accepting as one's own.)

A cuckoo. (2.1.125)
From Konrad Gesner, . . . *Historiae animalium* . . . (1585–1604).

FALSTAFF   Want no Mistress Ford, Master ⌐Brook;⌐ you
      shall want none. I shall be with her, I may tell you,
      by her own appointment. Even as you came in to
      me, her assistant or go-between parted from me. I   270
      say I shall be with her between ten and eleven, for
      at that time the jealous, rascally knave her hus-
      band will be forth. Come you to me at night. You
      shall know how I speed.

FORD, ⌐*as Brook*⌐   I am blessed in your acquaintance.   275
      Do you know Ford, sir?

FALSTAFF   Hang him, poor cuckoldly knave! I know
      him not. Yet I wrong him to call him poor. They
      say the jealous wittolly knave hath masses of
      money, for the which his wife seems to me well-   280
      favored. I will use her as the key of the cuckoldly
      rogue's coffer, and there's my harvest home.

FORD, ⌐*as Brook*⌐   I would you knew Ford, sir, that you
      might avoid him if you saw him.

FALSTAFF   Hang him, mechanical salt-butter rogue! I   285
      will stare him out of his wits. I will awe him with
      my cudgel; it shall hang like a meteor o'er the
      cuckold's horns. Master ⌐Brook,⌐ thou shalt know I
      will predominate over the peasant, and thou shalt
      lie with his wife. Come to me soon at night. Ford's   290
      a knave, and I will aggravate his style. Thou, Mas-
      ter ⌐Brook,⌐ shalt know him for knave and cuck-
      old. Come to me soon at night.   ⌐*Falstaff exits.*⌐

FORD   What a damned epicurean rascal is this! My
      heart is ready to crack with impatience. Who says   295
      this is improvident jealousy? My wife hath sent
      to him, the hour is fixed, the match is made.
      Would any man have thought this? See the hell of
      having a false woman: my bed shall be abused, my
      coffers ransacked, my reputation gnawn at. And   300
      I shall not only receive this villainous wrong but
      stand under the adoption of abominable terms,

304–5. **Amaimon, Lucifer, Barbason:** In manuscript conjuring books of the time, **Amaimon,** one of the four kings of the air, was a great ruler among the demons; **Lucifer** was one of the three principal demons. **Barbason** may be Shakespeare's own version of the more familiar Barbates or Barbares.

305. **additions:** titles

308. **secure:** overconfident

309–11. **Fleming, Welshman, Irishman:** conventional English stereotypes of neighboring peoples

311. **aquavitae:** strong spirits

312. **walk:** exercise

317. **prevent:** anticipate and forestall

318. **detect:** expose; accuse

319. **about it:** i.e., set about doing this

2.3 Dr. Caius responds furiously when Sir Hugh fails to meet him for their duel. The Host calms his anger by offering to take him to Anne Page.

A man with rapiers. (1.4.60; 2.3.13, 16)
From Giacomo di Grassi, . . . *True arte of defence* . . . (1594).

and by him that does me this wrong. Terms,
names! "Amaimon" sounds well, "Lucifer" well,
"Barbason" well; yet they are devils' additions, the   305
names of fiends. But "Cuckold," "Wittoll," "Cuckold"! The devil himself hath not such a name. Page
is an ass, a secure ass. He will trust his wife, he will
not be jealous. I will rather trust a Fleming with
my butter, Parson Hugh the Welshman with my   310
cheese, an Irishman with my aquavitae bottle, or
a thief to walk my ambling gelding, than my wife
with herself. Then she plots, then she ruminates,
then she devises; and what they think in their
hearts they may effect, they will break their hearts   315
but they will effect. ⌜God⌝ be praised for my jealousy! Eleven o'clock the hour. I will prevent this,
detect my wife, be revenged on Falstaff, and laugh
at Page. I will about it. Better three hours too soon
than a minute too late. Fie, fie, fie! Cuckold, cuck-   320
old, cuckold!

He exits.

Scene 3

Enter ⌜Doctor⌝ Caius ⌜and⌝ Rugby.

DOCTOR CAIUS   Jack Rugby.
RUGBY   Sir?
DOCTOR CAIUS   Vat is the clock, Jack?
RUGBY   'Tis past the hour, sir, that Sir Hugh promised
to meet.   5
DOCTOR CAIUS   By gar, he has save his soul dat he is no
come. He has pray his Pible well dat he is no come.
By gar, Jack Rugby, he is dead already if he be
come.
RUGBY   He is wise, sir. He knew your Worship would   10
kill him if he came.

12–13. **de herring . . . kill him:** Perhaps, "I will **kill him** deader than a **herring**." Proverbial: "as dead as a **herring**."

16. **Villainy:** i.e., villain

21. **morrow:** morning

24. **foin:** thrust, lunge

24–25. **traverse:** i.e., "**traverse** your ground," or move from side to side in fencing (the first of a number of technical terms from fencing [lines 26–27])

26. **pass:** lunge, thrust; **puncto:** cut or thrust with the point of a sword; **stock:** stoccado, or thrust; **reverse:** *punto riverso*, back-handed thrust

27. **distance:** observance of proper interval of space from an opponent; **montant:** upward thrust or blow; **he:** i.e., Sir Hugh; **Ethiopian:** i.e., swarthy one (literally, black African)

28. **Francisco:** perhaps, Frenchman

29. **Aesculapius:** Roman god of medicine; **Galien:** i.e., Galen, famous Greek physician from the second century C.E.; **heart of elder:** wordplay on *heart of oak*, a term for a man of courage (While the center or **heart** of an oak's trunk is very hard, the elder's is soft. The **elder** is also associated with Judas Iscariot, who hanged himself from an **elder** tree.)

30. **stale:** urine, which doctors analyze in making diagnoses

31. **jack-priest:** a term of contempt

33. **Castalion:** perhaps, a version of "Castilian" or Spanish (But see longer note, page 210.) **Urinal:** a glass vessel used to receive urine for medical examination (See picture, page 82.); also, a chamber pot; **Hector:** leader of the forces of Troy, not **Greece**

(continued)

80

DOCTOR CAIUS   By gar, de herring is no dead so as I vill
   kill him. Take your rapier, Jack. I vill tell you how I
   vill kill him.

RUGBY   Alas, sir, I cannot fence.   15

DOCTOR CAIUS   Villainy, take your rapier.

RUGBY   Forbear. Here's company.

Enter Page, Shallow, Slender, ⌐and⌐ Host.

HOST   ⌐God⌐ bless thee, bully doctor!

SHALLOW   ⌐God⌐ save you, Master Doctor Caius!

PAGE   Now, good Master Doctor!   20

SLENDER   Give you good morrow, sir.

DOCTOR CAIUS   Vat be all you, one, two, tree, four, come
   for?

HOST   To see thee fight, to see thee foin, to see thee traverse; to see thee here, to see thee there; to see   25
   ⌐thy⌐ pass, thy puncto, thy stock, thy reverse, thy
   distance, thy montant. Is he dead, my Ethiopian?
   Is he dead, my Francisco? Ha, bully? What says
   my Aesculapius, my Galien, my heart of elder, ha?
   Is he dead, bully stale? Is he dead?   30

DOCTOR CAIUS   By gar, he is de coward jack-priest of de
   vorld. He is not show his face.

HOST   Thou art a Castalion King Urinal Hector of
   Greece, my boy!

DOCTOR CAIUS   I pray you, bear witness that me have   35
   stay six or seven, two, tree hours for him, and he is
   no come.

SHALLOW   He is the wiser man, Master Doctor. He is a
   curer of souls, and you a curer of bodies. If you
   should fight, you go against the hair of your pro-   40
   fessions.—Is it not true, Master Page?

PAGE   Master Shallow, you have yourself been a great
   fighter, though now a man of peace.

SHALLOW   Bodykins, Master Page, though I now be old
   and of the peace, if I see a sword out, my finger   45

40. **against the hair of:** contrary to

44. **Bodykins:** God's (little) body

46. **make one:** join in

48. **salt:** i.e., savor, liveliness, freshness

57. **guest Justice:** i.e., Shallow, who is evidently, like Falstaff, staying at the Garter Inn

58. **Mockwater:** a word of unknown meaning, perhaps "urine"

63. **de Englishman:** i.e., any **Englishman; Scurvy:** worthless

65. **clapper-claw:** thrash, drub; **tightly:** soundly

70. **wag:** i.e., run for his life (literally, go or depart)

74. **eke:** also; **Cavaleiro:** i.e., courtly gentleman, gallant (See note to 2.1.193.)

75. **Frogmore:** a small village near Windsor

78. **about:** around

A urinal. (2.3.33; 3.1.14, 89)
From Robert Recorde, *The urinal of physick* . . . (1548).

itches to make one. Though we are justices and
doctors and churchmen, Master Page, we have
some salt of our youth in us. We are the sons of
women, Master Page.

PAGE   'Tis true, Master Shallow.   50

SHALLOW   It will be found so, Master Page.—Master
Doctor Caius, I am come to fetch you home. I am
sworn of the peace. You have showed yourself a
wise physician, and Sir Hugh hath shown himself
a wise and patient churchman. You must go with   55
me, Master Doctor.

HOST   Pardon, guest Justice. ⌐(*To Caius.*)⌐ A ⌐word,⌐
Monsieur Mockwater.

DOCTOR CAIUS   "Mockvater"? Vat is dat?

HOST   "Mockwater," in our English tongue, is "valor,"   60
bully.

DOCTOR CAIUS   By gar, then I have as much mockvater
as de Englishman. Scurvy jack-dog priest! By gar,
me vill cut his ears.

HOST   He will clapper-claw thee tightly, bully.   65

DOCTOR CAIUS   "Clapper-de-claw"? Vat is dat?

HOST   That is, he will make thee amends.

DOCTOR CAIUS   By gar, me do look he shall clapper-
de-claw me, for, by gar, me vill have it.

HOST   And I will provoke him to 't, or let him wag.   70

DOCTOR CAIUS   Me tank you for dat.

HOST   And moreover, bully—⌐(*He draws Shallow, Page,
and Slender aside.*)⌐ But first, Master guest, and
Master Page, and eke Cavaleiro Slender, go you
through the town to Frogmore.   75

PAGE   Sir Hugh is there, is he?

HOST   He is there. See what humor he is in; and I will
bring the doctor about by the fields. Will it do
well?

SHALLOW   We will do it.   80

PAGE, SHALLOW, and SLENDER   Adieu, good Master Doctor.   ⌐*Page, Shallow, and Slender exit.*⌐

84. **jackanape:** monkey (with reference to Slender)

89. **Cried game:** perhaps, a hunting cry

94. **adversary:** for "advocate" or for "emissary"

"Love like a shadow flies. . . ." (2.2.211–13)
From Geoffrey Whitney, *A choice of emblemes . . .* (1586).

DOCTOR CAIUS   By gar, me vill kill de priest, for he speak
   for a jackanape to Anne Page.

HOST   Let him die. Sheathe thy impatience; throw cold   85
   water on thy choler. Go about the fields with me
   through Frogmore. I will bring thee where Mistress Anne Page is, at a farmhouse a-feasting, and
   thou shalt woo her. Cried game! Said I well?

DOCTOR CAIUS   By gar, me dank you vor dat. By gar, I   90
   love you, and I shall procure-a you de good guest:
   de earl, de knight, de lords, de gentlemen, my pa-
   tients.

HOST   For the which I will be thy adversary toward
   Anne Page. Said I well?   95

DOCTOR CAIUS   By gar, 'tis good. Vell said.

HOST   Let us wag, then.

DOCTOR CAIUS   Come at my heels, Jack Rugby.

They exit.

THE
MERRY WIVES
OF WINDSOR

ACT 3

3.1 Page, Shallow, and Slender join Sir Hugh, who is waiting to fight Dr. Caius. When the Host brings Dr. Caius and Sir Hugh together, the two, prevented from dueling, reconcile in plotting revenge against the Host.

1–2. **servingman:** servant

4. **physic:** medicine

5. **Petty-ward:** in the direction of Windsor Little Park (**Petty** is from French *petit.*) **Park-ward:** in the direction of Windsor Great Park (See picture, page 160.)

6. **Old Windsor:** a village two or three miles south of Windsor

7. **the town way:** in the direction of Windsor itself

11. **cholers:** i.e., choler, bile (Sir Hugh may be using the word incorrectly, since in line 21 he expresses trepidation, not the anger supposedly caused by choler. However, his **trempling of mind** [line 12] could mean "angry agitation"; further, lines 13–15 clearly express anger.)

13. **melancholies:** i.e., melancholy, filled with black bile; **knog:** i.e., knock

14. **urinals:** See note to 2.3.33. **costard:** i.e., head (literally, a large apple)

16–26. **To shallow … madrigals:** Sir Hugh's song is based on Christopher Marlowe's well-known lyric "Come live with me and be my love," which contains the lines: "And we will sit upon the rocks, / Seeing the shepherds feed their flocks / By shallow rivers to whose falls / Melodious birds sing madrigals. / And I will make thee beds of roses, / And a

(continued)

ACT 3

Scene 1

Enter ⌜Sir Hugh⌝ Evans ⌜(with a book and a sword) and⌝ Simple ⌜(carrying Sir Hugh's gown).⌝

SIR HUGH I pray you now, good Master Slender's servingman and friend Simple by your name, which
way have you looked for Master Caius, that calls
himself doctor of physic?

SIMPLE Marry, sir, the ⌜Petty-ward,⌝ the Park-ward,   5
every way; Old Windsor way, and every way but
the town way.

SIR HUGH I most fehemently desire you, you will also
look that way.

SIMPLE I will, sir.   ⌜*He exits.*⌝   10

SIR HUGH Pless my soul, how full of cholers I am, and
trempling of mind! I shall be glad if he have deceived me. How melancholies I am! I will knog his
urinals about his knave's costard when I have good
opportunities for the 'ork. Pless my soul!   15
⌜(*Sings.*)⌝

> *To shallow rivers, to whose falls*
> *Melodious birds sings madrigals.*
> *There will we make our peds of roses*
> *And a thousand fragrant posies.*
> *To shallow—*   20

Mercy on me, I have a great dispositions to cry.

89

thousand fragrant posies." Into this love lyric Sir Hugh introduces a line ("Whenas I sat in Pabylon") derived from a metrical adaptation of Psalm 137.1, which reads: "Whenas we sat in Babylon the rivers round about, / And in remembrance of Sion the tears for grief burst out." **falls:** waterfalls, cascades

27. **he:** Doctor Caius

31. **There:** This set of characters would be coming from a different direction than Doctor Caius and his companions.

33. **stile:** a set of steps allowing one to climb over a fence

37–39. **Keep . . . wonderful:** i.e., it is as hard to **keep a** gambler away from dice as it is to **keep a good student from his book**

44. **the word:** i.e., **the word** of God, the Bible

46. **in . . . hose:** i.e., without your cloak or gown **doublet:** close-fitting jacket **hose:** breeches (See picture, page 92.)

47. **this raw rheumatic day:** i.e., in this damp and chilly weather that brings on rheumatism

⌜(Sings.)⌝
    Melodious birds sing madrigals—
    Whenas I sat in Pabylon—
    And a thousand vagram posies.
    To shallow rivers, to whose falls   25
    Melodious birds sings madrigals.

⌜*Enter Simple*⌝

SIMPLE Yonder he is, coming this way, Sir Hugh.
SIR HUGH He's welcome.
⌜(Sings.)⌝
    To shallow rivers, to whose falls—
Heaven prosper the right! What weapons is he?   30
SIMPLE No weapons, sir. There comes my master, Master Shallow, and another gentleman, from Frogmore, over the stile, this way.
SIR HUGH Pray you, give me my gown—or else keep it in your arms.   35

Enter Page, Shallow, ⌜and⌝ Slender.

SHALLOW How now, Master Parson? Good morrow, good Sir Hugh. Keep a gamester from the dice, and a good student from his book, and it is wonderful.
SLENDER, ⌜*aside*⌝ Ah, sweet Anne Page!   40
PAGE ⌜God⌝ save you, good Sir Hugh!
SIR HUGH ⌜God⌝ pless you from His mercy sake, all of you!
SHALLOW What, the sword and the word? Do you study them both, Master Parson?   45
PAGE And youthful still—in your doublet and hose this raw rheumatic day?
SIR HUGH There is reasons and causes for it.
PAGE We are come to you to do a good office, Master Parson.   50
SIR HUGH Fery well. What is it?

52. **reverend:** i.e., respected

52–53. **belike:** probably; possibly

57. **place:** social rank

58. **so wide of:** deviating so far from; **respect:** condition of being honored and respected

62. **Got's . . . heart:** Sir Hugh's confusion of "God's will," "God's passion," and "Passion of my heart"

62–63. **had as lief:** would as soon

63. **mess of porridge:** dish of stew

65. **Hibbocrates:** i.e., Hippocrates, Greek physician of the fifth century B.C.E.

69. **should:** i.e., who is to

82. **In good time:** to be sure; indeed

"In your doublet and hose." (3.1.46)
From [Robert Greene,] *A quip for an vpstart courtier* . . . (1620).

92

PAGE   Yonder is a most reverend gentleman who, belike having received wrong by some person, is at
most odds with his own gravity and patience that
ever you saw.   55

SHALLOW   I have lived fourscore years and upward. I
never heard a man of his place, gravity, and learning so wide of his own respect.

SIR HUGH   What is he?

PAGE   I think you know him: Master Doctor Caius, the   60
renowned French physician.

SIR HUGH   Got's will and His passion of my heart! I had
as lief you would tell me of a mess of porridge.

PAGE   Why?

SIR HUGH   He has no more knowledge in Hibbocrates   65
and Galen—and he is a knave besides, a cowardly
knave as you would desires to be acquainted
withal.

PAGE, ⌜*to Shallow*⌝   I warrant you, he's the man should
fight with him.   70

SLENDER, ⌜*aside*⌝   O, sweet Anne Page!

SHALLOW   It appears so by his weapons. Keep them
asunder. Here comes Doctor Caius.

Enter Host, ⌜Doctor⌝ Caius, ⌜and⌝ Rugby.
⌜*Caius and Sir Hugh offer to fight.*⌝

PAGE   Nay, good Master Parson, keep in your weapon.

SHALLOW   So do you, good Master Doctor.   75

HOST   Disarm them, and let them question. Let them
keep their limbs whole and hack our English.
⌜*Page and Shallow disarm Caius and Sir Hugh.*⌝

DOCTOR CAIUS, ⌜*to Sir Hugh*⌝   I pray you, let-a me speak
a word with your ear. Verefore vill you not
meet-a me?   80

SIR HUGH, ⌜*aside to Caius*⌝   Pray you, use your patience. ⌜(*Aloud.*)⌝ In good time.

DOCTOR CAIUS   By gar, you are de coward, de Jack dog,
John ape.

87. **you in friendship:** i.e., (to be) on friendly terms with you

89. **cogscomb:** i.e., head (A cockscomb is the cap of a professional Fool. See picture, page 120.)

96. **Gallia:** Wales (*Galles* in French); **Gaul:** France

100. **Machiavel:** schemer, intriguer (Niccolò Machiavelli's book *The Prince* [1513] counseled ruthless deceptiveness as the way to power.)

101. **potions:** liquid medicines acting as purges to induce bowel movements (**motions**)

104. **no-verbs:** of uncertain meaning; perhaps, nonwords (with reference to Sir Hugh's broken English); perhaps, thou-shalt-not's

106. **art:** learning

108. **burnt sack:** heated or mulled wine

109. **issue:** (only) outcome

116. **sot:** fool

117–18. **vlouting-stog:** flouting stock, object of mockery

A turtledove. (2.1.81)
From Konrad Gesner, . . . *Historiae animalium* . . . (1585–1604).

SIR HUGH, ⌐*aside to Caius*⌐ Pray you, let us not be   85
    laughing-stocks to other men's humors. I desire
    you in friendship, and I will one way or other
    make you amends. ⌐(*Aloud.*) By Jeshu,⌐ I will knog
    your urinal about your knave's cogscomb.

DOCTOR CAIUS *Diable!* Jack Rugby, mine Host de Jar-   90
    teer, have I not stay for him to kill him? Have I not,
    at de place I did appoint?

SIR HUGH As I am a Christians soul, now look you, this
    is the place appointed. I'll be judgment by mine
    Host of the Garter.   95

HOST Peace, I say, Gallia and Gaul, French and Welsh,
    soul-curer and body-curer!

DOCTOR CAIUS Ay, dat is very good, excellent.

HOST Peace, I say! Hear mine Host of the Garter. Am
    I politic? Am I subtle? Am I a Machiavel? Shall I   100
    lose my doctor? No, he gives me the potions and
    the motions. Shall I lose my parson, my priest, my
    Sir Hugh? No, he gives me the proverbs and the
    no-verbs. ⌐(*To Caius.*) Give me thy hand, terres-
    trial; so. (*To Sir Hugh.*)⌐ Give me thy hand, celes-   105
    tial; so. Boys of art, I have deceived you both. I
    have directed you to wrong places. Your hearts are
    mighty, your skins are whole, and let burnt sack be
    the issue. ⌐(*To Page and Shallow.*)⌐ Come, lay their
    swords to pawn. ⌐(*To Caius and Sir Hugh.*)⌐ Follow   110
    me, ⌐lads⌐ of peace, follow, follow, follow.
                                    ⌐*Host exits.*⌐

SHALLOW ⌐Afore God,⌐ a mad Host. Follow, gentlemen,
    follow.

SLENDER, ⌐*aside*⌐ O, sweet Anne Page!
                    ⌐*Shallow, Page, and Slender exit.*⌐

DOCTOR CAIUS Ha, do I perceive dat? Have you make-a   115
    de sot of us, ha, ha?

SIR HUGH This is well! He has made us his vlouting-
    stog. I desire you that we may be friends, and let

120. **scall:** i.e., scald, contemptible; **cogging:** cheating, wheedling; **companion:** fellow (a term of contempt)

125. **noddles:** i.e., noddle, head

3.2 Ford, knowing of Falstaff's visit to Mistress Ford, gathers as many men as he can to go with him to his house, promising them fine entertainment there.

———————

1. **keep your way:** i.e., go on (ahead), **keep** on **your way**

3. **Whether:** i.e., which of the two

12. **as she . . . together:** i.e., **as she** can be while still continuing to survive

13. **want:** lack

16. **had you:** did you find

18. **had him of:** i.e., got him from

us knog our prains together to be revenge on this
same scall, scurvy, cogging companion, the Host of   120
the Garter.

DOCTOR CAIUS   By gar, with all my heart. He promise
to bring me where is Anne Page. By gar, he deceive
me too.

SIR HUGH   Well, I will smite his noddles. Pray you,   125
follow.

⌐*Sir Hugh, Caius, Simple, and Rugby exit.*⌐

Scene 2

⌐*Enter*⌐ *Robin* ⌐*followed by*⌐ *Mistress Page.*

MISTRESS PAGE   Nay, keep your way, little gallant. You
were wont to be a follower, but now you are a
leader. Whether had you rather—lead mine eyes,
or eye your master's heels?

ROBIN   I had rather, forsooth, go before you like a man   5
than follow him like a dwarf.

MISTRESS PAGE   O, you are a flattering boy! Now I see
you'll be a courtier.

⌐*Enter*⌐ *Ford.*

FORD   Well met, Mistress Page. Whither go you?

MISTRESS PAGE   Truly, sir, to see your wife. Is she at   10
home?

FORD   Ay, and as idle as she may hang together, for
want of company. I think if your husbands were
dead, you two would marry.

MISTRESS PAGE   Be sure of that—two other husbands.   15

FORD   Where had you this pretty weathercock?

MISTRESS PAGE   I cannot tell what the dickens his name
is my husband had him of.—What do you call your
knight's name, sirrah?

ROBIN   Sir John Falstaff.   20

23. **league:** alliance, friendship; **goodman:** husband

26. **By your leave:** a polite request for permission (in this case to go to Mistress Ford)

31. **point-blank:** horizontally, in a direct line

32. **twelve score:** i.e., 240 yards or paces; **pieces out:** adds to

33. **folly:** wantonness; **motion:** urging, instigation; **advantage:** occasion, opportunity

35. **A man . . . wind:** i.e., it is easy to predict what will follow

37. **revolted:** i.e., faithless

40. **divulge:** publicly proclaim; **secure:** overconfident

41. **Acteon:** See notes to 2.1.118 and 122.

42. **cry aim:** i.e., encourage me (At archery contests, spectators would encourage contestants by crying out "**Aim!**")

49. **knot:** group of people; **cheer:** food and drink, fare

53–54. **break with her:** i.e., **break** my word to **her** (The expression also means "reveal my mind to her," something that Slender will prove incapable of doing.)

FORD   Sir John Falstaff!

MISTRESS PAGE   He, he. I can never hit on 's name.
There is such a league between my goodman and
he. Is your wife at home indeed?

FORD   Indeed, she is.   25

MISTRESS PAGE   By your leave, sir. I am sick till I see
her.   ⌜*Mistress Page and Robin exit.*⌝

FORD   Has Page any brains? Hath he any eyes? Hath
he any thinking? Sure they sleep; he hath no use
of them. Why, this boy will carry a letter twenty   30
mile as easy as a cannon will shoot point-blank
twelve score. He pieces out his wife's inclination.
He gives her folly motion and advantage. And now
she's going to my wife, and Falstaff's boy with her.
A man may hear this shower sing in the wind. And   35
Falstaff's boy with her! Good plots they are laid,
and our revolted wives share damnation together.
Well, I will take him, then torture my wife, pluck
the borrowed veil of modesty from the so-seeming
Mistress Page, divulge Page himself for a secure   40
and willful Acteon, and to these violent proceed-
ings all my neighbors shall cry aim. ⌜*A clock
strikes.*⌝ The clock gives me my cue, and my assur-
ance bids me search. There I shall find Falstaff. I
shall be rather praised for this than mocked, for it   45
is as positive as the earth is firm that Falstaff is
there. I will go.

⌜*Enter*⌝ *Page, Shallow, Slender, Host,* ⌜*Sir Hugh*⌝
Evans, ⌜*Doctor*⌝ *Caius,* ⌜*and Rugby.*⌝

SHALLOW, PAGE, etc.   Well met, Master Ford.

FORD   Trust me, a good knot. I have good cheer at
home, and I pray you all go with me.   50

SHALLOW   I must excuse myself, Master Ford.

SLENDER   And so must I, sir. We have appointed to dine
with Mistress Anne, and I would not break with
her for more money than I'll speak of.

55. **lingered about:** i.e., been dawdling over; or, perhaps, been kept waiting over

59. **stand wholly for:** entirely support

66. **holiday:** i.e., choice language

67. **carry 't:** i.e., **carry** it off, succeed

67–68. **in his buttons:** Editors have suggested that the phrase means "predestined," "written in his face," and "in the body enclosed by **his buttons.**" (The phrase is unknown except for this instance.)

70. **having:** wealth

71. **wild Prince and Poins:** The wildness of Prince Hal and his friend is to be found in Shakespeare's *Henry IV, Part 1* and *Part 2*. **region:** social station

72–73. **knit . . . substance:** i.e., use my wealth to prosper **substance:** wealth

74. **simply:** i.e., without a dowry

75. **waits on:** is subject to (as a servant who **waits on** his master is subject to him)

78. **dinner:** the midday meal

79. **sport:** entertainment, amusement

84. **anon:** soon

86. **canary:** wine from the Canary Islands (but also a lively dance, a sense with which Ford plays in lines 87–88)

87. **pipe-wine:** wine from a cask (with wordplay on **pipe** as the musical instrument that accompanies a **dance** [line 88])

89. **gentles:** i.e., gentlemen

SHALLOW   We have lingered about a match between   55
   Anne Page and my cousin Slender, and this day we
   shall have our answer.

SLENDER   I hope I have your good will, Father Page.

PAGE   You have, Master Slender. I stand wholly for
   you.—But my wife, Master Doctor, is for you alto-   60
   gether.

DOCTOR CAIUS   Ay, be-gar, and de maid is love-a me! My
   nursh-a Quickly tell me so mush.

HOST, ⌜*to Page*⌝   What say you to young Master Fenton? He capers, he dances, he has eyes of youth, he   65
   writes verses, he speaks holiday, he smells April
   and May. He will carry 't, he will carry 't. 'Tis in his
   buttons he will carry 't.

PAGE   Not by my consent, I promise you. The gentleman is of no having. He kept company with the   70
   wild Prince and Poins. He is of too high a region;
   he knows too much. No, he shall not knit a knot in
   his fortunes with the finger of my substance. If he
   take her, let him take her simply. The wealth I have
   waits on my consent, and my consent goes not that   75
   way.

FORD   I beseech you heartily, some of you go home
   with me to dinner. Besides your cheer, you shall
   have sport: I will show you a monster. Master Doctor, you shall go.—So shall you, Master Page.—   80
   And you, Sir Hugh.

SHALLOW   Well, fare you well. We shall have the freer
   wooing at Master Page's.
                    ⌜*Shallow and Slender exit.*⌝

DOCTOR CAIUS   Go home, John Rugby. I come anon.
                    ⌜*Rugby exits.*⌝

HOST   Farewell, my hearts. I will to my honest knight   85
   Falstaff, and drink canary with him.   ⌜*He exits.*⌝

FORD, ⌜*aside*⌝   I think I shall drink in pipe-wine first
   with him; I'll make him dance.—Will you go,
   gentles?

90. **Have with you:** i.e., let's go

3.3 Mistress Ford and Mistress Page begin their revenge against Falstaff. As Falstaff joins Mistress Ford, Mistress Page enters with news that Ford is approaching. Falstaff climbs into a large laundry basket and is hidden under dirty clothes and then carried out by servants instructed to throw the basket's contents into the river. As Ford searches in vain for Falstaff, the wives plot further revenge against both men.

———————

2. **buck-basket:** clothes basket, basket for dirty clothes (*Bucking* means "bleaching" and "soaking.")
6. **the charge:** i.e., their orders
7. **brief:** hasty, expeditious
9. **hard:** near
11. **staggering:** wavering, hesitation
13. **whitsters:** those who bleach clothes
13–14. **Datchet Mead:** a meadow near the Thames River
21. **eyas-musket:** young male sparrowhawk

PAGE, DOCTOR CAIUS, and SIR HUGH Have with you to   90
see this monster.

They exit.

Scene 3

Enter Mistress Ford ⌈and⌉ Mistress Page.

MISTRESS FORD   What, John! What, Robert!
MISTRESS PAGE   Quickly, quickly! Is the buck-basket—
MISTRESS FORD   I warrant.—What, ⌈Robert,⌉ I say!

⌈*Enter John and Robert with a large buck-basket.*⌉

MISTRESS PAGE   Come, come, come.
MISTRESS FORD   Here, set it down.   5
MISTRESS PAGE   Give your men the charge. We must be
brief.
MISTRESS FORD   Marry, as I told you before, John and
Robert, be ready here hard by in the brewhouse,
and when I suddenly call you, come forth, and   10
without any pause or staggering take this basket
on your shoulders. That done, trudge with it in all
haste, and carry it among the whitsters in Datchet
Mead, and there empty it in the muddy ditch close
by the Thames side.   15
MISTRESS PAGE   You will do it?
MISTRESS FORD   I ha' told them over and over. They lack
no direction.—Be gone, and come when you are
called.   ⌈*John and Robert exit.*⌉
MISTRESS PAGE   Here comes little Robin.   20

Enter Robin.

MISTRESS FORD   How now, my eyas-musket? What news
with you?
ROBIN   My master, Sir John, is come in at your back
door, Mistress Ford, and requests your company.

25. **Jack-a-Lent:** puppet (literally, the figure of a man set up during Lent to be pelted with stones by children)

29. **liberty:** i.e., freedom from service and employment

35. **remember you:** i.e., **remember**

36–37. **cue, act, hiss:** language from the theater (where, e.g., audiences hissed their disapproval)

39. **use:** deal with

40. **pumpion:** pumpkin (See picture, page 108.)

41. **turtles:** i.e., turtledoves (See note to 2.1.81.) **jays:** i.e., women in flashy clothing, prostitutes (called such after the European jay, a bird with striking plumage)

42. **Have . . . jewel:** a slight adaptation of the opening line of the Second Song in Sir Philip Sidney's sonnet sequence *Astrophil and Stella* (c. 1582)

44. **period:** goal

47. **cog:** fawn, wheedle

48. **would:** wish

56. **becomes:** suits; **ship-tire:** ornamental headdress in the form of a ship; **tire-valiant:** of uncertain meaning, but, perhaps, a fanciful headdress

57. **tire of Venetian admittance:** i.e., headdress regarded as fashionable in Venice (England copied Italian fashion.)

MISTRESS PAGE   You little Jack-a-Lent, have you been   25
    true to us?

ROBIN   Ay, I'll be sworn. My master knows not of your
    being here and hath threatened to put me into
    everlasting liberty if I tell you of it, for he swears
    he'll turn me away.   30

MISTRESS PAGE   Thou'rt a good boy. This secrecy of
    thine shall be a tailor to thee and shall make thee a
    new doublet and hose.—I'll go hide me.

MISTRESS FORD   Do so.—Go tell thy master I am alone.
    ⌜(*Robin exits.*)⌝ Mistress Page, remember you your   35
    cue.

MISTRESS PAGE   I warrant thee. If I do not act it, hiss
    me.   ⌜*She exits.*⌝

MISTRESS FORD   Go to, then. We'll use this unwhole-
    some humidity, this gross-wat'ry pumpion. We'll   40
    teach him to know turtles from jays.

Enter ⌜Sir John⌝ Falstaff.

FALSTAFF   "Have I caught thee, my heavenly jewel?"
    Why, now let me die, for I have lived long enough.
    This is the period of my ambition. O, this blessèd
    hour!   45

MISTRESS FORD   O, sweet Sir John!

FALSTAFF   Mistress Ford, I cannot cog. I cannot prate,
    Mistress Ford. Now shall I sin in my wish: I would
    thy husband were dead. I'll speak it before the best
    lord: I would make thee my lady.   50

MISTRESS FORD   I your lady, Sir John? Alas, I should be
    a pitiful lady.

FALSTAFF   Let the court of France show me such
    another. I see how thine eye would emulate the
    diamond. Thou hast the right arched beauty of the   55
    brow that becomes the ship-tire, the tire-valiant,
    or any tire of Venetian admittance.

MISTRESS FORD   A plain kerchief, Sir John. My brows
    become nothing else, nor that well neither.

60. **a tyrant:** i.e., cruel (with wordplay on **tire**)

61. **absolute courtier:** perfect (female) attendant of the queen (Lady Mary Wroth's *Urania* [1621] includes examples of uses of the word **courtier** for a female attendant at court.) **fixture:** i.e., placing

63. **semicircled farthingale:** petticoat hooped at the back, but flat in front; **thou wert:** i.e., you would have been; or, perhaps, you would be

64. **if Fortune . . . thy friend:** perhaps, if **Fortune were not** your foe (i.e., if you were fortunate enough to be highborn, or, perhaps, well married), for **Nature** is **thy friend** in making you beautiful (The passage is much discussed and often emended, although there seems general agreement on the sense.)

73. **Bucklersbury:** a street in London where herbs and herbal medicines were sold; **simple time:** i.e., summer, when herbs or simples are collected and sold

75. **betray:** deceive, mislead

78. **Counter gate:** i.e., prison **gate,** for prisons were notorious for their stench (**Counter** may refer specifically to a debtors' prison south of the Thames in London, but the name was also used for other prisons.)

82. **in that mind:** i.e., that opinion

86. **blowing:** puffing

87. **would needs:** must

88. **presently:** immediately

89. **ensconce me:** i.e., hide

90. **arras:** tapestry wall hanging

FALSTAFF   Thou art a tyrant to say so. Thou wouldst   60
make an absolute courtier, and the firm fixture of
thy foot would give an excellent motion to thy gait
in a semicircled farthingale. I see what thou wert,
if Fortune thy foe were not, Nature thy friend.
Come, thou canst not hide it.   65

MISTRESS FORD   Believe me, there's no such thing in
me.

FALSTAFF   What made me love thee? Let that persuade
thee. There's something extraordinary in thee.
Come, I cannot cog and say thou art this and that   70
like a many of these lisping hawthorn buds that
come like women in men's apparel and smell like
Bucklersbury in simple time. I cannot. But I love
thee, none but thee; and thou deserv'st it.

MISTRESS FORD   Do not betray me, sir. I fear you love   75
Mistress Page.

FALSTAFF   Thou mightst as well say I love to walk by
the Counter gate, which is as hateful to me as the
reek of a lime-kiln.

MISTRESS FORD   Well, heaven knows how I love you,   80
and you shall one day find it.

FALSTAFF   Keep in that mind. I'll deserve it.

MISTRESS FORD   Nay, I must tell you, so you do, or else
I could not be in that mind.

⌜*Enter Robin.*⌝

ROBIN   Mistress Ford, Mistress Ford! Here's Mistress   85
Page at the door, sweating and blowing and looking wildly, and would needs speak with you
presently.

FALSTAFF   She shall not see me. I will ensconce me behind the arras.   90

MISTRESS FORD   Pray you, do so. She's a very tattling
woman.   ⌜*Falstaff stands behind the arras.*⌝

95. **overthrown, undone:** ruined

98. **well-a-day:** alas

99. **honest:** worthy, upright; **to your:** i.e., as your

102. **Out upon you:** an expression of abhorrence and reproach

106. **officers:** i.e., office holders (referring perhaps to the parson Sir Hugh or Justice Shallow), although the meaning "bailiffs" is also present

108. **ill:** wicked

115. **clear:** innocent

116. **friend:** lover

117. **amazed:** i.e., paralyzed or frozen in bewilderment

124. **stand:** i.e., delay by saying

126. **Bethink you:** think; **conveyance:** contrivance; artifice; means of removing (him)

A pumpion. (3.3.40)
From John Gerard, *The herball . . .* (1597).

⌐*Enter Mistress Page.*⌐

What's the matter? How now?

MISTRESS PAGE   O Mistress Ford, what have you done?
You're shamed, you're overthrown, you're undone   95
forever!

MISTRESS FORD   What's the matter, good Mistress Page?

MISTRESS PAGE   O well-a-day, Mistress Ford, having an
honest man to your husband, to give him such
cause of suspicion!   100

MISTRESS FORD   What cause of suspicion?

MISTRESS PAGE   What cause of suspicion? Out upon you!
How am I mistook in you!

MISTRESS FORD   Why, alas, what's the matter?

MISTRESS PAGE   Your husband's coming hither, woman,   105
with all the officers in Windsor, to search for a gentleman that he says is here now in the house, by
your consent, to take an ill advantage of his absence. You are undone.

MISTRESS FORD   'Tis not so, I hope.   110

MISTRESS PAGE   Pray heaven it be not so, that you have
such a man here! But 'tis most certain your husband's coming, with half Windsor at his heels, to
search for such a one. I come before to tell you. If
you know yourself clear, why, I am glad of it. But if   115
you have a friend here, convey, convey him out. Be
not amazed! Call all your senses to you; defend
your reputation, or bid farewell to your good life
forever.

MISTRESS FORD   What shall I do? There is a gentleman,   120
my dear friend; and I fear not mine own shame so
much as his peril. I had rather than a thousand
pound he were out of the house.

MISTRESS PAGE   For shame! Never stand "you had
rather" and "you had rather." Your husband's here   125
at hand. Bethink you of some conveyance. In the

131. **bucking:** washing; **whiting time:** bleaching time

138. **Are ... letters:** i.e., is this your love letter (to me) (The word *letters* often referred to a single piece of correspondence.)

146. **cowlstaff:** a pole or staff used to carry heavy burdens, supported on the shoulders of two bearers (See picture below.) **drumble:** move sluggishly

154. **buck-washing:** process of washing coarse or very dirty linen (In his response Ford uses **buck** as the term for the male deer, the antlers of which are associated with the cuckold that Ford believes himself to be. **Buck** also meant "copulate.")

A cowlstaff. (3.3.146)
From Jean de Glen, *Des habits moeurs* . . . (1601).

house you cannot hide him. O, how have you deceived me! Look, here is a basket. If he be of any
reasonable stature, he may creep in here; and
throw foul linen upon him, as if it were going to   130
bucking. Or—it is whiting time—send him by your
two men to Datchet Mead.

MISTRESS FORD   He's too big to go in there. What shall I
do?   ⌈*Falstaff comes forward.*⌉

FALSTAFF   Let me see't, let me see't! O, let me see't! I'll   135
in, I'll in. Follow your friend's counsel. I'll in.

MISTRESS PAGE   What, Sir John Falstaff? ⌈*(Aside to
him.)*⌉ Are these your letters, knight?

FALSTAFF, ⌈*aside to Mistress Page*⌉   I love thee. Help me
away. Let me creep in here. I'll never—   140

⌈*Falstaff goes into the basket; they cover
him with dirty clothes.*⌉

MISTRESS PAGE, ⌈*to Robin*⌉   Help to cover your master,
boy.—Call your men, Mistress Ford.—You dissembling knight!   ⌈*Robin exits.*⌉

MISTRESS FORD   What, John! Robert! John!

⌈*Enter Robert and John.*⌉

Go, take up these clothes here quickly. Where's the   145
cowlstaff? Look how you drumble! Carry them to
the laundress in Datchet Mead. Quickly! Come.

Enter Ford, Page, ⌈*Doctor*⌉ *Caius,*
⌈*and Sir Hugh*⌉ *Evans.*

FORD   Pray you, come near. If I suspect without cause,
why then make sport at me. Then let me be your
jest; I deserve it.—How now? Whither bear you   150
this?

⌈ROBERT and JOHN⌉   To the laundress, forsooth.

MISTRESS FORD   Why, what have you to do whither they
bear it? You were best meddle with buck-washing!

157. **of the season:** i.e., in mating season, when the antlers are the largest

158. **tonight:** i.e., last night

159. **Ascend:** i.e., go upstairs to

161. **unkennel:** dislodge from its hole; **stop this way:** i.e., close this exit

162. **uncape:** perhaps, uncover (This puzzling and unsatisfactory word is variously emended.)

164. **too much:** extremely

171. **issue:** outcome, result

176. **taking:** state

178–79. **have need of washing:** i.e., having soiled himself in fear

182. **strain:** character, conduct

183. **special:** particular

185. **gross in his jealousy:** i.e., grossly or flagrantly jealous

186. **try:** test, examine

188. **scarce:** i.e., scarcely; **obey:** submit to, i.e., be cured by

189. **carrion:** a term of contempt (literally, dead flesh)

A greyhound. (1.1.88)
From Edward Topsell, *The historie of fourefooted beastes . . .* (1607).

FORD Buck? I would I could wash myself of the buck. 155
Buck, buck, buck! Ay, buck! I warrant you, buck,
and of the season too, it shall appear.
⌜*Robert and John exit with the buck-basket.*⌝
Gentlemen, I have dreamed tonight; I'll tell you my
dream. Here, here, here be my keys. Ascend my
chambers. Search, seek, find out. I'll warrant we'll 160
unkennel the fox. Let me stop this way first. ⌜(*He
locks the door.*)⌝ So, now uncape.

PAGE Good Master Ford, be contented. You wrong
yourself too much.

FORD True, Master Page.—Up, gentlemen. You shall 165
see sport anon. Follow me, gentlemen. ⌜*He exits.*⌝

SIR HUGH This is fery fantastical humors and jealousies.

DOCTOR CAIUS By gar, 'tis no the fashion of France. It is
not jealous in France. 170

PAGE Nay, follow him, gentlemen. See the issue of his
search. ⌜*Page, Sir Hugh, and Caius exit*⌝

MISTRESS PAGE Is there not a double excellency in this?

MISTRESS FORD I know not which pleases me better—
that my husband is deceived, or Sir John. 175

MISTRESS PAGE What a taking was he in when your
husband asked who was in the basket!

MISTRESS FORD I am half afraid he will have need of
washing, so throwing him into the water will do
him a benefit. 180

MISTRESS PAGE Hang him, dishonest rascal! I would all
of the same strain were in the same distress.

MISTRESS FORD I think my husband hath some special
suspicion of Falstaff's being here, for I never saw
him so gross in his jealousy till now. 185

MISTRESS PAGE I will lay a plot to try that, and we will
yet have more tricks with Falstaff. His dissolute
disease will scarce obey this medicine.

MISTRESS FORD Shall we send that foolish carrion Mis-

190. **excuse:** make excuses or explanations for; **throwing:** i.e., being thrown

196. **that:** i.e., that which; **compass:** achieve

199. **use:** treat

208. **presses:** cupboards

209. **the day of judgment:** Doomsday (See picture below.)

212. **suggests:** prompts; **imagination:** fantasy

213. **your distemper in this kind:** i.e., the sort of mental derangement from which you suffer

215. **my fault:** a blamable quality in me

"The day of judgment." (3.3.209)
From Thomas Fisher's etching of the wall painting of Doomsday
in the Guild Chapel at Stratford-upon-Avon (1807).

tress Quickly to him, and excuse his throwing into 190
the water, and give him another hope, to betray
him to another punishment?

MISTRESS PAGE   We will do it. Let him be sent for tomorrow eight o'clock to have amends.

⌐*Enter Ford, Page, Doctor Caius, and Sir Hugh.*¬

FORD   I cannot find him. Maybe the knave bragged of 195
that he could not compass.

MISTRESS PAGE, ⌐*aside to Mistress Ford*¬   Heard you
that?

MISTRESS FORD   You use me well, Master Ford, do you?

FORD   Ay, I do so. 200

MISTRESS FORD   Heaven make you better than your
thoughts!

FORD   Amen!

MISTRESS PAGE   You do yourself mighty wrong, Master
Ford. 205

FORD   Ay, ay. I must bear it.

SIR HUGH   If there be anypody in the house, and in the
chambers, and in the coffers, and in the presses,
heaven forgive my sins at the day of judgment!

DOCTOR CAIUS   Be gar, nor I too. There is nobodies. 210

PAGE   Fie, fie, Master Ford, are you not ashamed?
What spirit, what devil suggests this imagination?
I would not ha' your distemper in this kind for the
wealth of Windsor Castle.

FORD   'Tis my fault, Master Page. I suffer for it. 215

SIR HUGH   You suffer for a pad conscience. Your wife is
as honest a 'omans as I will desires among five
thousand, and five hundred too.

DOCTOR CAIUS   By gar, I see 'tis an honest woman.

FORD   Well, I promised you a dinner. Come, come, 220
walk in the park. I pray you, pardon me. I will
hereafter make known to you why I have done

228. a-birding: i.e., hunt small birds

229. hawk for the bush: i.e., sparrow **hawk** to drive the birds into the leafless bushes (to make it easier to shoot them)

3.4 Attempting to court Anne Page, Fenton is interrupted first by his rival Slender and then by a hostile Master and Mistress Page.

———————

1. **love:** i.e., approval
2. **turn:** refer, direct
4. **be thyself:** i.e., act independently (without reference to your father's wishes)
6. **my state . . . expense:** i.e., my estate having been depleted by my extravagance **state:** estate **galled:** chafed, irritated **expense:** extravagance, wastefulness

this.—Come, wife—come, Mistress Page, I pray
you, pardon me. Pray, heartily, pardon me.
⌐*Mistress Page and Mistress Ford exit.*¬

PAGE, ⌐*to Caius and Sir Hugh*¬ Let's go in, gentlemen.   225
But, trust me, we'll mock him. ⌐*(To Ford, Caius,
and Sir Hugh.)*¬ I do invite you tomorrow morning
to my house to breakfast. After, we'll a-birding together; I have a fine hawk for the bush. Shall it be
so?   230

FORD   Anything.

SIR HUGH   If there is one, I shall make two in the company.

DOCTOR CAIUS   If there be one or two, I shall make-a the
turd.   235

FORD   Pray you, go, Master Page.
⌐*Ford and Page exit.*¬

SIR HUGH   I pray you now, remembrance tomorrow on
the lousy knave mine Host.

DOCTOR CAIUS   Dat is good, by gar, with all my heart.

SIR HUGH   A lousy knave, to have his gibes and his   240
mockeries!

They exit.

Scene 4

Enter Fenton ⌐*and*¬ *Anne Page.*

FENTON
I see I cannot get thy father's love;
Therefore no more turn me to him, sweet Nan.

ANNE
Alas, how then?

FENTON   Why, thou must be thyself.
He doth object I am too great of birth,   5
And that, my state being galled with my expense,
I seek to heal it only by his wealth.

9. **riots:** dissipations, extravagances; **societies:** company

13. **speed me:** make me prosper

17. **stamps in gold:** gold coins

22. **suit:** petition

26. **make . . . bolt on 't:** proverbial for "do it one way or another" (A **shaft** is a long, slender arrow used with a longbow, a **bolt** a short, thick arrow used with a crossbow.) **'Slid:** by God's eyelid (a strong oath)

28. **dismayed:** overcome by fear

30. **but . . . afeard:** except **that I am** afraid

34. **ill-favored:** ugly

Book of Riddles. (1.1.196–97)
From *A new booke of merry riddles . . .* [1665].

Besides these, other bars he lays before me—
My riots past, my wild societies—
And tells me 'tis a thing impossible   10
I should love thee but as a property.

ANNE Maybe he tells you true.

⌐FENTON⌐
No, heaven so speed me in my time to come!
Albeit I will confess thy father's wealth
Was the first motive that I wooed thee, Anne,   15
Yet, wooing thee, I found thee of more value
Than stamps in gold or sums in sealèd bags.
And 'tis the very riches of thyself
That now I aim at.

ANNE   Gentle Master Fenton,   20
Yet seek my father's love, still seek it, sir.
If opportunity and humblest suit
Cannot attain it, why then—hark you hither.
                          ⌐*They talk aside.*⌐

Enter Shallow, Slender, ⌐*and Mistress*⌐ *Quickly.*

SHALLOW Break their talk, Mistress Quickly. My kinsman shall speak for himself.   25

SLENDER I'll make a shaft or a bolt on 't. 'Slid, 'tis but
venturing.

SHALLOW Be not dismayed.

SLENDER No, she shall not dismay me. I care not for
that, but that I am afeard.   30

MISTRESS QUICKLY, ⌐*to Anne*⌐ Hark ye, Master Slender
would speak a word with you.

ANNE
I come to him. ⌐*(Aside.)*⌐ This is my father's choice.
O, what a world of vile ill-favored faults
Looks handsome in three hundred pounds a year!   35

MISTRESS QUICKLY And how does good Master Fenton?
Pray you, a word with you.   ⌐*They talk aside.*⌐

SHALLOW, ⌐*to Slender*⌐ She's coming. To her, coz! O
boy, thou hadst a father!

44. **cousin:** i.e., nephew, kinsman

48. **come cut and longtail:** proverbial for "whatever happens" (**Cut** refers to a horse or dog whose tail has been docked, **longtail** to one with a full tail.)

48–49. **under the degree:** in the manner of the rank

50. **make:** provide

50–51. **a hundred . . . jointure:** i.e., a settlement that would (if and when she becomes a widow) provide her annually half his income (See line 35.)

57. **your will:** your wish, your pleasure

58. **'Od's heartlings:** by God's (little) heart (another strong oath); **pretty:** fine, excellent

65. **motions:** proposals

65–66. **happy man be his dole:** proverbial for "good luck to the winner"   **dole:** fate, destiny

A Fool wearing a coxcomb. (3.1.89; 5.5.146)
From Desiderius Erasmus, *Moria[e] enkomion . . .* (1676).

SLENDER   I had a father, Mistress Anne; my uncle can   40
  tell you good jests of him.—Pray you, uncle, tell
  Mistress Anne the jest how my father stole two
  geese out of a pen, good uncle.

SHALLOW   Mistress Anne, my cousin loves you.

SLENDER   Ay, that I do, as well as I love any woman in   45
  Gloucestershire.

SHALLOW   He will maintain you like a gentlewoman.

SLENDER   Ay, that I will, come cut and longtail, under
  the degree of a squire.

SHALLOW   He will make you a hundred and fifty   50
  pounds jointure.

ANNE   Good Master Shallow, let him woo for himself.

SHALLOW   Marry, I thank you for it. I thank you for that
  good comfort.—She calls you, coz. I'll leave you.

                           ⌈*He steps aside.*⌉

ANNE   Now, Master Slender.   55

SLENDER   Now, good Mistress Anne.

ANNE   What is your will?

SLENDER   My will? 'Od's heartlings, that's a pretty jest
  indeed! I ne'er made my will yet, I thank heaven. I
  am not such a sickly creature, I give heaven praise.   60

ANNE   I mean, Master Slender, what would you with
  me?

SLENDER   Truly, for mine own part, I would little or
  nothing with you. Your father and my uncle hath
  made motions. If it be my luck, so; if not, happy   65
  man be his dole. They can tell you how things go
  better than I can. You may ask your father.

        Enter Page ⌈*and*⌉ *Mistress Page.*

  Here he comes.

PAGE
  Now, Master Slender.—Love him, daughter Anne.—
  Why, how now? What does Master Fenton here?   70

73. **impatient:** i.e., angry (literally, irascible)

75. **match:** (1) potential mate; (2) equal

81. **for that:** because

83. **against ... manners:** i.e., in resistance to all rebuffs and **rebukes** (from the Page family) and contrary to my own good **manners**

84. **advance the colors:** lift up the flag or insignia (military language, continued in line 85 with **retire,** i.e., retreat)

87. **mean:** intend

89. **set quick:** buried alive (up to the neck)

94. **affected:** inclined, disposed

97. **gentle mistress:** i.e., Mistress Page (**Gentle** was used in polite or ingratiating address.)

An Elizabethan shilling. (1.1.151)
From Edward Hawkins, *The silver coins of England* . . . (1841).

You wrong me, sir, thus still to haunt my house.
I told you, sir, my daughter is disposed of.

FENTON
Nay, Master Page, be not impatient.

MISTRESS PAGE
Good Master Fenton, come not to my child.

PAGE   She is no match for you.   75

FENTON   Sir, will you hear me?

PAGE   No, good Master Fenton.—
Come Master Shallow.—Come, son Slender, in.—
Knowing my mind, you wrong me, Master Fenton.
⌜*Page, Shallow, and Slender exit.*⌝

MISTRESS QUICKLY, ⌜*to Fenton*⌝   Speak to Mistress Page.   80

FENTON
Good Mistress Page, for that I love your daughter
In such a righteous fashion as I do,
Perforce, against all checks, rebukes, and manners,
I must advance the colors of my love
And not retire. Let me have your good will.   85

ANNE
Good mother, do not marry me to yond fool.

MISTRESS PAGE
I mean it not; I seek you a better husband.

MISTRESS QUICKLY   That's my master, Master Doctor.

ANNE
Alas, I had rather be set quick i' th' earth
And bowled to death with turnips!   90

MISTRESS PAGE
Come, trouble not yourself.—Good Master Fenton,
I will not be your friend nor enemy.
My daughter will I question how she loves you,
And as I find her, so am I affected.
Till then, farewell, sir. She must needs go in;   95
Her father will be angry.

FENTON
Farewell, gentle mistress.—Farewell, Nan.
⌜*Mistress Page and Anne Page exit.*⌝

99–100. **a fool . . . physician:** Quickly's adaptation of the proverb "either **a fool** or **a physician**"

102. **once tonight:** sometime **tonight**

108. **in sooth:** indeed

111. **speciously:** confusion for "especially"

112. **must of:** i.e., **must** go on; **must** undertake

113. **slack:** neglect

3.5 Falstaff agrees once again to visit Mistress Ford and again informs "Brook" of his plans.

———————

3. **toast:** piece of bread toasted at the fire (often put in wine or beer)

4. **barrow:** barrow load

8. **'Sblood:** God's blood

"Tester I'll have in pouch. . . ." (1.3.90)
From *The araignment of John Selman . . .* (1611).

124

MISTRESS QUICKLY   This is my doing now. "Nay," said I,
"will you cast away your child on a fool and a
physician? Look on Master Fenton." This is my   100
doing.

FENTON
I thank thee; and I pray thee, once tonight
Give my sweet Nan this ring. There's for thy pains.
⌜*He gives her money and a ring.*⌝
MISTRESS QUICKLY   Now heaven send thee good fortune.
⌜*Fenton exits.*⌝
A kind heart he hath. A woman would run through   105
fire and water for such a kind heart. But yet I
would my master had Mistress Anne, or I would
Master Slender had her, or, in sooth, I would Mas-
ter Fenton had her. I will do what I can for them all
three; for so I have promised and I'll be as good as   110
my word—but speciously for Master Fenton. Well,
I must of another errand to Sir John Falstaff from
my two mistresses. What a beast am I to slack it!
⌜*She*⌝ *exits.*

Scene 5

Enter ⌜*Sir John*⌝ *Falstaff.*

FALSTAFF   Bardolph, I say!

Enter Bardolph.

BARDOLPH   Here, sir.
FALSTAFF   Go fetch me a quart of sack; put a toast in 't.
⌜*Bardolph exits.*⌝
Have I lived to be carried in a basket like a barrow
of butcher's offal, and to be thrown in the Thames?   5
Well, if I be served such another trick, I'll have my
brains ta'en out and buttered, and give them to a
dog for a New Year's gift. ⌜'Sblood,⌝ the rogues

9. **slighted:** of uncertain meaning (perhaps a combination of **slighted** [disdained] and *slid*); **remorse:** pity, compassion

10. **blind bitch's puppies:** perhaps, a deliberate comic inversion, for presumably the **puppies,** not the bitch, would be **blind**

13–14. **had been:** i.e., would have been

14. **shore:** bank; **shelvy:** sloped

18. **mummy:** i.e., mummified flesh, which was used as medicine

23. **reins:** kidneys

26. **cry you mercy:** beg your pardon

26–27. **Give . . . morrow:** i.e., **good** morning to **your Worship**

29. **brew:** prepare, concoct; **pottle:** half-gallon; **finely:** skillfully

31. **Simple of itself:** i.e., pure, unadulterated

32. **brewage:** concoction

40. **take on with:** rage at

41. **erection:** confusion for "direction"

A gibbet. (2.2.17)
From *Warhafftige . . . Verrätherey . . .* (1606).

slighted me into the river with as little remorse as
they would have drowned a blind bitch's puppies,   10
fifteen i' th' litter! And you may know by my size
that I have a kind of alacrity in sinking; if the bot-
tom were as deep as hell, I should down. I had
been drowned, but that the shore was shelvy and
shallow—a death that I abhor, for the water swells   15
a man, and what a thing should I have been when
I had been swelled! ⌜By the Lord,⌝ I should have
been a mountain of mummy.

⌜*Enter Bardolph with cups of sack.*⌝

BARDOLPH   Here's Mistress Quickly, sir, to speak with
you.   20
FALSTAFF   Come, let me pour in some sack to the
Thames water, for my belly's as cold as if I had
swallowed snowballs for pills to cool the reins. ⌜*He
drinks.*⌝ Call her in.
BARDOLPH   Come in, woman.   25

Enter ⌜*Mistress*⌝ *Quickly.*

MISTRESS QUICKLY   By your leave, I cry you mercy. Give
your Worship good morrow.
FALSTAFF, ⌜*to Bardolph*⌝   Take away these chalices. Go
brew me a pottle of sack finely.
BARDOLPH   With eggs, sir?   30
FALSTAFF   Simple of itself. I'll no pullet sperm in my
brewage.   ⌜*Bardolph exits.*⌝
How now?
MISTRESS QUICKLY   Marry, sir, I come to your Worship
from Mistress Ford.   35
FALSTAFF   Mistress Ford? I have had ford enough. I
was thrown into the ford, I have my belly full of
ford.
MISTRESS QUICKLY   Alas the day, good heart, that was
not her fault. She does so take on with her men;   40
they mistook their erection.

45. **yearn:** move to compassion

51. **his frailty:** i.e., man's **frailty** (Proverbial: "Flesh is frail.")

58. **not of:** i.e., not from

68. **sped you:** i.e., did you succeed

69. **ill-favoredly:** badly (*Ill-favored* means "ugly.")

72. **peaking:** sneaking; mean-spirited; **cornuto:** cuckold

74. **'larum:** i.e., state of alarm (literally, alarm, hubbub, uproar); **comes me in:** i.e., **comes in**

A cat-a-mountain. (2.2.26)
From Edward Topsell, *The historie of fourefooted beastes . . .* (1607).

128

FALSTAFF So did I mine, to build upon a foolish
woman's promise.

MISTRESS QUICKLY Well, she laments, sir, for it, that it
would yearn your heart to see it. Her husband goes   45
this morning a-birding; she desires you once more
to come to her, between eight and nine. I must
carry her word quickly. She'll make you amends, I
warrant you.

FALSTAFF Well, I will visit her. Tell her so. And bid her   50
think what a man is. Let her consider his frailty,
and then judge of my merit.

MISTRESS QUICKLY I will tell her.

FALSTAFF Do so. Between nine and ten, say'st thou?

MISTRESS QUICKLY Eight and nine, sir.   55

FALSTAFF Well, be gone. I will not miss her.

MISTRESS QUICKLY Peace be with you, sir.
⌜*Mistress Quickly exits.*⌝

FALSTAFF I marvel I hear not of Master ⌜Brook.⌝ He
sent me word to stay within. I like his money well.

Enter Ford ⌜disguised as Brook.⌝

O, here ⌜he⌝ comes.   60

FORD, ⌜*as Brook*⌝ ⌜God⌝ bless you, sir.

FALSTAFF Now, Master ⌜Brook,⌝ you come to know
what hath passed between me and Ford's wife.

FORD, ⌜*as Brook*⌝ That indeed, Sir John, is my business.   65

FALSTAFF Master ⌜Brook,⌝ I will not lie to you. I was at
her house the hour she appointed me.

FORD, ⌜*as Brook*⌝ And sped you, sir?

FALSTAFF Very ill-favoredly, Master ⌜Brook.⌝

FORD, ⌜*as Brook*⌝ How so, sir? Did she change her de-   70
termination?

FALSTAFF No, Master ⌜Brook,⌝ but the peaking cornuto
her husband, Master ⌜Brook,⌝ dwelling in a continual 'larum of jealousy, comes me in the instant of

76. **protested:** i.e., solemnly proclaimed (our love to each other)

79. **distemper:** deranged mental condition

86. **intelligence of:** information about

87. **invention:** inventiveness, ability to plan

92. **shirts and smocks:** men's and women's undergarments

96. **lay:** remained

100. **knaves, hinds:** literally, servants, but the words are also pejorative

101. **in the name:** under the designation

107. **held his hand:** i.e., **held** him back

110. **several:** separate, individual

Mount Etna. (3.5.128)
From Gabriel Rollenhagen, *Nucleus emblematum selectissimorum . . .* (1611).

our encounter, after we had embraced, kissed,   75
protested, and, as it were, spoke the prologue of
our comedy, and, at his heels, a rabble of his companions, thither provoked and instigated by his
distemper, and, forsooth, to search his house for
his wife's love.   80

FORD, ⌜*as Brook*⌝   What, while you were there?

FALSTAFF   While I was there.

FORD, ⌜*as Brook*⌝   And did he search for you and could
not find you?

FALSTAFF   You shall hear. As good luck would have it,   85
comes in one Mistress Page, gives intelligence of
Ford's approach, and, in her invention and Ford's
wife's distraction, they conveyed me into a buck-
basket.

FORD, ⌜*as Brook*⌝   A buck-basket!   90

FALSTAFF   ⌜By the Lord,⌝ a buck-basket! Rammed me
in with foul shirts and smocks, socks, foul stockings, greasy napkins, that, Master ⌜Brook,⌝ there
was the rankest compound of villainous smell that
ever offended nostril.   95

FORD, ⌜*as Brook*⌝   And how long lay you there?

FALSTAFF   Nay, you shall hear, Master ⌜Brook,⌝ what I
have suffered to bring this woman to evil for your
good. Being thus crammed in the basket, a couple
of Ford's knaves, his hinds, were called forth by   100
their mistress to carry me in the name of foul
clothes to Datchet Lane. They took me on their
shoulders, met the jealous knave their master in
the door, who asked them once or twice what they
had in their basket. I quaked for fear lest the lu-   105
natic knave would have searched it, but fate, or-
daining he should be a cuckold, held his hand.
Well, on went he for a search, and away went I for
foul clothes. But mark the sequel, Master ⌜Brook.⌝
I suffered the pangs of three several deaths: first,   110

111. **with:** i.e., by

112. **rotten bellwether:** leading sheep of a flock, suffering from the disease of sheep rot (with word-play on **bellwether** as "noisy person") For the possible connection of **bellwether** with cuckoldry, see longer note, page 211. **compassed:** bent into a circle or curve

113. **bilbo:** sword (from Bilbao, where swords were made to be so flexible that they could be bent **hilt to point**); **peck:** two-gallon vessel or basket

114. **stopped in:** shut up

115. **distillation:** vapor produced by means of heating a substance

115–16. **fretted:** corrupted

120. **bath:** state of being suffused with a liquid

123. **surge:** heavy or violent wave (one of many exaggerations in this speech)

125. **In good sadness:** i.e., in all seriousness

126. **suit:** courtship (of Mistress Ford)

127. **undertake:** engage with

128. **Etna:** a volcano in Sicily (See picture, page 130.)

131–32. **embassy of meeting:** message to meet (Falstaff again exaggerates, for an **embassy** is a message delivered by an ambassador.)

135. **address me:** i.e., **address** myself, make my way, betake myself

143. **There's a hole made in your best coat:** i.e., someone has the upper hand over you (proverbial)

146. **take:** capture, seize

an intolerable fright to be detected with a jealous
rotten bellwether; next, to be compassed, like a
good bilbo, in the circumference of a peck, hilt to
point, heel to head; and then, to be stopped in, like
a strong distillation, with stinking clothes that fret-   115
ted in their own grease. Think of that, a man of my
kidney—think of that—that am as subject to heat
as butter; a man of continual dissolution and thaw.
It was a miracle to 'scape suffocation. And in
the height of this bath, when I was more than half-   120
stewed in grease, like a Dutch dish, to be thrown
into the Thames and cooled, glowing hot, in that
surge, like a horseshoe! Think of that—hissing
hot—think of that, Master ⌜Brook.⌝

FORD, ⌜*as Brook*⌝   In good sadness, sir, I am sorry that   125
for my sake you have suffered all this. My suit,
then, is desperate. You'll undertake her no more?

FALSTAFF   Master ⌜Brook,⌝ I will be thrown into Etna,
as I have been into Thames, ere I will leave her
thus. Her husband is this morning gone a-birding.   130
I have received from her another embassy of meeting. 'Twixt eight and nine is the hour, Master
⌜Brook.⌝

FORD, ⌜*as Brook*⌝   'Tis past eight already, sir.

FALSTAFF   Is it? I will then address me to my appoint-   135
ment. Come to me at your convenient leisure,
and you shall know how I speed; and the conclusion shall be crowned with your enjoying her.
Adieu. You shall have her, Master ⌜Brook.⌝ Master
⌜Brook,⌝ you shall cuckold Ford.   ⌜*Falstaff exits.*⌝   140

FORD   Hum! Ha! Is this a vision? Is this a dream? Do I
sleep? Master Ford, awake! Awake, Master Ford!
There's a hole made in your best coat, Master
Ford. This 'tis to be married; this 'tis to have linen
and buck-baskets! Well, I will proclaim myself   145
what I am. I will now take the lecher. He is at my

148. **half-penny purse: purse** for small coins
151–52. **yet to be:** i.e., but being
152. **would not:** do not want to be
154. **horn-mad:** Proverbial: "He is **horn-mad**."
Horn-mad meant both "mad with rage" and "enraged at wearing the horns of the cuckold." See longer note to 2.1.122, page 209.

A cuckold. (2.1.122; 3.5.72)
From *Bagford ballads* (printed in 1878).

house. He cannot 'scape me. 'Tis impossible he
should. He cannot creep into a half-penny purse,
nor into a pepper-box. But lest the devil that
guides him should aid him, I will search impossi-   150
ble places. Though what I am I cannot avoid, yet to
be what I would not shall not make me tame. If I
have horns to make one mad, let the proverb go
with me: I'll be horn-mad.

⌜*He*⌝ *exits.*

THE
MERRY WIVES
OF WINDSOR

ACT 4

4.1 William, the young son of Master and Mistress Page, is briefly tested on his Latin by Sir Hugh.

3–4. **presently:** immediately

4. **courageous:** another of Quickly's confusions of words; perhaps, for "outrageously" or "ragingly"

6. **suddenly:** shortly, very soon

7. **by and by:** directly, at once

8. **young man:** Because he is only beginning to study Latin grammar, William Page would be about six or seven.

11–12. **Slender . . . play:** i.e., **Slender,** apparently considered a distinguished visitor, has asked that the schoolboys be given a holiday in his honor (an English custom)

16. **accidence:** rudiments of (Latin) grammar, or a book containing such a grammar (The book that underlies this scene is Lilly and Colet's often reprinted *A Shorte Introduction of Grammar,* the standard grammar-school text, probably in the 1577 edition, which William subsequently quotes.)

21. **numbers:** As Lilly notes, "In Nounes be **two Numbers,** the Singular and the Plurall."

ACT 4

Scene 1

Enter Mistress Page, ⌈Mistress⌉ Quickly, ⌈and⌉ William.

MISTRESS PAGE   Is he at Master Ford's already, think'st
thou?

MISTRESS QUICKLY   Sure he is by this, or will be presently. But truly he is very courageous mad about
his throwing into the water. Mistress Ford desires   5
you to come suddenly.

MISTRESS PAGE   I'll be with her by and by. I'll but bring
my young man here to school.

Enter ⌈Sir Hugh⌉ Evans.

Look where his master comes. 'Tis a playing day, I
see.—How now, Sir Hugh, no school today?   10

SIR HUGH   No. Master Slender is let the boys leave to
play.

MISTRESS QUICKLY   Blessing of his heart!

MISTRESS PAGE   Sir Hugh, my husband says my son
profits nothing in the world at his book. I pray you,   15
ask him some questions in his accidence.

SIR HUGH   Come hither, William. Hold up your head.
Come.

MISTRESS PAGE   Come on, sirrah. Hold up your head.
Answer your master. Be not afraid.   20

SIR HUGH   William, how many numbers is in nouns?

WILLIAM   Two.

24. **'Od's nouns:** i.e., by God's (Christ's) wounds; but, for Quickly, the phrase apparently means "odd (i.e., three) **nouns**"

25. **Peace your tattlings:** i.e., stop your prattling or chattering

27. **Pulcher:** Latin for "fair" (i.e., beautiful)

28. **Polecats:** small European weasels (not American **polecats** or skunks) Although the word is slang for prostitutes, the present context does not suggest that this meaning is relevant. **fairer:** more beautiful

30. **simplicity:** confusion for "simple" (i.e., foolish)

35. **It is lapis:** See longer note, page 211.

38. **he:** i.e., it

40–42. **Articles . . . hoc:** a direct quotation from the Lilly and Colet grammar book **hic, haec, hoc:** i.e., this (in the masculine, feminine, and neuter forms) For *this* as an article, and for the meanings of other Latin words here, see longer note, page 211.

44. **huius:** i.e., of this

45. **hinc:** Latin for "hence," "here," etc. (William should have replied *"hunc, hanc, hoc"*—or, as Sir Hugh pronounces it, **"hung, hang, hog"** [line 47].)

48. **bacon:** One method of curing pork (or **hog**) to produce **bacon** is to **hang** it.

50. **prabbles:** perhaps, quibbles

51. **focative:** This mispronunciation of "vocative" sounds like a vulgar word for copulation, thereby providing a context for vulgar double-meanings for a number of words that follow. **case:** (1) grammatical form; (2) vagina

(continued)

MISTRESS QUICKLY   Truly, I thought there had been one
    number more, because they say " 'Od's nouns."
SIR HUGH   Peace your tattlings!—What is "fair,"   25
    William?
WILLIAM   *Pulcher.*
MISTRESS QUICKLY   Polecats? There are fairer things
    than polecats, sure.
SIR HUGH   You are a very simplicity 'oman. I pray you,   30
    peace.—What is *lapis*, William?
WILLIAM   A stone.
SIR HUGH   And what is "a stone," William?
WILLIAM   A pebble.
SIR HUGH   No. It is *lapis*. I pray you, remember in your   35
    prain.
WILLIAM   *Lapis.*
SIR HUGH   That is a good William. What is he, William,
    that does lend articles?
WILLIAM   Articles are borrowed of the pronoun and be   40
    thus declined: *singulariter, nominativo, hic, haec,*
    hoc.
SIR HUGH   *Nominativo, hig, haeg, hog.* Pray you, mark:
    genitivo, huius. Well, what is your accusative case?
WILLIAM   *Accusativo, hinc.*   45
SIR HUGH   I pray you, have your remembrance, child.
    Accusativo, ⌜*hung,*⌝ *hang, hog.*
MISTRESS QUICKLY   "Hang-hog" is Latin for bacon, I
    warrant you.
SIR HUGH   Leave your prabbles, 'oman.—What is the   50
    focative case, William?
WILLIAM   O—*vocativo*—O—
SIR HUGH   Remember, William, focative is *caret.*
MISTRESS QUICKLY   And that's a good root.
SIR HUGH   'Oman, forbear.   55
MISTRESS PAGE, ⌜*to Mistress Quickly*⌝   Peace!
SIR HUGH   What is your genitive case plural, William?
WILLIAM   Genitive case?

52. **O:** (1) the sound William makes as he hesitates at a loss for an answer; (2) the interjection that often immediately precedes a vocative ("O, Romeo"); (3) the vagina

53. **focative is caret:** i.e., there is no vocative (of *hic*) (Literally, **caret** means "is wanting"; thus Sir Hugh's **"is caret"** is clumsily redundant.)

54. **root:** Quickly's confusion of **caret** for "carrot," which was slang for "phallus"

60. **horum, harum, horum:** i.e., of these (in the masculine, feminine, and neuter forms) Mistress Quickly confuses these words with **whore** (line 62).

61. **Vengeance of:** i.e., a plague on, to hell with; **Ginny's case: Ginny's** genitals

65. **to hick and to hack:** of somewhat uncertain meaning, although most probably **hack** is slang for "copulate"

77. **qui, quae, quod:** i.e., who, which, what, etc. (in the masculine, feminine, and neuter forms)

79. **preeches:** i.e., breeched, whipped on the buttocks (customary punishment for schoolboys who did not learn their Latin)

82. **sprag:** perhaps Sir Hugh's mispronunciation of "sprack" (The word *sprackly* meant "actively, smartly.")

4.2 Visiting Mistress Ford, Falstaff is again interrupted by Mistress Page, again with news of Ford's threatening approach. This time the women effect Falstaff's escape by dressing him as an old woman hated by Ford. This disguise gains Falstaff a beating from Ford.

_____

(continued)

SIR HUGH   Ay.

WILLIAM   Genitive: *horum, harum, horum.*   60

MISTRESS QUICKLY   Vengeance of Ginny's case! Fie on
her! Never name her, child, if she be a whore.

SIR HUGH   For shame, 'oman!

MISTRESS QUICKLY   You do ill to teach the child such
words.—He teaches him to hick and to hack,   65
which they'll do fast enough of themselves, and to
call "whorum."—Fie upon you!

SIR HUGH   'Oman, art thou lunatics? Hast thou no un-
derstandings for thy cases and the numbers of the
genders? Thou art as foolish Christian creatures as   70
I would desires.

MISTRESS PAGE, ⌜*to Mistress Quickly*⌝   Prithee, hold thy
peace.

SIR HUGH   Show me now, William, some declensions of
your pronouns.   75

WILLIAM   Forsooth, I have forgot.

SIR HUGH   It is *qui, quae, quod.* If you forget your *qui*'s,
your *quae*'s, and your *quod*'s, you must be
preeches. Go your ways and play, go.

MISTRESS PAGE   He is a better scholar than I thought he   80
was.

SIR HUGH   He is a good sprag memory. Farewell, Mistress Page.

MISTRESS PAGE   Adieu, good Sir Hugh.—Get you home,
boy. ⌜(*To Mistress Quickly.*)⌝ Come. We stay too   85
long.

They exit.

Scene 2

Enter ⌜Sir John⌝ Falstaff ⌜and⌝ Mistress Ford.

FALSTAFF   Mistress Ford, your sorrow hath eaten up
my sufferance. I see you are obsequious in your
love, and I profess requital to a hair's breadth, not

2. **sufferance:** suffering, trouble, wrong (Falstaff varies his language when attempting to seduce Mistress Ford. In this speech, he uses very elevated, Latinate diction.) **obsequious:** compliant

4. **office:** service, function

5. **accoutrement:** trappings; **compliment:** i.e., observances, formalities

8. **gossip:** friend (among women a form of address to a familiar acquaintance)

13. **people:** servants; family members (The distinction between the two was not as marked as today.)

21. **lunes:** fits of lunacy, tantrums; **takes on:** rages

23. **Eve's daughters:** i.e., women (The phrase implies that women have inherited **Eve's** duplicity.) **complexion:** disposition, physical constitution, appearance

25. **Peer out:** a command for his cuckold's horns to manifest themselves

34. **experiment:** trial

A coat of arms with luces. (1.1.16–17)
From Sir William Dugdale, *The antiquities of Warwickshire* . . . (1656).

only, Mistress Ford, in the simple office of love,
but in all the accoutrement, compliment, and cere-   5
mony of it. But are you sure of your husband now?

MISTRESS FORD   He's a-birding, sweet Sir John.

MISTRESS PAGE, ⌜*within*⌝   What ho, gossip Ford! What
ho!

MISTRESS FORD   Step into th' chamber, Sir John.   10
                              ⌜*Falstaff exits.*⌝

Enter Mistress Page.

MISTRESS PAGE   How now, sweetheart, who's at home
besides yourself?

MISTRESS FORD   Why, none but mine own people.

MISTRESS PAGE   Indeed?

MISTRESS FORD   No, certainly. ⌜*Aside to her.*⌝ Speak   15
louder.

MISTRESS PAGE   Truly, I am so glad you have nobody
here.

MISTRESS FORD   Why?

MISTRESS PAGE   Why, woman, your husband is in his   20
old ⌜lunes⌝ again. He so takes on yonder with my
husband, so rails against all married mankind, so
curses all Eve's daughters of what complexion soever, and so buffets himself on the forehead, crying
"Peer out, peer out!" that any madness I ever yet   25
beheld seemed but tameness, civility, and patience
to this his distemper he is in now. I am glad the fat
knight is not here.

MISTRESS FORD   Why, does he talk of him?

MISTRESS PAGE   Of none but him, and swears he was   30
carried out, the last time he searched for him, in a
basket; protests to my husband he is now here;
and hath drawn him and the rest of their company
from their sport to make another experiment of
his suspicion. But I am glad the knight is not here.   35
Now he shall see his own foolery.

38. **Hard:** near
39. **anon:** immediately
40. **undone:** ruined
42. **What:** what kind of
46. **bestow:** dispose of
53. **make you:** i.e., are you doing
57. **birding pieces:** small guns for shooting birds
58. **kiln-hole:** oven
61. **press:** cupboard
62. **abstract:** i.e., list (literally, summary); **for the remembrance of:** i.e., to remind himself about
63. **note:** a brief record written down to assist the memory
70. **gown:** i.e., dress

A country woman wearing a muffler. (4.2.71)
From John Speed, *The theatre of the empire of
Great Britaine . . .* (1627 [i.e., 1631]).

MISTRESS FORD   How near is he, Mistress Page?

MISTRESS PAGE   Hard by, at street end. He will be here anon.

MISTRESS FORD   I am undone! The knight is here.   40

MISTRESS PAGE   Why then, you are utterly shamed, and he's but a dead man. What a woman are you! Away with him, away with him! Better shame than murder.

MISTRESS FORD   Which way should he go? How should   45
I bestow him? Shall I put him into the basket again?

⌜*Enter Sir John Falstaff.*⌝

FALSTAFF   No, I'll come no more i' th' basket. May I not go out ere he come?

MISTRESS PAGE   Alas, three of Master Ford's brothers   50
watch the door with pistols, that none shall issue out. Otherwise you might slip away ere he came. But what make you here?

FALSTAFF   What shall I do? I'll creep up into the chimney.   55

MISTRESS FORD   There they always use to discharge their birding pieces.

⌜MISTRESS PAGE⌝   Creep into the kiln-hole.

FALSTAFF   Where is it?

MISTRESS FORD   He will seek there, on my word. Nei-   60
ther press, coffer, chest, trunk, well, vault, but he hath an abstract for the remembrance of such places, and goes to them by his note. There is no hiding you in the house.

FALSTAFF   I'll go out, then.   65

MISTRESS ⌜PAGE⌝   If you go out in your own semblance, you die, Sir John—unless you go out disguised.

MISTRESS FORD   How might we disguise him?

MISTRESS PAGE   Alas the day, I know not. There is no woman's gown big enough for him; otherwise he   70

71. **muffler:** scarf worn by women to cover the face and neck (See picture, page 146.)

73–74. **extremity:** extreme action or suffering

74. **mischief:** calamity; injury

76. **Brentford:** a village east of Windsor; **above:** upstairs

78. **thrummed:** fringed

81. **look:** search for

83. **straight:** straightway, immediately; **the while:** in the meantime

84. **would:** wish

85. **shape:** disguise

91. **in good sadness:** in earnest, no joking

92–93. **intelligence:** information

94. **try:** test

97. **presently:** immediately

102. **dishonest:** lewd, filthy; dishonorable

105. **honest:** chaste (This line challenges the then-accepted claim that chaste women were silent, not **merry.** There is an obvious allusion to the play's title.)

might put on a hat, a muffler, and a kerchief, and
so escape.

FALSTAFF Good hearts, devise something. Any extremity rather than a mischief.

MISTRESS FORD My maid's aunt, the fat woman of   75
Brentford, has a gown above.

MISTRESS PAGE On my word, it will serve him. She's as
big as he is. And there's her thrummed hat and her
muffler too.—Run up, Sir John.

MISTRESS FORD Go, go, sweet Sir John. Mistress Page   80
and I will look some linen for your head.

MISTRESS PAGE Quick, quick! We'll come dress you
straight. Put on the gown the while.
                                        ⌜*Falstaff exits.*⌝

MISTRESS FORD I would my husband would meet him
in this shape. He cannot abide the old woman of   85
Brentford. He swears she's a witch, forbade her my
house, and hath threatened to beat her.

MISTRESS PAGE Heaven guide him to thy husband's
cudgel, and the devil guide his cudgel afterwards!

MISTRESS FORD But is my husband coming?   90

MISTRESS PAGE Ay, in good sadness is he, and talks of
the basket too, howsoever he hath had intelligence.

MISTRESS FORD We'll try that; for I'll appoint my men
to carry the basket again, to meet him at the door   95
with it as they did last time.

MISTRESS PAGE Nay, but he'll be here presently. Let's go
dress him like the witch of Brentford.

MISTRESS FORD I'll first direct my men what they shall
do with the basket. Go up. I'll bring linen for him   100
straight.   ⌜*She exits.*⌝

MISTRESS PAGE Hang him, dishonest varlet! We cannot
misuse ⌜him⌝ enough.
  We'll leave a proof, by that which we will do,
  Wives may be merry and yet honest too.   105

106. **act:** i.e., behave unchastely

107. **Still . . . draff:** Proverbial: "It is the silent pigs that eat all the pigswill."

109. **hard at door:** right **at the door**

110. **dispatch:** make haste

113. **had lief as:** i.e., would as gladly

118. **knot:** band, group

119–20. **Now . . . shamed:** Proverbial: "Speak the truth and shame **the devil.**"

123. **passes:** goes to excess, beats everything

We do not act that often jest and laugh;
'Tis old but true: "Still swine eats all the draff."
⌜*She exits.*⌝

⌜*Enter Mistress Ford with Robert and John,*
who bring the buck-basket.⌝

MISTRESS FORD   Go, sirs, take the basket again on your
shoulders. Your master is hard at door. If he bid
you set it down, obey him. Quickly, dispatch.   110
⌜*She exits.*⌝

⌜ROBERT⌝   Come, come, take it up.
⌜JOHN⌝   Pray heaven it be not full of knight again.
⌜ROBERT⌝   I hope not. I had lief as bear so much lead.
⌜*They pick up the basket.*⌝

Enter Ford, Page, ⌜Doctor⌝ Caius, ⌜Sir Hugh⌝
Evans, ⌜and⌝ Shallow.

FORD   Ay, but if it prove true, Master Page, have you
any way then to unfool me again?—Set down the   115
basket, villain. ⌜*They put the basket down.*⌝ Some-
body call my wife. Youth in a basket! O, you pan-
derly rascals! There's a knot, a ⌜gang,⌝ a pack, a
conspiracy against me. Now shall the devil be
shamed.—What, wife, I say! Come, come forth!   120
Behold what honest clothes you send forth to
bleaching!
PAGE   Why, this passes, Master Ford! You are not to go
loose any longer; you must be pinioned.
SIR HUGH   Why, this is lunatics. This is mad as a mad   125
dog.
SHALLOW   Indeed, Master Ford, this is not well, indeed.
FORD   So say I too, sir.

⌜*Enter Mistress Ford.*⌝

Come hither, Mistress Ford.—Mistress Ford, the
honest woman, the modest wife, the virtuous crea-   130

135. **Hold it out:** keep it up

149. **Pluck me out: pluck out** for **me; linen:** i.e., clothes (specifically, undergarments and table linen)

153. **fidelity:** i.e., faith

156. **imaginations:** fantasies

161. **show no color:** i.e., deny that there is any plausible ground; **extremity:** extravagant behavior

162. **your table-sport:** i.e., the butt of the jokes you tell when you gather to eat and drink

164. **leman:** lover

Bearbaiting. (1.1.284)
From William Lily, *Antibossicon* (1521).

ture, that hath the jealous fool to her husband!—I
suspect without cause, mistress, do I?

MISTRESS FORD   Heaven be my witness you do, if you
suspect me in any dishonesty.

FORD   Well said, brazen-face. Hold it out.—Come   135
forth, sirrah.   ⌐*He pulls clothes out of the basket.*⌐

PAGE   This passes.

MISTRESS FORD   Are you not ashamed? Let the clothes
alone.

FORD   I shall find you anon.   140

SIR HUGH   'Tis unreasonable. Will you take up your
wife's clothes? Come, away.

FORD, ⌐*to the Servants*⌐   Empty the basket, I say.

MISTRESS FORD   Why, man, why?

FORD   Master Page, as I am a man, there was one con-   145
veyed out of my house yesterday in this basket.
Why may not he be there again? In my house I am
sure he is. My intelligence is true, my jealousy is
reasonable.—Pluck me out all the linen.

MISTRESS FORD   If you find a man there, he shall die a   150
flea's death.   ⌐*Robert and John empty the basket.*⌐

PAGE   Here's no man.

SHALLOW   By my fidelity, this is not well, Master Ford.
This wrongs you.

SIR HUGH   Master Ford, you must pray, and not follow   155
the imaginations of your own heart. This is jealousies.

FORD   Well, he's not here I seek for.

PAGE   No, nor nowhere else but in your brain.

FORD   Help to search my house this one time. If I find   160
not what I seek, show no color for my extremity.
Let me forever be your table-sport. Let them say of
me "As jealous as Ford, that searched a hollow
walnut for his wife's leman." Satisfy me once
more. Once more search with me.   165

⌐*Robert and John refill the basket and carry it off.*⌐

171. **quean:** hussy, harlot (a term of abuse for a woman); **cozening:** cheating, deceiving

172. **of errands:** i.e., on **errands**

175–76. **by th' figure:** i.e., (1) through predicting the future with a horoscope, or (2) through conjuring with diagrams and circles (There is, conceivably, an allusion instead to the wax figures of witchcraft.)

176. **daubery:** speciousness; dissembling

176–77. **our element:** the sphere in which we operate

183. **pratt her:** wordplay on the name "Mother Pratt"

184. **rag:** worthless thing (term of contempt)

184–85. **baggage, polecat, runnion:** terms of abuse for women (**Baggage** is, literally, rubbish; **polecat** was used for a prostitute; and **runnion** is known only as a Shakespearean coinage used here and in *Macbeth* [1.3.7].)

192. **By yea and no:** See note to 1.1.86.

196. **issue:** outcome

196–97. **cry out thus . . . trail:** yelp, like a hunting dog, when there is no quarry to be pursued

197. **open:** cry like a hound

MISTRESS FORD, ⌈*calling offstage*⌉ What ho, Mistress
  Page! Come you and the old woman down. My
  husband will come into the chamber.

FORD "Old woman"? What old woman's that?

MISTRESS FORD Why, it is my maid's aunt of Brentford. 170

FORD A witch, a quean, an old cozening quean! Have
  I not forbid her my house? She comes of errands,
  does she? We are simple men; we do not know
  what's brought to pass under the profession of
  fortune-telling. She works by charms, by spells, by 175
  th' figure, and such daubery as this is, beyond our
  element. We know nothing.— Come down, you
  witch, you hag, you! Come down, I say!
                    ⌈*Ford seizes a cudgel.*⌉

MISTRESS FORD Nay, good sweet husband!—Good gentlemen, let him ⌈not⌉ strike the old woman. 180

⌈*Enter Mistress Page and Sir John Falstaff disguised*
as an old woman.⌉

MISTRESS PAGE Come, Mother Pratt; come, give me
  your hand.

FORD I'll pratt her. ⌈*(He beats Falstaff.)*⌉ Out of my
  door, you witch, you rag, you baggage, you polecat, you runnion! Out, out! I'll conjure you, I'll 185
  fortune-tell you!   ⌈*Falstaff exits.*⌉

MISTRESS PAGE Are you not ashamed? I think you have
  killed the poor woman.

MISTRESS FORD Nay, he will do it.—'Tis a goodly credit
  for you. 190

FORD Hang her, witch!

SIR HUGH By yea and no, I think the 'oman is a witch
  indeed. I like not when a 'oman has a great peard.
  I spy a great peard under ⌈her⌉ muffler.

FORD Will you follow, gentlemen? I beseech you, fol- 195
  low. See but the issue of my jealousy. If I cry out
  thus upon no trail, never trust me when I open
  again.

199. **obey his humor:** i.e., humor him

203. **methought:** it seemed to me

209. **spirit of wantonness:** demon of lust

210–11. **fee simple:** absolute possession (a legal term)

211. **fine and recovery:** a legal phrase that describes one method of transferring property

212. **in the way of waste:** i.e., in a damaging way **waste:** damage to property not one's own; **attempt:** (1) endeavor to obtain; (2) try to seduce

214. **served:** treated

216. **figures:** imaginary forms, phantasms

219. **ministers:** agents

221. **period:** fitting conclusion

4.3 Some Germans want to hire the Host's horses. (See longer note, page 212.)

---

1. **have:** i.e., hire

A German nobleman. (4.3.1)
From John Speed, *A prospect of the most famous parts of the world . . .* (1631).

156

PAGE   Let's obey his humor a little further. Come, gen-
tlemen.   200
⌜*Ford, Page, Caius, Sir Hugh, and Shallow exit.*⌝
MISTRESS PAGE   Trust me, he beat him most pitifully.
MISTRESS FORD   Nay, by th' Mass, that he did not; he
beat him most unpitifully, methought.
MISTRESS PAGE   I'll have the cudgel hallowed and hung
o'er the altar. It hath done meritorious service.   205
MISTRESS FORD   What think you? May we, with the
warrant of womanhood and the witness of a good
conscience, pursue him with any further revenge?
MISTRESS PAGE   The spirit of wantonness is, sure,
scared out of him. If the devil have him not in fee   210
simple, with fine and recovery, he will never, I
think, in the way of waste, attempt us again.
MISTRESS FORD   Shall we tell our husbands how we
have served him?
MISTRESS PAGE   Yes, by all means—if it be but to scrape   215
the figures out of your husband's brains. If they
can find in their hearts the poor unvirtuous fat
knight shall be any further afflicted, we two will
still be the ministers.
MISTRESS FORD   I'll warrant they'll have him publicly   220
shamed, and methinks there would be no period to
the jest should he not be publicly shamed.
MISTRESS PAGE   Come, to the forge with it, then shape
it. I would not have things cool.
                                                          They exit.

Scene 3

Enter Host and Bardolph.

BARDOLPH   Sir, the ⌜Germans desire⌝ to have three of
your horses. The Duke himself will be tomorrow at
court, and they are going to meet him.

4. **comes:** i.e., who **comes**

9. **I'll sauce them:** of uncertain meaning, but probably equivalent to **I'll make them pay**

10. **at command:** available to use; at their disposal

11. **come off:** pay

4.4 Mistress Page and Mistress Ford, having fully disclosed their dealings with Falstaff to their husbands, conspire with them to humiliate Falstaff publicly that night in Windsor Forest. Master and Mistress Page each plan to take advantage of the occasion to marry their daughter to the suitor of their choice.

————————

1. **best discretions . . . 'oman:** confusion for, perhaps, "most discreet women"

3–4. **at an instant:** at the same time

7. **with cold:** i.e., of being **cold**

8. **wantonness:** lasciviousness, lustfulness

18. **that they:** i.e., **that** which **they**

HOST   What duke should that be comes so secretly? I
      hear not of him in the court. Let me speak with the   5
      gentlemen. They speak English?
BARDOLPH   Ay, sir. I'll call ⌐them⌐ to you.
HOST   They shall have my horses, but I'll make them
      pay. I'll sauce them. They have had my ⌐house⌐ a
      week at command; I have turned away my other   10
      guests. They must come off. I'll sauce them. Come.
                                          They exit.

Scene 4

Enter Page, Ford, Mistress Page, Mistress Ford, and
                  ⌐*Sir Hugh*⌐ *Evans.*

SIR HUGH   'Tis one of the best discretions of a 'oman as
      ever I did look upon.
PAGE   And did he send you both these letters at an
      instant?
MISTRESS PAGE   Within a quarter of an hour.   5
FORD
      Pardon me, wife. Henceforth do what thou wilt.
      I rather will suspect the sun with ⌐cold⌐
      Than thee with wantonness. Now doth thy honor
          stand,
      In him that was of late an heretic,   10
      As firm as faith.
PAGE   'Tis well, 'tis well. No more.
      Be not as extreme in submission as in offense.
      But let our plot go forward. Let our wives
      Yet once again, to make us public sport,   15
      Appoint a meeting with this old fat fellow,
      Where we may take him and disgrace him for it.
FORD
      There is no better way than that they spoke of.
PAGE   How, to send him word they'll meet him in the
      park at midnight? Fie, fie, he'll never come.   20

27. **use:** treat

30. **Sometime:** formerly; **keeper:** gamekeeper, officer in charge of a forest

32. **ragged:** uneven, irregular

33. **blasts:** blights; **takes:** magically seizes upon

34. **milch-kine:** milk cows

38. **eld:** people of olden time

39. **Received:** believed

41. **want:** lack

45. **meet with us:** Here many editors add a line from the Quarto: "Disguised like Herne [Quarto: Horne], with huge horns on his head." See longer note, page 212.

47. **in this shape:** in disguise as Herne the Hunter

Windsor and environs. (3.1.5; 4.4.81)
From John Speed, *The theatre of the empire of Great Britaine . . .* (1627 [i.e., 1631]).

SIR HUGH You say he has been thrown in the rivers
and has been grievously peaten as an old 'oman.
Methinks there should be terrors in him, that he
should not come. Methinks his flesh is punished;
he shall have no desires.   25

PAGE So think I too.

MISTRESS FORD
  Devise but how you'll use him when he comes,
  And let us two devise to bring him thither.

MISTRESS PAGE
  There is an old tale goes that Herne the Hunter,
  Sometime a keeper here in Windsor Forest,   30
  Doth all the wintertime, at still midnight,
  Walk round about an oak, with great ragged horns,
  And there he blasts the tree, and takes the cattle,
  And ⌜makes⌝ milch-kine yield blood, and shakes a
    chain   35
  In a most hideous and dreadful manner.
  You have heard of such a spirit, and well you know
  The superstitious idle-headed eld
  Received and did deliver to our age
  This tale of Herne the Hunter for a truth.   40

PAGE
  Why, yet there want not many that do fear
  In deep of night to walk by this Herne's oak.
  But what of this?

MISTRESS FORD   Marry, this is our device,
  That Falstaff at that oak shall meet with us.   45

PAGE
  Well, let it not be doubted but he'll come.
  And in this shape when you have brought him
    thither,
  What shall be done with him? What is your plot?

MISTRESS PAGE
  That likewise have we thought upon, and thus: 50
  Nan Page my daughter, and my little son,

52. **growth:** i.e., age, size

53. **urchins:** goblins, elves; **aufs:** elf or goblin children

54. **rounds:** rings

57. **sawpit:** a pit across which timber was laid to be sawed

58. **diffusèd:** disordered, confused

61. **pinch:** Fairies, goblins, elves and other supernatural creatures traditionally punished mortals with pinches that turned the mortals "black and blue" (*The Comedy of Errors* 2.2.203. See also *The Tempest* 1.2.390–94 and 2.2.3–7).

66. **sound:** soundly

69. **dis-horn the spirit:** i.e., remove from Falstaff the horns he wears in his disguise as Herne

74. **be . . . jackanapes:** i.e., act mischievously or impertinently (A *jackanape* is, literally, an ape or monkey.)

76. **vizards:** visors, masks (See picture below.)

81. **Eton:** a village across the Thames from Windsor (See picture, page 160.)

82. **straight:** straightaway, immediately

83. **to him:** i.e., go **to him**

Vizards. (4.4.76; 4.6.40)
From Guillaume de la Perrière, *Le théâtre des bons engins . . .* [1539?].

And three or four more of their growth we'll dress
Like urchins, aufs, and fairies, green and white,
With rounds of waxen tapers on their heads
And rattles in their hands. Upon a sudden,   55
As Falstaff, she, and I are newly met,
Let them from forth a sawpit rush at once
With some diffusèd song. Upon their sight,
We two in great amazedness will fly.
Then let them all encircle him about,   60
And, fairy-like, to pinch the unclean knight,
And ask him why, that hour of fairy revel,
In their so sacred paths he dares to tread
In shape profane.
FORD   And till he tell the truth,   65
Let the supposèd fairies pinch him sound
And burn him with their tapers.
MISTRESS PAGE   The truth being known,
We'll all present ourselves, dis-horn the spirit,
And mock him home to Windsor.   70
FORD   The children must
Be practiced well to this, or they'll ne'er do 't.
SIR HUGH   I will teach the children their behaviors, and
I will be like a jackanapes also, to burn the knight
with my taber.   75
FORD   That will be excellent. I'll go buy them vizards.
MISTRESS PAGE
My Nan shall be the queen of all the fairies,
Finely attirèd in a robe of white.
PAGE
That silk will I go buy. ⌈(*Aside.*)⌉ And in that time
Shall Master Slender steal my Nan away   80
And marry her at Eton.—Go, send to Falstaff
straight.
FORD
Nay, I'll to him again in name of ⌈Brook.⌉
He'll tell me all his purpose. Sure he'll come.

85. **properties:** stage props

86. **tricking for:** ornamentation for, supplies for dressing up

93. **well-landed:** rich because of the lands he holds

94. **affects:** likes, prefers

97. **crave:** beg for

4.5 The Host learns his horses have been stolen. Mistress Quickly approaches Falstaff with another invitation, this time to meet Mistress Ford and Mistress Page.

———————

1–2. **thickskin:** person dull or slow of feeling

2. **breathe:** speak; **discuss:** declare, pronounce

6. **There's:** The Host presumably points offstage. (Falstaff first speaks "within" [line 18] before entering at line 22.) **his house, his castle:** wordplay on the proverb "A man's **house** is **his castle**"

7. **standing-bed and truckle-bed:** A low bed on truckles or castors could be stored under a high bedstead or **standing-bed.**

7–8. **'Tis painted . . . Prodigal:** Either his **chamber** or his **standing-bed** is hung about with cloth on which is depicted the parable of the Prodigal Son from Luke 15. (See picture, page 170.)

9–10. **Anthropophaginian:** cannibal (See picture, page 166.)

12. **stay:** wait

MISTRESS PAGE
Fear not you that. Go get us properties   85
And tricking for our fairies.

SIR HUGH   Let us about it. It is admirable pleasures and
fery honest knaveries.
⌐*Page, Ford, and Sir Hugh exit.*⌐

MISTRESS PAGE   Go, Mistress Ford,
Send quickly to Sir John to know his mind.   90
⌐*Mistress Ford exits.*⌐
I'll to the doctor. He hath my good will,
And none but he, to marry with Nan Page.
That Slender, though well-landed, is an idiot,
And he my husband best of all affects.
The doctor is well-moneyed, and his friends   95
Potent at court. He, none but he, shall have her,
Though twenty thousand worthier come to crave her.
⌐*She exits.*⌐

Scene 5

Enter Host ⌐*and*⌐ *Simple.*

HOST   What wouldst thou have, boor? What, thick-
skin? Speak, breathe, discuss; brief, short, quick,
snap.

SIMPLE   Marry, sir, I come to speak with Sir John Falstaff from Master Slender.   5

HOST   There's his chamber, his house, his castle, his
standing-bed and truckle-bed. 'Tis painted about
with the story of the Prodigal, fresh and new. Go,
knock and call. He'll speak like an Anthropophaginian unto thee. Knock, I say.   10

SIMPLE   There's an old woman, a fat woman, gone up
into his chamber. I'll be so bold as stay, sir, till she
come down. I come to speak with her, indeed.

HOST   Ha? A fat woman? The knight may be robbed.
I'll call.—Bully knight! Bully Sir John! Speak from   15

17. **Ephesian:** i.e., drinking companion
19. **Bohemian Tartar:** The Host is playing extravagantly with language in this scene. Tartars are from central Asia; Bohemia was a kingdom in central Europe. **tarries:** awaits
21–22. **Privacy:** secret or private matters
24. **even:** just
25. **wise woman:** i.e., **woman** skilled in hidden arts, including fortune-telling; witch
27. **mussel-shell:** referring perhaps to Simple's gaping expression; or, perhaps, to his insignificance
27–28. **would you:** i.e., do you want
31. **beguiled:** cheated
36. **cozened:** cheated
43. **conceal:** confusion for "reveal"

A cannibal. (4.5.9–10)
From Conrad Lycosthenes, *Prodigiorum . . .* (1557).

thy lungs military. Art thou there? It is thine Host,
thine Ephesian, calls.

FALSTAFF, ⌜*within*⌝ How now, mine Host?

HOST Here's a Bohemian Tartar tarries the coming
    down of thy fat woman. Let her descend, bully, let   20
    her descend. My chambers are honorable. Fie! Pri-
    vacy? Fie!

Enter ⌜Sir John⌝ Falstaff.

FALSTAFF There was, mine Host, an old fat woman
    even now with me, but she's gone.

SIMPLE Pray you, sir, was 't not the wise woman of   25
    Brentford?

FALSTAFF Ay, marry, was it, mussel-shell. What would
    you with her?

SIMPLE My master, sir, my Master Slender, sent to her,
    seeing her go through the streets, to know, sir,   30
    whether one Nym, sir, that beguiled him of a chain,
    had the chain or no.

FALSTAFF I spake with the old woman about it.

SIMPLE And what says she, I pray, sir?

FALSTAFF Marry, she says that the very same man that   35
    beguiled Master Slender of his chain cozened him
    of it.

SIMPLE I would I could have spoken with the woman
    herself. I had other things to have spoken with her
    too from him.   40

FALSTAFF What are they? Let us know.

HOST Ay, come. Quick!

⌜SIMPLE⌝ I may not conceal them, sir.

HOST Conceal them, or thou diest.

SIMPLE Why, sir, they were nothing but about Mistress   45
    Anne Page, to know if it were my master's fortune
    to have her or no.

FALSTAFF 'Tis; 'tis his fortune.

SIMPLE What, sir?

53. **like who more bold:** i.e., **like** the boldest of the **bold**

56. **clerkly:** scholarly, learned

59. **wit:** wisdom, knowledge

60–61. **was paid:** i.e., with blows

62. **Out, alas:** a lamentation; **cozenage:** cheating, deception, fraud; **mere:** absolute

64. **Speak well:** i.e., tell me good news

64–65. **varletto:** varlet, rascal

70. **Doctor Faustuses:** In Christopher Marlowe's play *Doctor Faustus*, the German hero Faustus sells his soul to the devil.

75. **Have a care of:** i.e., pay attention to; **entertainments:** perhaps, guests whom you entertain; perhaps, hospitality

77. **cozen-Germans:** wordplay on "cozening" or cheating Germans and on "cousins german" (i.e., first cousins)

78. **Readings:** i.e., Reading (a town, like **Maidenhead** and **Colnbrook,** in the Thames Valley near Windsor)

80. **gibes:** flouts, jeers

80–81. **vlouting-stocks:** flouting stocks, objects of mockery

81. **convenient:** appropriate

Hector. (1.3.11; 2.3.33)
From [Guillaume Rouillé,] . . . *Prima pars promptuarii iconum* . . . (1553).

FALSTAFF To have her or no. Go. Say the woman told   50
    me so.
SIMPLE May I be bold to say so, sir?
FALSTAFF Ay, sir; like who more bold.
SIMPLE I thank your Worship. I shall make my master
    glad with these tidings.   ⌜*He exits.*⌝ 55
HOST Thou ⌜art⌝ clerkly, thou art clerkly, Sir John. Was
    there a wise woman with thee?
FALSTAFF Ay, that there was, mine Host, one that hath
    taught me more wit than ever I learned before in
    my life. And I paid nothing for it neither, but was   60
    paid for my learning.

Enter Bardolph.

BARDOLPH, ⌜*to Host*⌝ Out, alas, sir, cozenage, mere coz-
    enage!
HOST Where be my horses? Speak well of them, var-
    letto.   65
BARDOLPH Run away with the cozeners. For so soon as
    I came beyond Eton, they threw me off from be-
    hind one of them in a slough of mire, and set
    spurs, and away, like three German devils, three
    Doctor Faustuses.   70
HOST They are gone but to meet the Duke, villain. Do
    not say they be fled. Germans are honest men.

Enter ⌜Sir Hugh⌝ Evans.

SIR HUGH Where is mine Host?
HOST What is the matter, sir?
SIR HUGH Have a care of your entertainments. There is   75
    a friend of mine come to town tells me there is
    three cozen-Germans that has cozened all the
    hosts of Readings, of Maidenhead, of Colnbrook,
    of horses and money. I tell you for good will, look
    you. You are wise, and full of gibes and vlouting-   80
    stocks, and 'tis not convenient you should be coz-
    ened. Fare you well.   ⌜*He exits.*⌝

87. **grand:** great

88. **Jamanie:** Germany; **trot:** i.e., troth

90. **Hue and cry:** i.e., give the "hue and cry" to capture the criminals

93. **would:** wish

98. **liquor:** grease or oil (to make waterproof)

100. **dried pear:** i.e., **pear** fallen from its tree and **dried** up

101–2. **forswore myself at primero:** i.e., cheated at cards **forswore:** swore falsely

102. **my wind . . . enough:** i.e., **if** I had **enough** breath (The Quarto here adds "to say my prayers.")

107. **bestowed:** disposed of

112. **speciously:** confusion for "especially"

The story of the Prodigal Son. (4.5.7–8)
From [Guillaume Guéroult], *Figures de la Bible . . .* (1565–70).

Enter ⌐Doctor⌐ Caius.

DOCTOR CAIUS   Vere is mine Host de Jarteer?

HOST   Here, Master Doctor, in perplexity and doubtful
dilemma.   85

DOCTOR CAIUS   I cannot tell vat is dat. But it is tell-a me
dat you make grand preparation for a duke de
Jamanie. By my trot, dere is no duke that the court
is know to come. I tell you for good will. Adieu.
                                                            ⌐He exits.⌐

HOST, ⌐to Bardolph⌐   Hue and cry, villain, go!—Assist   90
me, knight. I am undone.—Fly, run; hue and cry,
villain! I am undone.   ⌐Host and Bardolph exit.⌐

FALSTAFF   I would all the world might be cozened, for I
have been cozened and beaten too. If it should
come to the ear of the court how I have been trans-   95
formed, and how my transformation hath been
washed and cudgeled, they would melt me out of
my fat drop by drop, and liquor fishermen's boots
with me. I warrant they would whip me with their
fine wits till I were as crestfallen as a dried pear. I   100
never prospered since I forswore myself at
primero. Well, if my wind were but long enough, I
would repent.

Enter ⌐Mistress⌐ Quickly.

Now, whence come you?

MISTRESS QUICKLY   From the two parties, forsooth.   105

FALSTAFF   The devil take one party, and his dam the
other, and so they shall be both bestowed. I have
suffered more for their sakes, more than the villainous inconstancy of man's disposition is able to
bear.   110

MISTRESS QUICKLY   And have not they suffered? Yes, I
warrant, speciously one of them. Mistress Ford,

117. **was like to be:** narrowly missed being, came near to being

121. **stocks:** an instrument of punishment and public shaming that imprisoned the ankles in a wooden frame (See picture below.)

125. **somewhat:** something

128. **crossed:** thwarted

4.6 The Host is asked to arrange for a vicar to marry Anne to Fenton that night.

---

2. **heavy:** i.e., with sorrow; **give over all:** abandon everything

7. **keep your counsel:** not divulge what you say

10. **answered:** requited, returned

11. **So far forth:** i.e., insofar

A man in the stocks.
From August Casimir Redel, *Apophtegmata symbolica* . . . (n.d.).

good heart, is beaten black and blue that you cannot see a white spot about her.

FALSTAFF What tell'st thou me of black and blue? I was   115
beaten myself into all the colors of the rainbow,
and I was like to be apprehended for the witch of
Brentford. But that my admirable dexterity of wit,
my counterfeiting the action of an old woman, delivered me, the knave constable had set me i' th'   120
stocks, i' th' common stocks, for a witch.

MISTRESS QUICKLY Sir, let me speak with you in your
chamber. You shall hear how things go, and, I warrant, to your content. Here is a letter will say
somewhat. ⌜*She gives him a paper.*⌝ Good hearts,   125
what ado here is to bring you together! Sure, one
of you does not serve heaven well, that you are so
crossed.

FALSTAFF Come up into my chamber.

They exit.

Scene 6

Enter Fenton ⌜and⌝ Host.

HOST Master Fenton, talk not to me. My mind is
heavy. I will give over all.

FENTON
Yet hear me speak. Assist me in my purpose,
And, as I am a gentleman, I'll give thee
A hundred pound in gold more than your loss.   5

HOST I will hear you, Master Fenton, and I will, at the
least, keep your counsel.

FENTON
From time to time I have acquainted you
With the dear love I bear to fair Anne Page,
Who mutually hath answered my affection,   10
So far forth as herself might be her chooser,

14. **mirth whereof:** i.e., entertainment or sport contained in it; **larded:** interspersed; **my matter:** i.e., what I'm concerned about

17. **scene:** part of a play; **image:** form

18. **at large:** in detail

21. **present:** act the part of

23. **something:** somewhat; **rank:** abundantly; **on foot:** in motion, astir

29. **shuffle:** smuggle, remove in a surreptitious manner

30. **sports:** diversions, amusements; **tasking of:** occupying

31. **dean'ry:** residence of a church official; **attends:** is present in readiness

32. **Straight:** straightway, immediately

34. **it rests:** i.e., is what remains for you to do

35. **means:** intends

36. **habit:** costume

39. **denote her to:** i.e., distinguish her for

40. **masked and vizarded:** i.e., **masked**

41. **quaint:** elegantly, fashionably, prettily; **loose:** loosely

42. **flaring:** streaming

43. **spies his vantage ripe:** i.e., observes for himself an opportune moment **vantage:** opportunity **ripe:** arrived at a fitting time for some purpose

44. **token:** signal

Even to my wish. I have a letter from her
Of such contents as you will wonder at,
The mirth whereof so larded with my matter
That neither singly can be manifested   15
Without the show of both. Fat Falstaff
Hath a great scene; the image of the jest
I'll show you here at large. ⌈*He shows the Host a
     paper.*⌉ Hark, good mine Host:
Tonight at Herne's oak, just 'twixt twelve and one,   20
Must my sweet Nan present the Fairy Queen—
The purpose why is here—in which disguise,
While other jests are something rank on foot,
Her father hath commanded her to slip
Away with Slender, and with him at Eton   25
Immediately to marry. She hath consented. Now, sir,
Her mother, ⌈ever⌉ strong against that match
And firm for Doctor Caius, hath appointed
That he shall likewise shuffle her away,
While other sports are tasking of their minds,   30
And at the dean'ry, where a priest attends,
Straight marry her. To this her mother's plot
She, seemingly obedient, likewise hath
Made promise to the doctor. Now, thus it rests:
Her father means she shall be all in white,   35
And in that habit, when Slender sees his time
To take her by the hand and bid her go,
She shall go with him. Her mother hath intended
The better to ⌈denote⌉ her to the doctor—
For they must all be masked and vizarded—   40
That quaint in green she shall be loose enrobed,
With ribbons pendent flaring 'bout her head;
And when the doctor spies his vantage ripe,
To pinch her by the hand, and on that token
The maid hath given consent to go with him.   45

48. **here it rests:** i.e., here's what I need from you, here's what remains to be done

49. **stay:** wait

51. **give . . . ceremony:** i.e., unite **our hearts** ceremonially

52. **husband:** manage well, make the most of (perhaps with wordplay on **husband** as a noun)

53. **Bring you:** if **you bring; maid:** young woman

54. **bound:** obligated

55. **present:** immediate

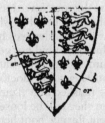

A coat of arms quartered. (1.1.24–26)
From Sir William Dugdale, *The antiquities of Warwickshire . . .* (1656).

HOST
    Which means she to deceive, father or mother?
FENTON
    Both, my good Host, to go along with me.
    And here it rests, that you'll procure the vicar
    To stay for me at church 'twixt twelve and one,
    And, in the lawful name of marrying,   50
    To give our hearts united ceremony.
HOST
    Well, husband your device. I'll to the vicar.
    Bring you the maid, you shall not lack a priest.
FENTON
    So shall I evermore be bound to thee;
    Besides, I'll make a present recompense.   55

                                        They exit.

THE
MERRY WIVES
OF WINDSOR

ACT 5

5.1 Falstaff, having agreed to meet Mistress Page and Mistress Ford, promises success to "Brook."

---

1. **hold:** i.e., keep the appointment
1–2. **This . . . time:** The **third time** was proverbially lucky. (Proverbial: "The **third time** pays for all.")
2–3. **I hope . . . numbers:** Proverbial: "There is **luck in odd numbers.**"
3. **divinity:** divine power
3–4. **odd numbers:** here, odd-numbered days
8. **wears:** i.e., passes away, is running out

Acteon and Diana. (2.1.118, 122; 3.2.41)
From Henry Peacham, *Minerua Britanna* . . . [1612].

ACT 5

Scene 1

Enter ⌐Sir John⌐ Falstaff ⌐and Mistress⌐ Quickly.

FALSTAFF   Prithee, no more prattling. Go. I'll hold. This
is the third time; I hope good luck lies in odd numbers. Away, go. They say there is divinity in odd
numbers, either in nativity, chance, or death.
Away.   5

MISTRESS QUICKLY   I'll provide you a chain, and I'll do
what I can to get you a pair of horns.

FALSTAFF   Away, I say! Time wears. Hold up your head,
and mince.   ⌐*Mistress Quickly exits.*⌐

Enter Ford ⌐disguised as Brook.⌐

How now, Master ⌐Brook!⌐ Master ⌐Brook,⌐ the   10
matter will be known tonight or never. Be you in
the park about midnight, at Herne's oak, and you
shall see wonders.

FORD, ⌐*as Brook*⌐   Went you not to her yesterday, sir, as
you told me you had appointed?   15

FALSTAFF   I went to her, Master ⌐Brook,⌐ as you see,
like a poor old man, but I came from her, Master
⌐Brook,⌐ like a poor old woman. That same knave
Ford, her husband, hath the finest mad devil of
jealousy in him, Master ⌐Brook,⌐ that ever gov-   20
erned frenzy. I will tell you, he beat me grievously,
in the shape of a woman; for in the shape of man,

181

23–24. **Goliath . . . weaver's beam:** It was said of **Goliath,** the great Philistine warrior: "And the shaft of his spear was like **a weaver's beam**" (1 Samuel 17.7). **weaver's beam:** one of the wooden rollers on a loom

24. **life is a shuttle:** Job 7.6: "My days pass over more speedily than **a** weaver's **shuttle." shuttle:** weaver's tool that, as cloth is woven, carries the thread back and forth across the loom so quickly as to be almost invisible

26. **plucked geese:** perhaps **plucked** feathers from live **geese**

27. **whipped top:** made a **top** spin by whipping it (See picture, page 184.)

31. **in hand:** in process, being dealt with

5.2 Slender prepares to elope with Anne Page.

———————

1. **couch:** lie hidden

5. **nayword:** i.e., code word (literally, password, watchword)

6. **mum, budget:** "Mumbudget" is thought to have been a children's game that required silence.

8. **what needs:** i.e., what is the need for

9. **decipher:** indicate

11. **become:** suit

12. **prosper:** be propitious to; **means:** intends

14. **horns:** Proverbial: "**The devil** is known **by his horns.**"

(continued)

Master ⌜Brook,⌝ I fear not Goliath with a weaver's
beam, because I know also life is a shuttle. I am in
haste. Go along with me; I'll tell you all, Master   25
⌜Brook.⌝ Since I plucked geese, played truant, and
whipped top, I knew not what 'twas to be beaten
till lately. Follow me. I'll tell you strange things of
this knave Ford, on whom tonight I will be revenged, and I will deliver his wife into your hand.   30
Follow. Strange things in hand, Master ⌜Brook!⌝
Follow.

They exit.

Scene 2

Enter Page, Shallow, ⌜and⌝ Slender.

PAGE   Come, come. We'll couch i' th' castle ditch till we
see the light of our fairies.—Remember, son Slender, my—
SLENDER   Ay, forsooth, I have spoke with her, and we
have a nayword how to know one another. I come   5
to her in white and cry "mum," she cries "budget,"
and by that we know one another.
SHALLOW   That's good too. But what needs either your
"mum" or her "budget"? The white will decipher
her well enough. It hath struck ten o'clock.   10
PAGE   The night is dark. Light and spirits will become
it well. Heaven prosper our sport! No man means
evil but the devil, and we shall know him by his
horns. Let's away. Follow me.

They exit.

Scene 3

Enter Mistress Page, Mistress Ford, ⌜and Doctor⌝ Caius.

MISTRESS PAGE   Master Doctor, my daughter is in
green. When you see your time, take her by the

5.3 Dr. Caius waits to elope with Anne Page. Mistress Page and Mistress Ford follow their plan to torment Falstaff.

---

4. **before:** ahead
8. **abuse:** ill-usage
14. **pit:** sawpit (with possible wordplay on **pit** as "hell" suggested by the reference to Sir Hugh as **the Welsh devil**)
18. **cannot ... amaze:** i.e., must terrify or bewilder
20, 21. **mocked:** (1) disappointed; deceived; (2) ridiculed
23. **lewdsters:** lewd persons

5.4 Sir Hugh and the "fairies" approach.

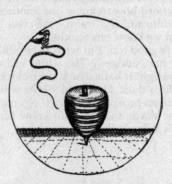

A whipped top. (5.1.27)
From Giovanni Ferro, *Teatro d'imprese . . .* (1623).

hand; away with her to the deanery, and dispatch
it quickly. Go before into the park. We two must go
together.   5

DOCTOR CAIUS   I know vat I have to do. Adieu.

MISTRESS PAGE   Fare you well, sir.   ⌈*Caius exits.*⌉
My husband will not rejoice so much at the abuse
of Falstaff as he will chafe at the doctor's marrying
my daughter. But 'tis no matter. Better a little chid-   10
ing than a great deal of heartbreak.

MISTRESS FORD   Where is Nan now, and her troop of
fairies, and the Welsh devil ⌈Hugh?⌉

MISTRESS PAGE   They are all couched in a pit hard by
Herne's oak, with obscured lights, which, at the   15
very instant of Falstaff's and our meeting, they will
at once display to the night.

MISTRESS FORD   That cannot choose but amaze him.

MISTRESS PAGE   If he be not amazed, he will be
mocked. If he be amazed, he will every way be   20
mocked.

MISTRESS FORD   We'll betray him finely.

MISTRESS PAGE
Against such lewdsters and their lechery,
Those that betray them do no treachery.

MISTRESS FORD   The hour draws on. To the oak, to the   25
oak!

They exit.

Scene 4

Enter ⌈*Sir Hugh*⌉ *Evans and* ⌈*boys disguised,
like him, as*⌉ *Fairies.*

SIR HUGH   Trib, trib, fairies! Come, and remember
your parts. Be pold, I pray you. Follow me into the
pit, and when I give the watch-'ords, do as I pid
you. Come, come; trib, trib.   *They exit.*

5.5 Falstaff is tormented by the "fairies" and then publicly humiliated. Slender and Dr. Caius enter in turn to report that each has been deceived into eloping with a disguised boy instead of Anne Page. Finally Fenton and Anne Page enter, married. Fenton and Falstaff are forgiven, and the party moves to the home of Master and Mistress Page.

---

0 SD. **buck's head:** This term is drawn from the stage direction in the Quarto. It can mean either the whole head of a buck, which would entirely mask Falstaff's face, or only the buck's antlers.

3. **Jove:** in mythology, king of the gods

4. **Europa:** Enamored of **Europa, Jove** transformed himself into **a bull** and carried her off to Crete. (See picture, page 198.)

5. **a beast a man:** perhaps, an animalistic **man** (into) a fully human one

6. **Jupiter:** another name for **Jove**

7. **Leda:** a princess raped by **Jupiter** as a swan

8. **complexion:** (1) appearance; (2) nature

10. **fault:** sin

12. **have hot backs:** i.e., are lustful

13. **For:** i.e., as **for**

14. **rut-time:** mating season

15. **piss my tallow:** excrete my fat (as bucks during mating season were supposed to do)

17. **deer:** with wordplay on *dear*

19. **scut:** tail (with wordplay on sexual parts)

20. **potatoes:** i.e., sweet **potatoes,** regarded as an aphrodisiac; **Greensleeves:** a popular love song

(continued)

Scene 5

Enter ⌜Sir John⌝ Falstaff ⌜wearing a buck's head.⌝

FALSTAFF   The Windsor bell hath struck twelve. The
minute draws on. Now, the ⌜hot-blooded⌝ gods assist me! Remember, Jove, thou wast a bull for thy
Europa; love set on thy horns. O powerful love,
that in some respects makes a beast a man, in   5
some other a man a beast! You were also, Jupiter,
a swan for the love of Leda. O omnipotent love,
how near the god drew to the complexion of a
goose! A fault done first in the form of a beast; O
Jove, a beastly fault! And then another fault in the   10
semblance of a fowl; think on't, Jove, a foul fault.
When gods have hot backs, what shall poor men
do? For me, I am here a Windsor stag, and the fat-
test, I think, i' th' forest. Send me a cool rut-time,
Jove, or who can blame me to piss my tallow?   15

Enter Mistress Page ⌜and⌝ Mistress Ford.

Who comes here? My doe?
MISTRESS FORD   Sir John? Art thou there, my deer, my
male deer?
FALSTAFF   My doe with the black scut! Let the sky rain
potatoes, let it thunder to the tune of "Greensleeves,"   20
hail kissing-comfits, and snow eryngoes; let there
come a tempest of provocation, I will shelter me
here.   ⌜*He embraces her.*⌝
MISTRESS FORD   Mistress Page is come with me, sweetheart.   25
FALSTAFF   Divide me like a bribed buck, each a haunch.
I will keep my sides to myself, my shoulders for
the fellow of this walk, and my horns I bequeath
your husbands. Am I a woodman, ha? Speak I like
Herne the Hunter? Why, now is Cupid a child of   30
conscience; he makes restitution. As I am a true
spirit, welcome.   ⌜*A noise of horns within.*⌝

21. **kissing-comfits:** perfumed candies for sweetening the breath; **eryngoes:** candied seaholly roots (then regarded as an aphrodisiac)

22. **provocation:** (sexual) stimulation

26. **bribed:** i.e., stolen; or, obtained through bribery of the gamekeeper

28. **fellow . . . walk:** gamekeeper in charge of this part of the forest (who got the **shoulders** as part of his fee)

29. **woodman:** (1) hunter; (2) womanizer

30–31. **now . . . conscience:** i.e., **Cupid** seems to have developed a **conscience**

31–32. **As I am a true spirit:** wordplay on the common expression "As I am a true man"

39. **else:** otherwise; **cross:** thwart

39 SD. **Mistress Quickly, Pistol:** See longer note, page 212.

41. **shades:** specters, phantoms

42. **You . . . destiny:** See longer note, page 213.

43. **Attend:** look after; **your office:** the performance of your duty; **quality:** business, occupation

44. **Crier:** as in "town **crier**"; **Hobgoblin:** mischievous spirit, also called Puck or Robin Goodfellow; **oyes:** hear ye, the conventional call of the **crier**

45. **list:** listen for; **airy:** insubstantial; **toys:** a slighting or contemptuous form of address

47. **unraked:** not raked up in a pile and therefore liable to go out before dawn

49. **bilberry:** a berry of deep blue-black color

50. **sluts:** slovenly kitchen maids (without particular reference to sexual activity); **sluttery:** sluttishness, slovenliness

51. **He that:** i.e., whoever

(continued)

188

MISTRESS PAGE   Alas, what noise?
MISTRESS FORD   Heaven forgive our sins!
FALSTAFF   What should this be?   35
MISTRESS FORD and MISTRESS PAGE   Away, away.
                                  ⌈*The two women run off.*⌉

FALSTAFF   I think the devil will not have me damned,
   lest the oil that's in me should set hell on fire. He
   would never else cross me thus.

   Enter ⌈*Mistress*⌉ *Quickly, Pistol,* ⌈*Sir Hugh*⌉ *Evans,*
   Anne Page ⌈*and boys, all disguised as*⌉ *Fairies* ⌈*and*
                       carrying tapers.⌉

MISTRESS QUICKLY, ⌈*as Fairy Queen*⌉
   Fairies black, gray, green, and white,   40
   You moonshine revelers and shades of night,
   You orphan heirs of fixèd destiny,
   Attend your office and your quality.
   Crier Hobgoblin, make the fairy oyes.
PISTOL, ⌈*as Hobgoblin*⌉
   Elves, list your names. Silence, you airy toys!—   45
   Cricket, to Windsor chimneys shalt thou leap,
   Where fires thou find'st unraked and hearths
      unswept.
   There pinch the maids as blue as bilberry.
   Our radiant queen hates sluts and sluttery.   50
FALSTAFF, ⌈*aside*⌉
   They are fairies. He that speaks to them shall die.
   I'll wink and couch. No man their works must eye.
                    ⌈*He crouches down and covers his eyes.*⌉
SIR HUGH, ⌈*as a fairy*⌉
   Where's Bead? Go you, and where you find a maid
   That ere she sleep has thrice her prayers said,
   Raise up the organs of her fantasy;   55
   Sleep she as sound as careless infancy.
   But those as sleep and think not on their sins,
   Pinch them, arms, legs, backs, shoulders, sides, and
      shins.

52. **wink:** close my eyes; **couch:** lie hidden

55. **the organs of her fantasy:** her imagination (i.e., in dreams)

56. **careless:** carefree

62. **aufs:** elf or goblin children

63. **perpetual doom:** i.e., Doomsday, which in Christianity marks the end of the world

64. **state as wholesome:** as sound condition; **as in . . . fit:** i.e., as is appropriate to its great dignity

65. **Worthy:** i.e., **worthy** of; **owner it:** i.e., **owner** worthy of **it**

66. **several . . . order:** i.e., the individual stalls assigned to each knight of the Garter. (Each stall had a stall-plate bearing the knight's **coat** of arms; above each stall appeared the knight's **crest,** and above these his banner, emblazoned with his **coat** of arms, on a stave projecting from the wall.) See longer note, page 214.

67. **juice of balm:** fragrant oil

68. **Each fair installment:** i.e., may **each** splendid stall; **coat:** i.e., **coat** of arms; **sev'ral:** individual, separate

69. **blazon:** coat of arms, or banner bearing the coat of arms

71. **compass:** circular shape

72. **Th' expressure . . . bears:** i.e., the look the fairy **ring** bears   **expressure:** expression

74. **Honi . . . pense:** "Evil be to him who evil thinks"—the motto of the Order of the Garter (See picture, page 200, and longer note to 1.1.137, page 205.)

(continued)

MISTRESS QUICKLY, ⌐*as Fairy Queen*¬ About, about!   60
  Search Windsor Castle, elves, within and out.
  Strew good luck, aufs, on every sacred room,
  That it may stand till the perpetual doom
  In state as wholesome as in state 'tis fit,
  Worthy the owner, and the owner it.   65
  The several chairs of order look you scour
  With juice of balm and every precious flower.
  Each fair installment, coat, and sev'ral crest
  With loyal blazon evermore be blest!
  And nightly, meadow fairies, look you sing,   70
  Like to the Garter's compass, in a ring.
  Th' expressure that it bears, green let it be,
  ⌐More¬ fertile-fresh than all the field to see;
  And *Honi soit qui mal y pense* write
  In em'rald tufts, flowers purple, blue, and white,   75
  Like sapphire, pearl, and rich embroidery,
  Buckled below fair knighthood's bending knee.
  Fairies use flowers for their charactery.
  Away, disperse! But till 'tis one o'clock,
  Our dance of custom round about the oak   80
  Of Herne the Hunter let us not forget.
SIR HUGH, ⌐*as a fairy*¬
  Pray you, lock hand in hand. Yourselves in order set;
  And twenty glowworms shall our lanterns be,
  To guide our measure round about the tree.
  But stay! I smell a man of middle earth.   85
FALSTAFF, ⌐*aside*¬ Heavens defend me from that Welsh
  fairy, lest he transform me to a piece of cheese.
PISTOL, ⌐*as Hobgoblin, to Falstaff*¬
  Vile worm, thou wast o'erlooked even in thy birth.
MISTRESS QUICKLY, ⌐*as Fairy Queen, to Sir Hugh*¬
  With trial-fire touch me his finger-end.
  If he be chaste, the flame will back descend   90
  And turn him to no pain. But if he start,
  It is the flesh of a corrupted heart.

76–77. **Like . . . knee:** Members of the order wore a blue garter below the **knee**; the motto was usually, but not always, in gold lettering

78. **charactery:** writing, script

80. **dance of custom:** customary **dance**

84. **measure:** dance

85. **man of middle earth:** i.e., mortal **man** (Middle English *middelerd* signified that Earth was between heaven and hell.)

86–87. **Welsh fairy:** Falstaff's identification of him as **Welsh** may indicate that an actor playing Sir Hugh should somehow maintain the character's earlier speech pattern.

88. **o'erlooked:** bewitched

89. **touch me:** i.e., **touch**

98 SD. **Here . . . Page:** This stage direction, based on that of the Quarto, has been adapted to the details of the Folio text's plot, in which Doctor Caius is told to find Anne Page in **white,** and Slender to find her in **green.**

100. **luxury:** lasciviousness

101. **bloody fire:** i.e., **fire** made of blood

103. **aspire:** rise up

105. **mutually:** jointly, in common

109. **watched you:** i.e., caught you (literally, kept you under surveillance to prevent escape)

111. **hold up:** sustain, keep up; **higher:** i.e., further, longer

PISTOL, ⌜*as Hobgoblin*⌝
  A trial, come!
SIR HUGH, ⌜*as a fairy*⌝   Come, will this wood take fire?

⌜*Sir Hugh puts a taper to Falstaff's finger, and he starts.*⌝

FALSTAFF   O, O, O!   95
MISTRESS QUICKLY, ⌜*as Fairy Queen*⌝
  Corrupt, corrupt, and tainted in desire!
  About him, fairies. Sing a scornful rhyme,
  And, as you trip, still pinch him to your time.

⌜*Here they pinch him and sing about him, and Doctor
Caius comes one way and steals away a boy in white.
And Slender comes another way; he takes a boy in
green. And Fenton steals Mistress Anne Page.*⌝

⌜FAIRIES *sing*⌝
    Fie on sinful fantasy!
    Fie on lust and luxury!   100
    Lust is but a bloody fire
    Kindled with unchaste desire,
    Fed in heart whose flames aspire
    As thoughts do blow them higher and higher.
    Pinch him, fairies, mutually;   105
    Pinch him for his villainy.
  Pinch him and burn him and turn him about,
  Till candles and starlight and moonshine be out.

⌜*A noise of hunting is made within, and all the fairies
run away from Falstaff, who pulls off his buck's head
and rises up.*⌝ Enter Page, ⌜*Mistress Page,
Mistress Ford and*⌝ Ford.

PAGE, ⌜*to Falstaff*⌝
  Nay, do not fly. I think we have watched you now.
  Will none but Herne the Hunter serve your turn?   110
MISTRESS PAGE
  I pray you, come, hold up the jest no higher.—
  Now, good Sir John, how like you Windsor wives?

113. **yokes:** i.e., horns (presumably so called because they resemble the yoke of a plow)

119. **but:** except

121. **arrested:** i.e., seized (by legal warrant) as security

127. **Both the proofs:** presumably, proof that you are **both an ass** in your stupidity and **an ox** with your horns

130. **surprise of:** attack on

131. **grossness:** enormity; **foppery:** absurdity, foolishness

132. **received:** accepted, approved; **in despite of the teeth of:** i.e., in defiance of

133. **rhyme and reason:** proverbial ("Neither **rhyme** nor **reason.**")

134. **wit:** intelligence; **Jack-a-lent:** i.e., a target for everyone to throw at (See note to 3.3.25.)

144. **wants matter:** lacks means

145. **ridden with:** i.e., **ridden** by

146. **coxcomb:** hat worn by a professional Fool (See picture, page 120.) **frieze:** coarse woolen cloth (which Falstaff associates with Wales)

⌈*She points to the horns.*⌉
See you these, husband? Do not these fair yokes
Become the forest better than the town?

FORD, ⌈*to Falstaff*⌉ Now, sir, who's a cuckold now?   115
 Master ⌈Brook,⌉ Falstaff's a knave, a cuckoldly
 knave. Here are his horns, Master ⌈Brook.⌉ And,
 Master ⌈Brook,⌉ he hath enjoyed nothing of Ford's
 but his buck-basket, his cudgel, and twenty
 pounds of money, which must be paid to Master   120
 ⌈Brook.⌉ His horses are arrested for it, Master
 ⌈Brook.⌉

MISTRESS FORD Sir John, we have had ill luck. We
 could never meet. I will never take you for my love
 again, but I will always count you my deer.   125

FALSTAFF I do begin to perceive that I am made an ass.

FORD Ay, and an ox too. Both the proofs are extant.

FALSTAFF And these are not fairies. I was three or four
 times in the thought they were not fairies; and yet
 the guiltiness of my mind, the sudden surprise of   130
 my powers, drove the grossness of the foppery into
 a received belief, in despite of the teeth of all
 rhyme and reason, that they were fairies. See now
 how wit may be made a Jack-a-Lent when 'tis upon
 ill employment.   135

SIR HUGH Sir John Falstaff, serve Got and leave your
 desires, and fairies will not pinse you.

FORD Well said, Fairy Hugh.

SIR HUGH And leave you your jealousies too, I pray
 you.   140

FORD I will never mistrust my wife again till thou art
 able to woo her in good English.

FALSTAFF Have I laid my brain in the sun and dried it,
 that it wants matter to prevent so gross o'erreach-
 ing as this? Am I ridden with a Welsh goat too?   145
 Shall I have a coxcomb of frieze? 'Tis time I were
 choked with a piece of toasted cheese.

152. **decay:** downfall

152–53. **late walking:** i.e., going out **late** at night

153. **through:** throughout

159. **hodge-pudding:** a kind of sausage made of a variety of ingredients

160. **puffed:** inflated, swollen, distended

161. **intolerable:** excessive; insupportable

162. **slanderous as Satan:** i.e., as prone to lying as the devil (For the devil as the father of lies, see John 8.44.)

163. **poor as Job:** In the Book of Job, God allows **Job** to be stripped of property, children, and health.

164. **wicked as his wife:** Job's **wife** advises him to curse God (Job 2.9).

166. **metheglins:** Metheglin is spiced mead, originally a Welsh concoction.

167. **starings:** glaring

167–68. **pribbles and prabbles:** i.e., brabbles (brawls)

169. **start of:** advantage over

170. **dejected:** overthrown; disheartened

171. **flannel:** woolen cloth, originally made in Wales

171–72. **Ignorance . . . o'er me:** i.e., **Ignorance** (in the figure of Sir Hugh) has plumbed my very depths (See longer note, page 214.)

172. **Use:** treat

175. **should:** were to

176. **that:** i.e., **that** which

178. **eat:** take, imbibe; **posset:** See note to 1.4.8.

182. **Doctors doubt that:** Proverbial: "The **doctors doubt** of **that,** . . . for I am of a different opinion."

183. **this:** i.e., **this** time

SIR HUGH   Seese is not good to give putter. Your belly is
   all putter.

FALSTAFF   "Seese" and "putter"? Have I lived to stand at   150
   the taunt of one that makes fritters of English?
   This is enough to be the decay of lust and late
   walking through the realm.

MISTRESS PAGE   Why, Sir John, do you think though we
   would have thrust virtue out of our hearts by the   155
   head and shoulders, and have given ourselves
   without scruple to hell, that ever the devil could
   have made you our delight?

FORD   What, a hodge-pudding? A bag of flax?

MISTRESS PAGE   A puffed man?   160

PAGE   Old, cold, withered, and of intolerable entrails?

FORD   And one that is as slanderous as Satan?

PAGE   And as poor as Job?

FORD   And as wicked as his wife?

SIR HUGH   And given to fornications, and to taverns,   165
   and sack, and wine, and metheglins, and to drink-
   ings and swearings and starings, pribbles and
   prabbles?

FALSTAFF   Well, I am your theme. You have the start of
   me. I am dejected. I am not able to answer the   170
   Welsh flannel. Ignorance itself is a plummet o'er
   me. Use me as you will.

FORD   Marry, sir, we'll bring you to Windsor to one
   Master ⌈Brook,⌉ that you have cozened of money,
   to whom you should have been a pander. Over and   175
   above that you have suffered, I think to repay that
   money will be a biting affliction.

PAGE   Yet be cheerful, knight. Thou shalt eat a posset
   tonight at my house, where I will desire thee to
   laugh at my wife, that now laughs at thee. Tell her   180
   Master Slender hath married her daughter.

MISTRESS PAGE, ⌈*aside*⌉ Doctors doubt that. If Anne
   Page be my daughter, she is, by this, Doctor Caius'
   wife.

186–87. **dispatched:** concluded the business

189. **on 't:** i.e., of it

190. **Of what:** i.e., know **of what**

192. **lubberly:** loutish, clumsy

193. **swinged:** beaten

196. **post-master's boy: boy** who serves the **post-master** (the man who provides post-horses for rapid travel, or who is the official responsible for post-messengers)

200. **for all:** even though

201. **had him:** i.e., accepted him as a wife (or, consummated the marriage with him)

205. **white:** The Folio inexplicably reverses **white** and **green** (as set up in 4.6 and 5.2), both here and at lines 210 and 217.

214. **un paysan:** a peasant

Jove as a bull, abducting Europa. (5.5.3–4)
From Gabriele Simeoni, *La vita . . . d'Ouidio . . .* (1559).

Enter Slender.

SLENDER Whoa, ho, ho, Father Page!   185
PAGE Son, how now! How now, son! Have you dispatched?
SLENDER "Dispatched"? I'll make the best in Glouces-
  tershire know on 't. Would I were hanged, la, else!
PAGE Of what, son?   190
SLENDER I came yonder at Eton to marry Mistress
  Anne Page, and she's a great lubberly boy. If it had
  not been i' th' church, I would have swinged him,
  or he should have swinged me. If I did not think it
  had been Anne Page, would I might never stir! And 195
  'tis a post-master's boy.
PAGE Upon my life, then, you took the wrong—
SLENDER What need you tell me that? I think so, when
  I took a boy for a girl. If I had been married to him,
  for all he was in woman's apparel, I would not 200
  have had him.
PAGE Why, this is your own folly. Did not I tell you
  how you should know my daughter by her gar-
  ments?
SLENDER I went to her in ⌜white,⌝ and cried "mum," 205
  and she cried "budget," as Anne and I had appointed, and yet it was not Anne, but a post-
  master's boy.
MISTRESS PAGE Good George, be not angry. I knew of
  your purpose, turned my daughter into ⌜green,⌝ 210
  and indeed she is now with the doctor at the deanery, and there married.

Enter ⌜Doctor⌝ Caius.

DOCTOR CAIUS Vere is Mistress Page? By gar, I am cozened! I ha' married *un garçon,* a boy; *un paysan,* by
  gar, a boy. It is not Anne Page. By gar, I am coz- 215
  ened.

226. **maid:** term of address to a young, unmarried woman

227. **amaze:** bewilder (i.e., by asking her two questions at once)

229. **proportion held:** i.e., agreement

230. **contracted:** engaged, betrothed

231. **sure:** i.e., bound (together)

234. **unduteous title:** undutifulness

235. **evitate:** avoid

239. **guide the state:** i.e., rule

240. **wives . . . fate:** Proverbial: "Marriage is destiny."

242. **stand:** place from which hunters shoot

245. **What . . . embraced:** Proverbial: **"What cannot be** cured **must be** endured."

The badge of the Garter Herald. (5.5.74)
From Elias Ashmole, *The institution, laws & ceremonies of the . . . Order of the Garter . . .* (1672).

MISTRESS PAGE   Why? Did you take her in ⌜green?⌝
DOCTOR CAIUS   Ay, be gar, and 'tis a boy. Be gar, I'll raise
  all Windsor.
FORD   This is strange. Who hath got the right Anne?   220

Enter Fenton and Anne Page.

PAGE   My heart misgives me. Here comes Master Fen-
  ton.— How now, Master Fenton!
ANNE   Pardon, good father. Good my mother, pardon.
PAGE   Now, mistress, how chance you went not with
  Master Slender?   225
MISTRESS PAGE
  Why went you not with Master Doctor, maid?
FENTON
  You do amaze her. Hear the truth of it.
  You would have married her most shamefully,
  Where there was no proportion held in love.
  The truth is, she and I, long since contracted,   230
  Are now so sure that nothing can dissolve us.
  Th' offense is holy that she hath committed,
  And this deceit loses the name of craft,
  Of disobedience, or unduteous title,
  Since therein she doth evitate and shun   235
  A thousand irreligious cursèd hours
  Which forcèd marriage would have brought upon her.
FORD, ⌜*to Page and Mistress Page*⌝
  Stand not amazed. Here is no remedy.
  In love the heavens themselves do guide the state.
  Money buys lands, and wives are sold by fate.   240
FALSTAFF   I am glad, though you have ta'en a special
    stand to strike at me, that your arrow hath
    glanced.
PAGE
  Well, what remedy? Fenton, heaven give thee joy.
  What cannot be eschewed must be embraced.   245

247. muse: complain; marvel

Queen Elizabeth I at Windsor for an investiture
of Knights of the Garter.
From Elias Ashmole, *The institution, laws & ceremonies
of the . . . Order of the Garter . . .* (1672).

FALSTAFF
    When night-dogs run, all sorts of deer are chased.
MISTRESS PAGE
    Well, I will muse no further.—Master Fenton,
    Heaven give you many, many merry days.—
    Good husband, let us every one go home
    And laugh this sport o'er by a country fire—   250
    Sir John and all.
FORD   Let it be so, Sir John.
    To Master ⌜Brook⌝ you yet shall hold your word,
    For he tonight shall lie with Mistress Ford.
                                        They exit.

Longer Notes

1.1.2. Star-Chamber: The Court of Star Chamber consisted principally of members of the monarch's Privy Council. Originally a court of appeal, it began in the sixteenth century to hear cases that had not been heard by lower courts. At the same time, its mandate expanded to include instances of public disorder or **riot** (line 35). The Court of Star Chamber was named for the star pattern painted on the ceiling of the hall at Westminster Palace where its meetings were held.

1.1.137. Garter: The Order of the **Garter** (a knightly order composed of 25 knights and the monarch) was founded in the mid–fourteenth century by King Edward III. From the earliest days of the order, Windsor Castle was its center, with one of the towers of the castle named the Garter Tower. (For Windsor and its castle, see longer note to 2.2.62, page 210.) The Garter Ceremony is held annually at Windsor. Among the references to the Order of the Garter in the play are the name of the Garter Inn and the quotation of the order's motto, *Honi soit qui mal y pense* (5.5.74).

1.1.161. humors: In early usage, *humor* referred to the bodily fluids of blood, phlegm, black bile, and yellow bile; later, the term referred to the dispositions, character traits, or moods thought to be caused by these fluids, and then to moods or whims in general. In Nym's language, the word becomes so vague as to have no real meaning.

1.1.196–97. Book of Riddles: The earliest record of a book with such a title dates from 1511. The use to which such books could be put is indicated by the title page of one printed in 1620: *A Helpe to Discourse or A Miscelany of Merriment. Consisting of wittie, Philosophicall and Astronomicall Questions and Answers. As also, Of Epigrams, Epitaphs, Riddles, and Iests. . . .*

1.3.9. Keiser: This is the first of a number of titles or proper names in the Host's speeches that seem malformed. See also "Cavaleiro" (2.1.193, etc.), "Galien" (2.3.29), and "Castalion" (2.3.33). In all these cases, the malformations may indicate comic mispronunciations. Here, for example, "Keiser" could be pronounced "Keeser" to rhyme with "Caesar." It is possible to find several instances of this kind of comic mispronunciation in plays usually dated in the 1570s and 1580s, the two decades that preceded that of *Merry Wives'* composition. See, for instance, George Whetstone's *Promos and Cassandra* 2: "Casgandra" for *Cassandra* and "Ramstrugio" for *Andrugio* (4.2); and Robert Wilson's *Coblers Prophesie:* "Markedy" for *Mercury* (sig. B1) and "Shebiter" for *Jupiter* (B1v).

1.3.70. Guiana: This part of northeastern South America had been described by Sir Walter Ralegh in *The discouerie of the large, rich, and bevvtiful empire of Guiana, with a relation of the great and Golden Citie of Manoa (which the spanyards call El Dorado)* printed in 1596—the title, like the work itself, exaggerating the desirability of colonizing the region.

1.3.86. French thrift . . . page: There is little evidence that the **French** actually practiced such **thrift** in limiting attendants to a **page.** However, George Chapman, in his play *Monsieur D'Olive* (printed 1606), writes "With our great lords, followers abroad and hospitality at home are out of date. The world's now grown thrifty. He that fills a whole page in folio with his style [i.e., someone with so many titles that they occupy the largest of printed pages] thinks it veriest noble to be manned with one bare page and a pander."

1.3.102–4. **Ford . . . yellowness:** There is a good deal of uncertainty in the text about which of Falstaff's revolted men, Pistol or Nym, is to be associated with which of the husbands whose wives Falstaff is pursuing. Initially, at 1.3.35, Pistol is associated with Ford; yet here, at the end of the same scene, Nym, rather than Pistol, plans to approach Ford while Pistol will talk to Page. Later, however (2.1.110–38), Falstaff's men will switch back: Pistol will approach Ford and Nym Page. Some editors attempt to straighten out the text's double reversal by emending it. They exchange the names of Page and Ford (1.3.96, 98, and 102) so that Pistol plans from the beginning to go to Ford and Nym to Page. But the text is not so easily straightened out. The exchange of names would have Nym say "I will incense Page to deal with poison. I will possess him with **yellowness**," thus associating Page with the jealousy that is uniquely Ford's.

We believe that the text is better not emended in this way. Throughout the play, both in its action and its dialogue, Ford is the jealous husband, a role that he exclusively occupies, while Page is repeatedly presented as in no way inclined to jealousy and quite invulnerable to temptation towards it. To emend 1.3.102–4 and have Nym say of Page "I will possess him with yellowness" is therefore to correct a minor problem in the play's text at the cost of introducing a much greater inconsistency.

1.4.14. **peevish:** Editors have noted the apparent inappropriateness of calling Rugby either "silly" or "perverse" for praying. The humor of many of Mistress Quickly's speeches arises from their utter lack of logic combined with her misuse of particular words.

1.4.64. **Qu'ai-j'oublié:** In the Folio text, this French expression, like much of Doctor Caius's French, is filled with errors. (See the Textual Notes for more examples.) It is printed as "Que ay ie oublie," thus failing to elide "Que ay" (i.e., *Que ai*) and "ie oublie" (i.e., *je oublie*). Such elision was already in place in French writings published in England in the sixteenth century. The failure to elide cannot be blamed on a copyist or a compositor unfamiliar with French, because such an agent could not have known to expand "Qu" to *Que* or "i" to *ie;* both *Que* and *ie* are proper French words, their forms wrong only in context because elisions are required. (Note that "ay" would then have been acceptable for *ai* and "i" for *j*.) Thus the failure to elide must be Shakespeare's. Even so, in keeping with our editorial policy in printing foreign languages in the plays, we have elided the expressions. Our policy is to modernize and, where necessary, correct passages in foreign languages, unless an error in the early printed text can be reasonably explained as a joke. It seems unlikely to us that Doctor Caius is to be represented as comically mangling French as well as English.

1.4.78. **phlegmatic:** Mistress Quickly here, and perhaps again at line 96, attempts to place Doctor Caius within the humoral system of personalities, but her language, as so often, fails. A man who is **phlegmatic,** according to humoral psychology, is dominated by the bodily humor of phlegm (the cold, moist humor) and is thus apathetic and indolent. A choleric man, in contrast, is dominated by choler (the hot, dry humor), and thus prone to anger. The **melancholy** man (line 96) is dominated by black bile (the cold, dry humor) and thus prone to sullenness, sadness, and mental gloom. Both **phlegmatic** and **melancholy** may, then, be Mistress Quickly's mistakes for *choleric*. Since, however, **melancholy** also occasionally meant irascible or angry, Mistress Quickly may not be erring in using that term to describe Doctor Caius. (In *King John*, Shakespeare has a character refer to "that surly spirit, **melancholy**" [3.3.44].)

2.1.122. **horn:** The association of cuckolds with horns growing from the man's forehead goes back to ancient times and may originate with the early and prevalent practice of "grafting the spurs of a castrated cock on the root of the excised comb, where they grew and became horns, sometimes of several inches long" (*OED*, "horn" 7a). The cuckold and his horns led to the commonplace connection between cuckolds and beasts with horns, a connection often alluded to in Shakespeare's plays, as is the link between the cuckoo and the cuckold (as in 2.1.125–26).

2.1.175. **very rogues:** The word *rogue* came into English in 1561, first as the name given a beggar who uses as his excuse for being on the road the tale that he has come to seek a kinsman, and then, in addition, as the name for a beggar who got money by pretending to be sick. By 1572 *rogue* had become the term used in legal statutes to refer to those who, though healthy, were unemployed and who had no source of income. To be a rogue—i.e., to be unemployed and destitute— was to be a criminal liable to severe punishment.

2.1.212. **Brook:** Throughout the First Folio text, this name appears as "Broome"; the name **Brook** (or

"Brooke," to be precise) is taken from the Quarto. "Brooke" was the name of a prominent and powerful aristocratic family. Editors adopt the Quarto reading of the name not only because of the suspicion of a kind of censorship but also because of the wordplay associated with it. For example, at 2.2.151–52 Falstaff says "Such Brooks are welcome to me that o'erflows such liquor." Here Falstaff plays on "Brooks" and *brooks*. The name "Broome" would not do here, for obvious reasons. There seems little doubt, then, that the Quarto preserves in **Brook** Ford's original disguise name, which at some later time was altered to "Broome," the Folio disguise name.

2.2.62. **lay at Windsor:** The royal palace of **Windsor** Castle was in Shakespeare's day one of the chief residences of the English sovereign, as it had been since the time of William the Conqueror. It was prized by centuries of monarchs for its royal hunting preserve (Windsor Forest) and for its parks and gardens. The royal court resided sometimes at Windsor, sometimes at other royal palaces such as Whitehall and (until the early sixteenth century) Westminster, and sometimes as guests at the estates of noblemen. Mistress Quickly's speech (lines 61–78) presents a vivid picture of **Windsor** with the court in residence, especially as viewed by a citizen of the town. Of special interest is the suggestion that noble lords sought the favors of the wives of local citizens like Master Ford.

2.3.33. **Castalion:** If the Host's **Castalion King** refers to the Castilian **King,** the reference would be to Philip II, who had sent a great fleet or armada against England in 1588, and who continued to threaten it long after. However, **Castalion** may instead be a version of *Castalian*, with reference to Castalia, the sacred spring of the Muses on Mount Parnassus in Greece. Editors also note that *Castalion* was a contemporary spelling of the name of the well-known writer Castiglione, famous especially for his book *Il Cortegiano*, translated into English in 1561 as *The Courtier*.

3.5.112. **bellwether:** A **bellwether**—a sheep that wears a bell and leads the other sheep, as Ford leads the **rabble of his companions** (lines 77–78)—can be a ram, and therefore horned, as is the image of the cuckold. (See longer note to 2.1.122, above, and picture, page 134.) In *As You Like It* Shakespeare refers to a "bell-wether" as "a crooked-pated old cuckoldy ram" (3.2.81, 82).

4.1.35. **It is lapis:** Lilly and Colet instructed schoolmasters to have their pupils translate English words into Latin and then translate the Latin words back into English: "Furthermore, we see many understand Latine, that cannot speake it, and when they read the Latine word in the booke, can tell you the English thereof at any time; but when they haue laid away their bookes, they cannot contrariwise tell you for the English the Latine againe, whensoeuer you will aske them. And therefore this exercise helpeth this sore well, and maketh those words which he understandeth, to be readiest by use unto him."

4.1.40–42. **Articles . . . hoc:** According to Lilly, **articles are thus declined: singulariter:** i.e., singly, or, in the singular; **nominativo:** i.e., in the nominative, the case in which the subject of a sentence appears, just as **genitivo** means "in the genitive," or possessive; **accusativo:** "in the accusative," the case in which the object of a sentence appears; and **vocativo:** "in the vocative," the case for direct address to someone or something.

4.3. Scene Heading: This brief and puzzling scene, which alludes to an equally puzzling "Duke," is widely thought to begin a plot of revenge by Doctor Caius and Sir Hugh against the Host. That plot seems to involve accomplices who have impersonated German visitors to Windsor for the purpose of stealing horses from the Host.

4.4.45. **meet with us:** Editors have long since felt that something was missing from the Folio text after the line "That Falstaff at that oak shall meet with us." Lewis Theobald, in his edition of 1733, found some lines in the Quarto that seemed to him to fill that gap. Many editors today continue to use one of the lines that Theobald imported into his text, a line that reads "Disguised like Herne [Quarto: Horne], with huge horns on his head." The problem for us arises in the fact that the line appears in the Quarto in a context that has a low level of convergence with the Folio's language. The Quarto reads:

> Now that *Falstaffe* hath bene so deceiued,
> As that he dares not venture to the house,
> Weele send him word to meet vs in the field,
> *Disguised like Horne, with huge horns on his head,*
> The houre shalbe iust betweene twelue and one,
> And at that time we will meet him both.

Because the verbal contexts are so different, we do not include the Quarto line.

5.5.39 SD. **Mistress Quickly, Pistol:** The appearance of these characters among the fairies marks an unexplained departure from the plans detailed in earlier scenes. At 4.4.51–53, Mistress Page had spoken of the fairies being played by her daughter Anne, son William, and "three or four more" of their age and size. Then at 4.4.77 Mistress Page had embroidered the scheme to have Anne play "the queen of all the fairies," the role that Fenton also told the Host she was to play (4.6.21). There is no preparation for the appearance of Mistress Quickly and Pistol as fairies, and no preparation for Mistress Quickly taking the role of the queen from Anne. Yet Mistress Quickly seems to play the queen: she speaks first, and the import of all her speeches is to give the fairies orders. It has long been noted that neither Mistress Quickly nor Pistol retains in this scene the speech mannerisms that have vividly distinguished them throughout the play. The absence of those mannerisms has led to the further suggestion that the fairies' roles are taken not by the characters themselves but only by the actors who previously presented them, and who are simply being designated in stage directions and speech prefixes by the names of the characters they had previously played. While this possibility cannot be ruled out, it actually makes no difference. Whether we assume that the characters (Mistress Quickly and Pistol) are playing the fairies or that the actors who previously played these roles are now doubling as fairies, the audience will be aware only that the Quickly and Pistol actors/characters are now in new roles as fairies. Since the Quickly/Pistol actors have their final exit in their fairy roles, there is no opportunity for them to reveal themselves as the characters played earlier, or to demonstrate that they have abandoned their earlier roles. (For the possible significance of Mistress Quickly's personating the Fairy Queen, see "A Modern Perspective," pages 237–38.)

5.5.42. **You . . . destiny:** In this much-debated line, the word **orphan** perhaps refers to the belief that fairies come into being without parents, and **heirs of fixèd destiny** indicates either that each of the fairies has been prescribed a specific duty (to the performance of which each is now being sent), or that fairies are permitted (and thus destined) to appear only at night.

5.5.66. several . . . order: This long speech of the "Fairy Queen," most of it irrelevant to the action of the play, has suggested to some scholars that *The Merry Wives of Windsor* may have been written for performance on an occasion associated with the knights of the Garter. In a 1931 book, *Shakespeare and Shallow,* Leslie Hotson developed the theory that the play's occasion was the Garter Feast celebrated in the royal Whitehall Palace on April 23 (St. George's Day) in 1597, because that was the year of election of George Carey, Lord Hunsdon, then patron of the acting company to which Shakespeare belonged. The formal installation of Hunsdon (and the other newly elected knights) would have taken place a month later at the annual Garter Ceremony held in St. George's Chapel at Windsor Castle—the chapel described in Mistress Quickly's speech. However, no surviving evidence validates Hotson's elaborate theory.

5.5.171–72. Ignorance . . . o'er me: Another way of reading this line sees Falstaff as saying "the depth of my ignorance is so great that it cannot be fathomed; and, even the ignorant (e.g., Sir Hugh) are **o'er** or above me." There may also be wordplay on the fact that a **plummet**—a weight attached to a line and used for measuring the depth of water—is usually made of lead, which is associated with stupidity.

Textual Notes

The reading of the present text appears to the left of the square bracket. Unless otherwise noted, the reading to the left of the bracket is from F, the First Folio text (upon which this edition is based). The earliest sources of readings not in F are indicated as follows: **Q** is the Quarto of 1602; **Q3** is the Quarto of 1630; **F2** is the Second Folio of 1632; **F3** is the Third Folio of 1663–64; **Ed.** is an earlier editor of Shakespeare, beginning with Rowe in 1709. No sources are given for emendations of punctuation or for corrections of obvious typographical errors, like turned letters that produce no known word. **SD** means stage direction; **SP** means speech prefix; *uncorr.* means the first or uncorrected state of the First Folio; *corr.* means the second or corrected state of the First Folio; ~ stands in place of a word already quoted before the square bracket; ʌ indicates the omission of a punctuation mark.

1.1   0. SD *Enter ... Evans*] Ed.; *Enter Iustice*
           Shallow, Slender, *Sir* Hugh Euans,
           Master Page, Falstoffe, Bardolph,
           Nym, Pistoll, Anne Page, *Mistresse*
           Ford, *Mistresse* Page, Simple. F; *Enter*
           Iustice Shallow, *Syr* Hugh, *Maister*
           Page, *and* Slender. Q
     2. matter of it.]~~~, F
    19 *and hereafter.* SP SIR HUGH] This ed.;
           Euans F
    22. fresh fish. The salt fishʌ] ~~, ~~~, F
    28. py'r Lady] F (per-lady)

215

33–34. compromises] F (compremises)
   46. Thomas] F
   65 *and repeatedly but not invariably here-
       after.* Master] F (Mr *and also* Mr. *and*
       M.)
   73 *and hereafter in this scene.* SP PAGE]
       Ed.; *Mr. Page.* (*elsewhere in this scene
       also M., Ma.*) F
   74. Got's] F (go't's)
  105. hath;] ~, F
  106. SD *Enter . . . Pistol.*] Q (*Enter Syr* Iohn
       Falstaffe, Pistoll, Bardolfe, *and* Nim.)
  137. Garter] Gater F
  139. goot] F (goo't)
  156. latten] Q (laten); F (Latine)
  175. careers] F (Car-eires)
  176. Latin] F (Latten)
  181. virtuous] vertuons F
  183. SD *Enter . . . wine.*] Ed.; *Enter Mis-
       tresse* Foord, *Mistresse* Page, *and her
       daughter* Anne. Q
  189. SD *He kisses her.*] Q (*Syr* Iohn kisses
       her.); *not in* F
  192. SD *All . . . exit.*] Ed.; *Exit all, but* Slen-
       der *and mistresse* Anne. Q; *not in* F
  209. motions, Master Slender.] ~; (~~) F
  218. Mistress] F (Mi.)
  225. can] F (cã)
  226. the] F (ỹ)
  248. discretion answer] discetion-answere
       F
  258. absence] F (absēce)
  293. SD *Enter Page.*] Q (*Enter Maister*
       Page.); *not in* F

1.2   5. wringer] F (Ringer)
           9. acquaintance] F (acquaintãce)

1.3	14.	lime] Q; liue F
	14.	SD *Host exits.*] Q; *not in* F
	19.	thou] F (ẙ)
	20.	SD *Bardolph exits.*] Q; *not in* F
	21–22.	conceited] F (cõceited)
	40.	waist] F (waste)
	52.	legion] Ed.; legend F
	60.	oeillades] Ed.; illiads F
	85.	humor] Q; honor F
	86.	SD *Falstaff . . . exit.*] Q (*Exit Falstaffe, and the Boy.*); *not in* F
1.4	0.	SD *Enter . . . Simple.*] Q; *Enter Mistris Quickly, Simple, Iohn Rugby, Doctor, Caius, Fenton.* F
	1	*and hereafter.* SP MISTRESS QUICKLY] Ed.; *Qu.* F
	39.	SD *Simple exits.*] Ed.; *He steps into the Counting-house.* Q; *not in* F
	44	*and hereafter.* SP DOCTOR CAIUS] Ed.; *Ca.* F
	45–46.	*un boîtier vert*] Ed.; vnboyteene verd F
	52.	*Ma*] mai F
	52–53.	*fort chaud. Je m'en vais à la cour—la grande affaire*] Ed.; *for ehando, Ie man voi a le Court la grand affaires* F
	55.	*Oui, mets-le à*] Ouy mette le au F
	55.	*Dépêche*] de-peech F
	59.	and] aad F
	64.	*Qu'ai-j'oublié*] que ay ie oublie F
	70.	*Larron*] Ed.; La-roone F
	92.	*baille*] Ed.; ballow F
	93.	SD *Rugby . . . writes.*] Q (*The Doctor writes.*); *not in* F
	97.	you] F (yoe)
	99.	the] F (ẙ)
	101.	wring] F (ring)

127. goodyear] F (good-ier)
132. SD *Caius . . . exit.*] *Exit Doctor.* Q; *not in* F
150. Fenton] *Feuton* F
170. him] hiim F

2.1   0. SD *Enter Mistress Page reading a letter.*] Ed.; Enter *Mistris* Page, *Mistris* Ford, *Master* Page, *Master* Ford, Pistoll, Nim, Quickly, Host, Shallow. F; *Enter Mistresse* Page, *reading of a letter.* Q
1. I] Q3; *omit* F
2. holiday] F (holly-day)
20. Jewry] F (*Iurie*)
31. SD *Enter Mistress Ford.*] Q
36. believe] beleeee F
57. praised] Ed.; praise F
62. Hundredth Psalm] Ed.; hundred Psalms F
108. SD *Enter . . . Nym.*] Enter Ford, Page, Pistoll and Nym. Q
128. SD *He exits.*] Q (*Exit Pistoll*); *not in* F
138. SD *He exits.*] Q (*Exit Nym.*); *not in* F
150. Whither] F (Whether)
159. SD *Enter Mistress Quickly.*] Q *after equivalent of line 150*
167. SD *Mistress . . . exit.*] Q (*Exit Mistresse* Ford, *Mis.* Page, *and* Quickly.); *not in* F
187. SD *Enter Host.*] Enter Host and Shallow. Q
202. SD *The Host . . . aside.*] Ford *and the* Host talkes. Q; *not in* F
210. SP FORD] Q; *Shal.* F
212 *and hereafter.* Brook] Q; Broome F
216. ameers] Ed.; An-heires F
228. SD *Page . . . exit.*] Exit Host and Shallow. Q; *not in* F

230. wife's] F (wiues)
235. SD *He exits.*] *Exeunt.* F; *Exit omnes.* Q

2.2   0. SD *Enter . . . Pistol.*] Ed.; *Enter Syr Iohn, and Pistoll.* Q; *Enter Falstaffe, Pistoll, Robin, Quickly, Bardolffe, Ford.* F

22. honor] hononor F
23, 52. God] Q; heauen F
32. SD *Enter Mistress Quickly.*] Q
115. infection] F (infectiō)
133–34. SD *Mistress . . . exit.*] Ed.; *Exit Mistresse Quickly.* Q; *not in* F
144. SD *Enter . . . wine.*] Q (*Enter Bardolfe.*); *not in* F
154. SD *Enter . . . Brook.*] *Enter Foord disguised like* Brooke. Q
155. God bless] Ed.; 'Blesse F; God saue Q
240. exchange] enchange F
293. SD *Falstaff exits.*] Q; *not in* F
313. ruminates] rumiuates F
316. God] Q; Heauen F
321. SD *He exits.*] *Exti.* F

2.3   0. SD *Enter . . . Rugby.*] Ed.; *Enter the Doctor and his man.* Q; *Enter Caius, Rugby, Page, Shallow, Slender, Host.* F

17. SD *Enter . . . Host.*] *Enter Shallow, Page, my Host, and Slender.* Q
18. God bless] Q; 'Blesse F
19. God save] Q (*where speech is attributed to* Page); 'Saue F
26. thy] Ed.; thee F
33. Urinal∧] ~: F
38. Doctor] Docto)r F
57. word] Q; *not in* F
81. SP PAGE, SHALLOW, and SLENDER] Ed.; *All.* F

82. SD *Page . . . exit.*] Q (*Exit all but the Host and Doctor.*); not in F

3.1   0. SD *Enter . . . gown.*] Ed.; *Enter Euans, Simple, Page, Shallow, Slender, Host, Caius, Rugby.* F; *Enter Syr Hugh and Simple.* Q

5. Petty-ward] Ed.; pittie-ward F

16. *rivers*] *Ruiers* F

25–26. *To shallow rivers, to whose falls | Melodious birds sings madrigals.*] Ed.; *To shallow, &c.* F

41. God save] Q; 'Saue F

42. God pless] Q; 'Plesse F

67. acquainted] acquaiuted F

73. SD *Enter . . . fight.*] Ed.; *Enter Doctor and the Host, they offer to fight.* Q

81–82. patience.] ∼∧ F

88. By Jeshu] Q; not in F

98. excellent] excellant F

104–5. Give me thy hand, terrestrial; so.] Q (Giue me thy hand terestiall, So∧); not in F

111. lads] Q; Lad F

111. SD *Host exits.*] Q; not in F

112. Afore God] Q; Trust me F

126. SD *Sir Hugh . . . exit.*] Q (*Exit omnes*); not in F

3.2   0. SD *Enter . . . Mistress Page.*] Ed.; *Mist. Page, Robin, Ford, Page, Shallow, Slender, Host, Euans, Caius.* F

9. Whither] F (whether)

32. wife's] F (wiues)

43. cue] F (Qu)

47. SD *Enter . . . Rugby.*] *Enter Shallow, Page, host, Slender, Doctor, and sir Hugh.* Q

83. SD *Shallow . . . exit.*] Q; *not in* F

86. SD *He exits.*] Q (*Exit host.*); *not in* F

90. SP PAGE, DOCTOR CAIUS, and SIR HUGH]
    Ed.; *All.* F

3.3   0. SD *Enter . . . Mistress Page.*] Ed.; *Enter
    M. Ford, M. Page, Seruants, Robin,
    Falstaffe, Ford, Page, Caius, Euans.* F;
    *Enter Mistresse Ford, with two of her
    men, and a great buck busket.* Q

3. Robert] Ed.; Robin F

12. That] F (ỹ)

13. haste] F (hast)

13. Datchet] Ed.; Dotchet F

19. SD *John . . . exit.*] Ed.; *Exit seruant.* Q

24, 47, 98, 142, 189–90. Mistress] F
    (Mist.)

36. cue] F (Qu)

41. SD *Enter . . . Falstaff.*] Q (*Enter Sir
    Iohn.*)

72. like∧] ~. F

73. Bucklersbury] Ed.; Bucklers-berry F

76. Mistress] F (M.)

79. lime-kiln] F (Lime-kill)

92. SD 1–2. *Falstaff . . . Page.*] Q (*"Enter
    Mistresse Page." after line 79,* Q *omit-
    ting lines 80–90; "Falstaffe stands be-
    hind the aras.");* not *in* F

105. hither] F (hether)

137. Falstaff] *Faistaffe* F

137–38. SD (*Aside to him.*)] Q (*Aside*); *not in* F

140. SD *Falstaff . . . clothes.*] Q (*Sir Iohn
    goes into the basket, they put cloathes
    ouer him, the two men carries it away:
    Foord meetes it, and all the rest, Page,
    Doctor, Priest, Slender, Shallow.*); *not
    in* F

150, 153. Whither] F (Whether)

152. SP ROBERT and JOHN] Ed.; *Ser.* F

155, 213. the] F ($\tilde{y}$)

172. SD *Page . . . exit.*] *Exit omnes.* Q

189. foolish] foolishion F

194. SD *Enter . . . Sir Hugh.*] Ed.; *Enter all.* Q

211. ashamed] ash em'd F

217. 'omans] F (o'mans)

223. Mistress] F (Mi.)

224. heartily] F (hartly)

3.4   0. SD *Enter . . . Anne Page.*] Ed.; *Enter Fenton, Anne, Page, Shallow, Slender, Quickly, Page, Mist. Page.* F; *Enter M. Fenton, Page, and mistresse Quickly.* Q

13. SP FENTON] Q3; *not in* F

40. Mistress] F (M.)

42, 81. Mistress] F (Mist.)

70. Fenton] *Fenter* F

74. Fenton,] ~. F

104. SD *Fenton exits.*] *Exit Fen.* Q

113. SD *She exits.*] Q (*Exit.*); *Exeunt* F

3.5   0. SD *Enter Sir John Falstaff.*] Q; *Enter Falstaffe, Bardolfe, Quickly, Ford.* F

8. 'Sblood] Q; *not in* F

17. By the Lord] Q; *not in* F

19, 35. Mistress] F (M.)

25. SD *Enter Mistress Quickly.*] Q

31. sperm] Spersme F

36, 86. Mistress] F (Mist.)

57. SD *Mistress Quickly exits.*] Q; *not in* F

59. SD *Enter . . . Brook.*] Ed.; *Enter Brooke.* Q

60. he] F3; be F

61. God] Q; *not in* F

80, 88.	wife's] F (wiues)
91.	By the Lord] Q; Yes F
140.	SD *Falstaff exits.*] Q
154.	SD *He exits.*] Ed.; *Exeunt.* F; *Exit omnes.* Q

4.1

0.	SD *Enter . . . William.*] Ed.; *Enter Mistris Page, Quickly, William, Euans.* F
30, 50, 55, 63, 68.	'oman] F (o'man)
35.	remember] remeuber F
47.	*hung*] Ed.; *hing* F
67.	whorum] F (*horum*)
68.	lunatics] Lunaties F
77.	*quae*] Ed.; *que* F
78.	*quae*'s] Ed.; *Ques* F
82–83.	Mistress] F (*Mis.*)

4.2

0.	SD *Enter . . . Mistress Ford.*] Ed.; *Enter Falstoffe, Mist. Ford, Mist. Page, Seruants, Ford, Page, Caius, Euans, Shallow.* F; *Enter misteris Ford and her two men.* ("*Enter Syr Iohn.*" 4 Q lines later) Q
1.	Mistress] F (*Mi.*)
4.	Mistress] F (Mist.)
5.	compliment] F (complement)
10.	SD 1. *Falstaff exits.*] *He steps behind the arras.* Q
10.	SD 2. *Enter Mistress Page.*] Q
11.	who's] F (whose)
21.	lunes] Ed.; lines F
58.	SP MISTRESS PAGE] Ed.; *not in* F
58.	kiln-hole] F (Kill-hole)
66.	SP PAGE] Ed.; *Ford* F
76	*and hereafter.* Brentford] Ed.; F (*Brainford*)
80.	Mistress] *Mistriis* F
83.	SD *Falstaff exits.*] Ed.; *Exit Mis. Page, & Sir Iohn.* Q; *not in* F

99. direct] direct direct F
103. him] F2; *omit* F
111, 113. SP ROBERT] Ed.; I *Ser.* F
112. SP JOHN] Ed.; 2 *Ser.* F
113. SD *Enter . . . Shallow.*] Q (*Enter M. Ford, Page, Priest, Shallow, the two men carries the basket, and Ford meets it.*)
118. gang] Ed.; gin F; ging F2
127. this] thi F
142, 164. wife's] F (wiues)
180. not] Q3; *omit* F
180. SD *Enter . . . old woman.*] Q (*Enter Falstaffe disguised like an old woman, and misteris Page with him, Ford beates him, and hee runnes away.*)
192, 193. 'oman] F (o'man)
194. her] Q; his F
200. SD *Ford . . . exit.*] Q (*Exit omnes.*)

4.3
1. Germans desire] Ed.; Germane desires F
7. them] Q; him F
9. house] Q; houses F

4.4
1, 22. 'oman] F (o'man)
6. thou] F (ỹ)
7. cold] Ed.; gold F
27. when] F (whẽ)
28, 48. thither] F (thether)
34. makes] F2; make F
44. device] F (deuise)
53. aufs] F (Ouphes)
88. SD *Page . . . exit.*] *Exit omnes.* Q; *not in* F

4.5
0. SD *Enter . . . Simple.*] Q; *Enter Host, Simple, Falstaffe, Bardolfe, Euans, Caius, Quickly.* F

1–2. have, boor? What, thick-skin?] Ed.;
       ~? (~)~? (~~) F
  22. SD *Enter Sir John Falstaff.*] *Enter Sir
       Iohn.* Q (*after line 24*)
  30. through] F (thorough)
  43. SP SIMPLE] Ed.; *Fal.* F
  56. Thou art] Q; Thou are F
  61. SD *Enter Bardolph.*] Q
  78. Readings] F (Readins)
  78. Colnbrook] Cole-brooke F
  92. SD *Host . . . exit.*] Ed.; *Exit.* Q; *not in* F
 103. SD *Enter Mistress Quickly.*] Q

4.6
   5. gold∧] ~, F
  27. ever] Ed.; euen F
  39. denote] Ed.; deuote F
  50. in] F *corr.*; id F *uncorr.*

5.1
   0. SD *Enter . . . Mistress Quickly.*] Ed.;
       Enter Falstoffe, Quickly, and Ford. F
   6. SP MISTRESS QUICKLY] *Qai.* F
  23. Goliath] Goliah F
  25. haste] F (hast)
  26. Brook.] *Broome:)* F
  32. SD *They exit.*] Ed.; *Exennt.* F

5.2
  10. struck] F (strooke)
  10. o'clock] F (a' clocke)

5.3
   0. SD *Mistress*] F (*Mist.*) (*twice*)
  13. Hugh] Ed.; Herne F

5.5
   0. SD *Enter . . . head.*] *Enter sir Iohn with
       a Bucks head vpon him.* Q; *Enter Fal-
       staffe, Mistris Page, Mistris Ford,
       Euans, Anne Page, Fairies, Page, Ford,
       Quickly, Slender, Fenton, Caius, Pis-
       toll.* F
   1. struck] F (stroke)
   2. hot-blooded] Ed.; hot-bloodied F
  11. foul] F (fowle)

15. SD *Enter ... Mistress Ford.*] Q

32, 36. SDD *A noise of horns within. The two women run off.*] Ed.; Q (*There is a noise of hornes, the two women run away.*); not in F

39. SD *Enter ... tapers.*] Ed. *Enter sir Hugh like Satyre, and boyes drest like Fayries, mistresse Quickly, like the Queene of Fayries: they sing a song about him, and afterward speake.* Q; *Enter Fairies.* F

62. aufs] F (Ouphes)

71. ring.] ~, F

73. More.] F2; Mote F

79. o'clock] F (a clocke)

94. SD *Sir Hugh ... starts.*] Ed.; *They put the Tapers to his fingers, and he starts.* Q

98. SD *Here ... Anne Page.*] Ed.; *Here they pinch him, and sing about him, & the Doctor comes one way & steales away a boy in red. And Slender another way he takes a boy in greene: And Fenton steales misteris Anne, being in white. And a noyse of hunting is made within: and all the Fairies runne away. Falstaffe pulles of his bucks head, and rises vp. And enters M. Page, M. Ford, and their wiues, M. Shallow, Sir Hugh.* Q

99. SP FAIRIES *sing*] Ed.; *The Song.* F

115. who's] F (whose)

136. SP SIR HUGH] *Euant.* F

205. white] Ed.; greene F

210, 217. green] Ed.; white F

214. *un garçon*] oon Garsoon F

214. *un paysan*] oon pesant F

220. SD *Enter ... Anne Page.*] Q (*Enter Fenton and Anne.*); not in F

The Merry Wives of Windsor:
A Modern Perspective

Natasha Korda

The Merry Wives of Windsor is often described as unique in the Shakespearean canon because of its contemporaneity—its quality of here-and-now-ness—which "create[s] the impression of life in an English provincial town as it is being lived at the moment of the play's first performance."[1] The world of the play is indeed quite different from the far-off never-never lands of Illyria, Arden, or Belmont. It is given a local habitation and a name, Windsor, whose recognizable topography is rendered in homely detail, Park-ward and Petty-ward, from Frogmore to Datchet Mead. This quality has in turn led to the play's designation as the "most realistic of Shakespeare's comedies."[2] The play seems to stand apart in offering what might be called its own modern perspective on small-town life in early modern England.

In applying the phrase "modern perspective" to the play, I am taking the word *modern* in its very Shakespearean sense, which derives from the Latin roots *modus* (manner, fashion) and *hodiernus* (of the present time). Its early modern usage was closely related to the word *mode*, which denoted in English "a prevailing fashion, custom, practice or style . . . characteristic of a particular place or period," and in French "a collective

227

manner of living or thinking proper to a country or age" (*OED*). As used by Shakespeare, the word commonly refers to the everyday, ordinary, or commonplace. The realism or modern-ity that sets *Merry Wives* apart is constructed through a variety of techniques that ground the world of the play in the particularity and texture of everyday life: references to popular customs (hue and cry, shaming rituals, bearbaiting); folk and fairy lore (Herne the Hunter, the Fairy Queen, Hobgoblin, elves, aufs, urchins, nymphs); everyday objects (seacoal, cowlstaffs, coffers, chests, trunks, presses, halfpenny purses, pepperboxes, buck-baskets, foul shirts and smocks, greasy napkins); food and drink (hot venison pasties, Banbury cheese, burned sack, salt fish, stewed prunes, pippins, pumpions, possets); routines of housewifery (washing, wringing, brewing, baking, bleaching, scouring); domestic architecture (lodges, brew houses, kiln holes, closets); coins (groats, millsixpences, Edward shovel-boards); fashions in apparel, both elite (jerkins, fans, semicircled farthingales, Venetian head-tires) and ordinary (mufflers, plain kerchiefs, thrummed hats); idiomatic speech, including such red-lattice phrases or slurs as "Froth and scum, thou liest," "mechanical salt-butter rogue!" "peaking cornuto," "old cozening quean!" "you rag, you baggage, you polecat, you runnion!"; the foreign accents of Sir Hugh and Doctor Caius; class idiolects both elite (Fenton's blank verse) and vulgar (Mistress Quickly's bawdy malapropisms); and throughout, a higher percentage of prose than in any other play by Shakespeare. It is perhaps the play's situatedness in Shakespeare's England that has led scholars to seek a specific occasion for which it was written, and to suggest numerous topical allusions to particular events or persons hidden in the text.

Yet the notion that *Merry Wives* holds, as it were, a

mirror up to everyday life "as it was lived in a small country town round about the year 1600,"[3] or that it points to a particular event, occasion, or person, diverts our attention away from the complexity of the text itself and of its relation to its various historical contexts, both past and present. For the play does not merely record small-town life, popular customs, and domestic routines during the historical moment defined as Shakespeare's present. Rather, it calls such customs and routines into question by situating them in relation to England's historical past and its *political* present. What has often been called the play's "anachronism," its mixing of past and present elements, serves as a constant reminder that more is at stake than the simple present, if only because the town of Windsor is populated by a cast of characters who themselves have a past in Shakespeare's chronicle history plays. Shakespeare thus situates the comedy within the orbit of a constellation of plays that are deeply concerned with issues of political legitimacy and historical engagement. It is thus not entirely accurate to describe *Merry Wives* as modern, for its concerns are confined neither to the present nor to the everyday lives of ordinary citizens. Shakespeare was in fact profoundly mistrustful of such modern perspectives narrowly construed. In *Othello*, he refers to them as the "thin habits and poor likelihoods / Of modern seeming" (1.3.127–28). As the phrase "modern seeming" suggests, and as *Merry Wives* and *Othello* (as well as a host of other early modern plays) make abundantly clear, everyday appearances can be dangerously misleading. Both plays explore the potentially dire consequences of a jealousy that feeds on "thin habits and poor likelihoods," or what might be described as an overly narrow or myopic, uncritical view of the present.

As we begin to unravel the complexity of Shakespeare's engagement with the modern in *Merry Wives*, it would help to acknowledge that the play is neither his only nor his first exploration of contemporary English small-town life. In *The Taming of the Shrew*'s Induction, too, we are likewise given a glimpse of the here-and-now that is far from simple—and that bears little resemblance to anything that might be described as "merry olde England." Rather, as in *Merry Wives*, we are introduced to the class and gender conflicts that characterized a period of momentous social, political, and economic change. That such conflicts reach beyond the domestic sphere is suggested by the Induction's concluding description of the play itself: it is not simply a "comonty"—the drunken Sly's term for a comedy concerned with everyday life, common customs, and "household stuff"—but rather "a kind of history" (Ind.2.140, 143–44). Throughout the 1590s, Shakespeare explored the generic boundaries of the comedy and the history play, and, as always, he delighted in mixing things up. When Petruchio, the shrew tamer, confides to his audience "Thus have I *politicly* begun my reign" (4.1.188; my emphasis), he makes clear that the domestic sphere was not perceived to be isolated from the political sphere. Rather, the governance of the former was explicitly modeled on that of the latter: "Thy husband" is "thy lord, thy king, thy governor," Kate reminds her female audience in her final speech (5.2.162, 154). It is thus only partly true to say that comedies such as *Shrew* and *Merry Wives* are concerned with "money and marriages, not crowns and kingdoms"[4]—with the private, not the political—for the two were viewed as inseparable.[5]

Yet the analogy between the governance of the household and the state became more difficult to sustain during the period in which both *Shrew* and *Merry*

Wives were written, when England was ruled by a *female* monarch—which is perhaps why both plays are concerned with defining the wife's role in the governance of the household and with the specter of the unruly woman-on-top. During the first half of the sixteenth century, there had been no need to consider the implications of female rule with respect to marital hierarchy, or vice versa. A domestic treatise of the period thus easily establishes the confinement of female governance within the domestic sphere: "[Think] you it was for nothing that wise men forbade you [women] rule and governance of countries . . . ? All this same meaneth that you shall not meddle with matters of realms or cities. Your own house is a city great enough for you."[6] But with the accession of Mary I in 1553, and with her marriage to Philip II of Spain, female governance of the state became a reality; political theorists were faced with the problem of reconciling wives' ordinary domestic duties with a married queen regnant's extraordinary political duties. Matters were further complicated by the legal status of wives under the English Common Law: according to "coverture," a woman's legal identity was subsumed, and her property rights forfeited, to her husband during marriage. Although it had been established since the reign of Edward III that a queen regnant was to be treated as a single woman with regard to her legal status and property rights, this precedent had never been put to the test. A contemporary political theorist voiced the anxieties of English subjects that their "liberties, laws, commodities, and fruits" would be "given in to the power and distribution of others by the reason of [Mary's] marriage."[7]

Mary's reign therefore left a legacy of doubt regarding the ability of a married queen regnant to enforce her exemption from the law of coverture. This legacy weighed heavily on Elizabeth I and her subjects during the early part of her reign, while she still entertained the idea of marriage.[8] Legal theorists who wished to defend her right to rule argued at times for her exceptional status (i.e., although an ordinary woman "must be subject," a queen "may be her husband's head"), and thus for a discontinuity between women's domestic and political roles; at other times they pointed to a continuity between them (i.e., women often manage affairs within the household, "and an household is a little commonwealth"; therefore you cannot "debar them of all rule").[9] The apparent contradiction between these two arguments arose from the disparity between legal theory and actual practice. For as contemporary commentators frequently noted, in fact women exerted considerable control over domestic affairs.

The comic intrigue of *Merry Wives* mines these cultural anxieties surrounding female domestic and political rule, inviting us to consider the implications of the former with respect to the latter. Initially offering a modern perspective on wives' active, managerial role in everyday domestic affairs, it then progresses beyond the boundaries of the domestic sphere to examine the implications of this role at court in its concluding masque, which centers on the figure of the Fairy Queen. That the wives' domestic management has political resonance is suggested early in the play when we learn that they have "all the rule" of their husbands' purses (1.3.51–52, 69–70)—a state of affairs running directly against the law of coverture. Importantly, however, the world of the play is presented not as one of topsy-turvy misrule or shrewish inversion, as in many of Shakespeare's comedies, but as a glimpse into the everyday lives of common citizens. We are told, for example, the mundane details of the domestic routines that define Mistress Page's household management:

"Do what she will, say what she will, take all, pay all, go to bed when she list, rise when she list—all is as she will. And, truly, she deserves it" (2.2.117–20). Yet the defensive tone of Quickly's "truly, she deserves it" indicates that women's managerial control over the domestic sphere was still a matter of contention. It is therefore crucial that the play portrays both wives not as unruly or overbearing shrews, but rather as ordinary housewives who protect the propriety of their domestic domains.

The contemporary debate over wives' domestic duties surfaces in the conflicting attitudes displayed by Ford and Page. Whereas Page demonstrates absolute trust in his wife's self-governance ("I would turn her loose to him," he says of Falstaff, "and what he gets more of her than sharp words, let it lie on my head" [2.1.181–83]), Ford pries into every aspect of his wife's domestic management, viewing Page as "an ass, a secure ass. He will trust his wife. . . . I will rather trust a Fleming with my butter, . . . an Irishman with my aquavitae bottle, or a thief to walk my ambling gelding, than my wife with herself. Then she plots, then she ruminates, then she devises" (2.2.308–14). Ford's mistrust, although ostensibly grounded in the obvious, or what counts as common sense, is spun out of a web of "modern seeming." His reasoning smacks of a narrowminded provincialism ("We are simple men. . . . We know nothing" [4.2.173, 177], he later declares) that epitomizes the "thin habits" of collective wisdom (which is often characterized by caricatures, biased beliefs, recycled rumors, and slanderous slurs). "Rumor is a pipe / Blown by surmises, jealousies, conjectures," we are told in *Henry IV, Part 2* by Rumor itself, who delivers the Induction speech in a costume "painted full of tongues" (Ind. 15–16, SD 0). "Upon my tongues continual slanders ride," Rumor further boasts, "Stuffing the ears of men with false reports" (6, 8). Ford's own surmises, jealousies, and conjectures regarding his wife make clear that slanderous, false reports could be as damaging in domestic affairs as in affairs of state.[10]

The play reveals Ford's mistrust to be misplaced, and he is publicly ridiculed for it: "Fie, fie, Master Ford, are you not ashamed?" Page reproves his friend. "What spirit, what devil suggests this imagination?" (3.3.211–12). Ford is cast as both uncharitably suspicious of and as unnecessarily meddlesome in his wife's domestic affairs as he obsessively searches every square inch of his household for Falstaff. The length of Mistress Ford's list of potential hiding places habitually inspected by her husband underscores the excessiveness of his domestic surveillance ("Neither press, coffer, chest, trunk, well, vault, but he hath an abstract for the remembrance of such places, and goes to them by his note" [4.2.60–63]), as does the minuteness of the objects (from a halfpenny purse to a pepperbox) in which he seeks the gargantuan knight. Ford's search for Falstaff in his wife's buck-basket is likewise castigated by the community as inappropriate meddling: "Why, this passes, Master Ford!" says Page. "You are not to go loose any longer; you must be pinioned" (4.2.123–24). Sir Hugh likewise cautions, "Why, this is lunatics. This is mad as a mad dog" (125–26), to which Shallow adds, "Indeed, Master Ford, this is not well, indeed" (127). Domestic advice manuals of the period similarly warned husbands against meddling in their wives' domestic management: husbands "must be accounted over-curious, or rather mean spirited," *The Ladies Dictionary* chides, who "must be peeping, prying, and finding fault with the Feminine Jurisdiction."[11]

Merry Wives playfully assuages male anxiety surrounding wives' ability to supervise both house and hold by making the stranger who threatens to infiltrate them quite literally unhideable. The purely comedic aspect of the wives' plans for revenge revolves around the practical impossibility of hiding Falstaff, who simply won't fit into any of the household's available recesses or repositories. His monumental proportions are thereby turned to comic advantage, making him not only an unlikely gallant ("I had rather be a giantess," says Mistress Page, "and lie under Mount Pelion" [2.1.79–80]) but an extremely inconvenient one as well. Because "There is no hiding [Falstaff] in the house" (4.2.63–64), the wives must come up with inventive ways of conveying him—past Ford and his search party—out of it. Their first scheme relies on a literal act of housekeeping that removes the "stain" of impropriety (i.e., the threats of theft, adultery, and slander), embodied by the fat, "greasy" knight, out of the household with their dirty linens to be "bucked" or bleached in the Thames. Particularly ingenious in the wives' demonstration of their ability to govern the "Feminine Jurisdiction" is the choice of weapons they deploy: a buck-basket, a cowlstaff, and dirty linens. All were household objects commonly used during the period in public shaming rituals to punish unruly or wayward wives and their hapless husbands. In *ridings*, for example, adulteresses, cuckolds, and wife-beaten husbands were hoisted on a cowlstaff while accompanied through town by a boisterous procession of jeering neighbors; in *charivari*, victims were dragged out of the house, covered with mud and filth, and then washed in a lake or river on a cucking stool. The play thus dramatically appropriates and transforms the tools of communal shaming: here, they are used not to punish wayward wives but rather to vindicate the wives' honesty as they are wielded against a would-be seducer. In the second scheme of revenge, Falstaff is coerced into disguising himself as "the fat woman of Brentford" (4.2.75–76) and thereby into parodying another shaming ritual called Skimmington, in which husbands who had been beaten or cuckolded by their wives were made to dress in their wives' clothing and to ride the cowlstaff while being beaten by a neighbor. The merry wives effectively convert the tools of such public spectacles into a more discreet form of punishment that succeeds in warding off the prying gaze of the community while displaying themselves as chaste and chary housewives. The play thus offers a complex, if not critical, perspective on the general thinking, fashions, and customs that constitute modern, everyday life.

In their final scheme of revenge, the wives once again appropriate and redeploy elements of public shaming. The "rough music," mocking rhymes, and cacophony produced by beating pots and pans, common to such rituals, reappear as the "rattles" (4.4.55) and "scornful rhyme[s]" (5.5.97) used to discipline "the unclean knight" (4.4.61); moreover, Falstaff's buck's horns, ordinarily used to shame cuckolded husbands, are here worn by the would-be cuckolder instead. Ford gloats over this propitious reversal of the typical terms of the ritual: "Now, sir," he chides Falstaff, "who's a cuckold now? . . . Falstaff's a knave, a cuckoldy knave. Here are his horns" (5.5.115–17). Indeed, the husband actually enjoys the shaming ritual concocted by the wives because it is not directed at him. The whole community has already discovered through the agency of the wives that Ford is not a cuckold and that his wife, in Sir Hugh's words, "is as honest a 'omans as I will desires among five thousand, and five hundred too" (3.3.216–18).

In moving beyond the bounds of the domestic sphere into the public environs of Windsor Castle, the final masque likewise invites us to consider the wives' governance of the "Feminine Jurisdiction" in relation to

Queen Elizabeth's governance of the state. The masque begins by casting the "Fairy Queen" as a scrupulous housekeeper, proclaiming "Our radiant queen hates sluts and sluttery" (5.5.50). While the obvious referent of this pronouncement is Elizabeth's status as "the Virgin queen," the terms *slut* and *sluttery* denoted slovenliness and insufficiently scrupulous housekeeping (the elves have just found the fires "unraked and hearths unswept" [5.5.47–48]). The Fairy Queen herself employs the language of housewifery, ordering her elfish subjects to "Search Windsor Castle . . . within and out," and to "scour" her knights' "chairs of order" to ensure that all is "fit, / Worthy the owner, and the owner it" (5.5.61, 66, 64–65). The Fairy Queen is portrayed as a fastidious housewife who commands her servants to investigate every nook and cranny of her household so as properly to order and protect her property. Yet the property over which the queen presides, unlike that of an ordinary housewife, is her own, both because she is queen and because she is unmarried. Unlike many of the court entertainments performed for Elizabeth during the early part of her reign, Shakespeare's masque culminates not in the Fairy Queen's marriage but in her punishment of the unclean knight's "lust and luxury" (5.5.100).

In the latter part of her reign, Elizabeth's self-presentation as a royal housewife who had "given herself in Marriage to her Kingdom"[12] had given way to the cult of the Virgin Queen, whose iconography was showing increasing signs of strain during the social and economic crises of the 1590s (the period in which *Merry Wives* was written). England's population was under a heavy tax burden to pay for foreign wars and had experienced frequent plague outbreaks; in addition, a succession of agricultural and climatic disasters had resulted in dire food shortages, inflation, and an upsurge in poverty and rioting. Towns were hit hard, as dearth threatened the domestic comforts of the middling sort. Elizabeth's reputation likewise suffered, as many blamed the queen for the desperate state of the economy. Nor did the crisis leave the court untouched, as Elizabeth was forced to cut down on court expenditures and the distribution of patronage. Images of Elizabeth produced by her courtiers during the 1590s were at best ambivalent and at worst iconoclastic.

Shakespeare's masque seems to suggest that like the merry wives, Elizabeth must sift and scour all corners to make ends meet and safeguard the property and propriety of her own "Feminine Jurisdiction." Yet in casting the unmarried Mistress Quickly as the Fairy Queen, the masque also calls attention to Elizabeth's resolute status as single. The audience's startled expectations on discovering Quickly instead of Anne Page playing the queen may well have been akin to those of Elizabeth's own subjects, who had been expecting their maiden queen to marry a suitable suitor—even if, like Anne, she insisted he be someone of her own choosing—but who, by the end of her reign, were ruled by an aging queen who was neither a wife nor a mother; instead, she was, like Quickly, a "dry nurse" (1.2.4) to her subjects. Yet to understand the modern perspective of *Merry Wives* in its historical context, we need not read the play as a political allegory or polemic. Rather, if the play offers a modern perspective on everyday life in England at the close of the sixteenth century, it is one that explores the comedic potential of the complex and pervasive contemporary preoccupation with the reality and legitimacy of female domestic and political rule. It is, in this sense, "a kind of history."

1. Walter Cohen, introduction to *The Merry Wives of Windsor*, in *The Norton Shakespeare*, ed. Stephen

Greenblatt (New York: W. W. Norton, 1997), p. 1225. Anne Barton likewise describes *Merry Wives* as "a play apart[,] . . . unique among the comedies in that it is set explicitly in an English town well known to members of Shakespeare's audience"; it offers "a stage picture of ordinary, middle-class life in a small country town, among innkeepers and doctors, country magistrates, parsons, citizens and their wives and children" (introduction to *The Merry Wives of Windsor,* in *The Riverside Shakespeare,* ed. G. Blakemore Evans, 2nd ed. [Boston: Houghton Mifflin, 1997], p. 320.)

2. Barton, introduction, p. 323.

3. G. R. Hibbard, introduction to *The Merry Wives of Windsor,* ed. Hibbard (New York: Penguin Books, 1973), p. 14.

4. Ibid.

5. The complex connections between the private and the political are staged in the history plays as well, through interposed scenes of comic, everyday life in the Boar's Head tavern in Eastcheap, or on Justice Shallow's country estate.

6. Juan Luis Vives, *Instruction of a Christen Woman,* trans. Richard Hyrd (London, 1529), sig. C4v (spelling modernized).

7. John Knox, *The First Blast of the Trumpet against the Monstrous Regiment of Women* [1558], in *The Works of John Knox,* ed. David Laing (Edinburgh: J. Thin, 1895), 3:411 (spelling modernized).

8. For a more extended discussion of these matters, see Constance Jordan, "Woman's Rule in Sixteenth-Century British Political Thought," *Renaissance Quarterly* 40 (1987): 421–51, an essay to which I am indebted.

9. Quotations from John Aylmer, *An Harborowe for Faithful and Trewe Subjectes* (London, 1559), sig. C4v, D1r (spelling modernized).

10. Ford's comparison of his wife to a "thief" further suggests that what was at stake in trusting one's wife was not only sexual fidelity but the safeguarding of household property. His fears are in this respect not far-fetched; Falstaff makes clear from the beginning that his main motive in cuckolding Ford is pecuniary: "They say the jealous wittolly knave hath masses of money, for the which his wife seems to me well-favored. I will use her as the key of the cuckoldly rogue's coffer" (2.2.278–82). Ford's mistrust of his wife is likewise expressed in terms that make clear the interdependence of social, sexual and economic "trust": "See the hell of having a false woman: my bed shall be abused, my coffers ransacked, my reputation gnawn at" (2.2.298–300). In the credit economy of early modern England, the term *trust* suggested not simply placing one's confidence or reliance in a person but giving a person credit for goods supplied, or committing the safety of one's property to another. Trust, credit, and reputation all functioned as forms of currency that were grounded in "a system of judgments about trustworthiness" circulating within a community. The trustworthiness of wives was particularly important because of their role in managing the household economy. See Craig Muldrew, *The Economy of Obligation: The Culture of Credit and Social Relations in Early Modern England* (New York: St. Martin's Press, 1998), p. 148.

11. N.H., *The Ladies Dictionary* (London: John Dunton, 1694), p. 203.

12. William Camden, *The History of the Most Renowned and Victorious Princess Elizabeth Late Queen of England*, ed. Wallace MacCaffrey (Chicago: University of Chicago Press, 1970), p. 30.

Further Reading

The Merry Wives of Windsor

Abbreviations: *Ado* = *Much Ado about Nothing;*
AYL = *As You Like It; Ham.* = *Hamlet; H4* = *Henry*
IV; 2H4 = *Henry IV, Part 2; H5* = *Henry V; MND* =
A Midsummer Night's Dream; Rom. = *Romeo and*
Juliet; Wiv. = *The Merry Wives of Windsor*

Brown, Pam Allen. "Near Neighbors, Women's Wars,
and 'Merry Wives.'" In her *Better a Shrew Than a*
Sheep: Women, Drama, and the Culture of the Jest in
Early Modern England, pp. 33–55. Ithaca: Cornell University Press, 2003.

Brown detects in the "jesting women" of early modern drama a keen awareness that being the object of
any sexual overture puts them on trial before a jury of
neighbors and relatives. The "undercover women's
war" waged by the Windsor wives against slander, sexual assault, and jealousy is designed to appeal to female audiences by demonstrating that when faced with
sexual aggressors and unwanted seducers, women, if
they were to cope in the "court of neighborhood,"
would need to form good alliances and to acquire performance skills. Although there is no actual adultery in
the play, the wives' willingness to endanger their repu-
tations and their obvious delight in secrecy and merry
deceit call into question the prevailing view that *Wiv.* is
an uncomplicated celebration of innocent female
mirth.

Cotton, Nancy. "Castrating (W)itches: Impotence and Magic in *The Merry Wives of Windsor*." *Shakespeare Quarterly* 38 (1987): 321–26.

Citing the widely held belief in the early modern era that witches had the power to castrate, Cotton examines Shakespeare's emphasis in *Wiv.* on images relating to impotence and magic. She uses this causally connected imagery to read the play as a projection of a masculine view that regards any woman "as a potential witch, or Mother Prat, because of her power to reject and/or deceive any man who desires her." The main plot is governed by Ford's dual obsession with cuckoldry and witchcraft, phobias that can be traced to his "unconscious sense of failure" at not producing an heir. Cotton interprets all three tricks perpetrated against Falstaff "as forms of emasculation." She discusses the final scene at length since it offers not only the most dramatic of "symbolic castrations" inflicted on Falstaff and the failed suitors of Anne Page but also the "most vivid ... stage image ... of the women as witches": the wives' action figures a witches' sabbath, and the fairy disguise of Mistress Quickly and Anne furthers the link between women and magical power. The masculine association of impotence with female sorcery is finally dismissed when the wives use their female "craft" in support of their husbands' power, "metamorphosing deceit into merriment."

Erickson, Peter. "The Order of the Garter, the Cult of Elizabeth, and Class–Gender Tension in *The Merry Wives of Windsor*." In *Shakespeare Reproduced: The Text in History and Ideology*, edited by Jean Howard and Marion F. O'Connor, pp. 116–40. New York: Methuen, 1987.

In his examination of the class–gender dynamic in *Wiv.*, Erickson draws on such contextual materials as the garter ceremony, Elizabeth I's Petrarchan politics, and Elizabethan uses of pastoral. Instead of reading the play as a positive celebration of female, middle-class power, he contends that both class and gender are "strongly marked by a conservative valence: neither supports an enlightened egalitarian image of the play." Central to his argument is the figure of Fenton, whose marriage to Anne redistributes wealth upward (hence revitalizing the aristocratic class) and qualifies the power of the wives (Mrs. Page being beaten at her own game). Of the two ideological components, however, the treatment of gender is ultimately more complicated than that of class. Like the Queen at court, the Windsor wives display superior wit and exercise controlling power, thereby arousing male uneasiness; and, as their constant insistence on marital chastity attests, they, like the Virgin Queen, clearly operate within a male-centered universe. Displaying an ironic and troubled ratification of female power, *Wiv.* reveals a patriarchal ideology that is not "monolithic but multivalent."

Evans, Bertrand. "For the Love of Mockery: Approach to the Summit." In his *Shakespeare's Comedies,* pp. 68–117, esp. 98–117. Oxford: Clarendon Press, 1960.

Evans focuses on Shakespeare's manipulation of "discrepant awarenesses"—i.e., the gaps between the levels of awareness of the characters in the play and the audience outside it—to argue for a complexity not usually attributed to *Wiv.* Between the apex of awarenesses in Mistress Quickly (the play's "nearest equivalent" to the all-knowing Portia and Rosalind) and the "nether depth" of Falstaff range the other major figures whose practices and counterpractices (Evans counts eleven in all) provide the comic action. With all the characters being both deceivers and victims of deception, and with discrepancies furthering plot development and arising not only from an ignorance of tricks but also from character traits (e.g., the natural folly of Sir Hugh and Doctor Caius and the jealous nature of Master Ford), the play emerges as a worthy forerunner to the brilliance of *Ado* and *AYL*. The surprise substitution of Mistress Quickly for Anne Page as the queen of fairies in 5.5 is a departure from Shakespeare's usual practice of permitting the audience to know everything.

Freedman, Barbara. "Shakespearean Chronology, Ideological Complicity, and Floating Texts: Something Is Rotten in Windsor." *Shakespeare Quarterly* 45 (1994): 190–201.

Freedman uses the plethora of topical references found in *Wiv.* to argue against the currently held view that it is an occasionalist play, the occasion being the election of Lord Hunsdon to the Order of the Garter in April 1597. The question is not whether Garter references exist but how to read them. Freedman's objections to the 1597 date include (1) the lack of proof that theatrical events were ever commissioned for Garter ceremonies; (2) the difficulty in imagining how a queen, reportedly concerned about her own age and fading beauty, would have been flattered by the performance of a play with overt references to age and fading attractiveness; and (3) the nagging question of why Lord Hunsdon (or the Queen), on the occasion of his election to the Garter after many failed attempts, would commission a play that lampoons him in the vain and pompous character of Falstaff. Freedman finds entirely plausible both a date of 1598 and a public audience well acquainted with the Garter ceremony. She concludes that the play's "free-floating topicality" and the "unabashed presence" of two variant conclusions in the Quarto and Folio texts lend credence to recent arguments "for a revisionist Shakespeare whose topicality was more inclusive than exclusive."

Gurr, Andrew. "Intertextuality at Windsor." *Shakespeare Quarterly* 38 (1987): 189–200.

Gurr explores the rivalry between Henslowe's Admiral's company and the Lord Chamberlain's Players (Shakespeare's company) in the period between May 1594 and 1600, when they were the only companies competing for London playgoing audiences. The rivalry, at first simply imitative (i.e., the repertories offered plays different but of the same type), gradually grew more complex, especially in plays dealing with sex and marriage, which is where *Wiv.* becomes "a peculiarly interesting test case." A comparison of Shakespeare's play with Henry Porter's *The Two Angry Women of Abingdon*, possibly on the playbills early in 1597 and thus precipitating *Wiv.*, illustrates how Shakespeare "deliberately altered the priorities between love and marriage as Porter and the other plays in the rival repertory offered them." In contrast to the triumph of the fathers' wishes over the mothers' regarding the marital prospects of their children in the Porter play, young love prevails in Shakespeare's subplot involving the marriage of Anne Page to Fenton, Anne triumphing over the wishes of both of her parents. This difference in the treatment of generational conflict where romantic desire and parental authority collide becomes a "real divergence" between the two companies around the turn of the century, when theatrical groups proliferated and prompted a rivalry radically different in kind. Gurr's discovery "hint[s] at some of the intertextual influences at work in the drama of Shakespeare and others in the last years of the 16th century."

Helgerson, Richard. "The Buck Basket, the Witch, and the Queen of Fairies." In his *Adulterous Alliances: Home, State, and History in Early Modern European Drama and Painting*, pp. 57–76. Chicago: University of Chicago Press, 2000. (An earlier version of the chapter, titled "The Buck Basket, the Witch, and the Queen of Fairies: The Women's World of Shakespeare's Windsor," appeared in *Renaissance Culture and the Everyday*, edited by Patricia Fumerton and Simon Hunt [Philadelphia: University of Pennsylvania Press, 1999], pp. 162–82.)

Helgerson is concerned with the prehistory of a cultural shift from aristocracy to a cult of domesticity. His New Historicist reading of *Wiv.* views Shakespeare's Windsor as providing "not simply . . . an adjunct of state power but . . . an alternative to it" in the "expression of a local and domestic and female authority that stood for a significantly different England than the one based on patriarchy and royal dynastic succession." The three devices used by the Windsor wives to defeat the aristocratic sexual predator who invades their specifically middle-class and female domestic space "situate . . . the local and domestic differently": the laundry basket shows the autonomy of the female-controlled household, the disguise of Falstaff as the witch of Brentford suggests "a regional network of subversive female gossips," and the masque of the fairies (especially in the person of the Fairy Queen) implies a covert connection between the Windsor women and Elizabeth I. The wives prevail against one prodigal courtier, Falstaff, but not against his "younger doppelganger," Fenton, who acquires Windsor's wealth through marriage to a Windsor woman. With its final resolution of class tensions favoring the aristocracy, *Wiv.* can be seen as a comedy focused on "the intersection of home, state, and history, a comedy in which the home's marginality is both questioned and reaffirmed."

Kegl, Rosemary. " 'The adoption of abominable terms': Middle Class, Merry Wives, and the Insults That Shape Windsor." In her *The Rhetoric of Concealment: Figuring Gender and Class in Renaissance Literature*, pp. 77–125. Ithaca: Cornell University Press, 1994. (For a shorter version of the essay, titled " 'The adoption of abominable terms': The Insults That Shape Windsor's Middle Class," see *ELH* 61 [1994]: 253–78.)

Focusing on passages of abuse in *Wiv.*, Kegl concludes that insults are "central to the process of naming the relationships among Windsor's inhabitants." An examination of Robert Shallow and Sir Hugh Evans—a justice of the peace and a parson—of the history of Windsor and of its castle, and of early modern struggles over the nature of women's activity enables her to locate *Wiv.*'s network of insults within a larger social process that generated "shifting authority relations" among state, local, and ecclesiastical officials on the public level, and among husbands, wives, and children in the domestic sphere. The play's "abominable terms" (2.2.302) establish political alliances and reinforce categories (e.g., "townsmen" and "gentlemen") through which the various groups of characters "experience their political identities" and pursue their "multiple and often contradictory short- and long-term interests."

Korda, Natasha. " 'Judicious oeillades': Supervising Marital Property in *The Merry Wives of Windsor*." In her *Shakespeare's Domestic Economies: Gender and Property in Early Modern England*. Philadelphia: University of Pennsylvania Press, 2002. (The chapter originally appeared under the same title in *Marxist Shakespeares*, edited by Jean Howard and Scott Cutler Shershow [London: Routledge, 2001], pp. 82–103.)

Korda's materialist-feminist reading of *Wiv.* relates the play to the rise of a consumer culture that "distinguished the household-as-container from the stuff it contained," i.e., goods or movable properties requiring efficient management. With the redefinition of *household,* early modern housewives emerged as more than "passive objects of exchange between men to assume a more active role as 'keepers' of household properties." Such supervisory power, however, as noted in treatises like Robert Cleaver's *A Godlie Forme of Householde Government* (1598), could breed "much disquieteness" if perceived as a threat to the husband's authority. In *Wiv.,* Korda argues, "the 'disquietnesse' surrounding the housewife's supervisory role with respect to marital property is fully explored, and ultimately dispelled, by the wives' self-discipline." Through a literal act of housekeeping (throwing Falstaff out of the house with the dirty linens), the wives punish the invader, exhibit managerial skills, and safeguard their sexual modesty, thereby assuaging male anxiety. The public punishment of Falstaff entrusted to them by their husbands in Act 5 stands as a culmination of the wives' diligent domestic supervision.

Leggatt, Alexander. "The Comedy of Intrigue: Adultery." In his *Citizen Comedy in the Age of Shakespeare,* pp. 125–49, esp. 146–49. Toronto: University of Toronto Press, 1973.

Popular between 1585 and 1625, "citizen comedy," as defined by Leggatt, is set in England within a predominantly middle-class milieu; at its core are social issues, class awareness, sexual and financial intrigue, and domestic locations. Courtship and romance, if present at all, operate in a world of hard economic bargaining. While Ford and Page are not given specific occupations such as shopkeeper, merchant, or craftsman, they appear to occupy a middle station on the social scale, between the court and aristocracy at one end and the lowest class of laborers, servants, and vagabonds at the other. Noting how the intrigue of adultery is a major feature of this type of comedy, Leggatt singles out *Wiv.* as one of the more ambitious of citizen comedies in its combination of "moral and social commentary with the amoral fun of trickery." He praises the balanced treatment of both Falstaff and Ford, both of whom are put in their places but in a lighthearted manner. "Even in a genre he touched only once Shakespeare set standards that his contemporaries found hard to match": in *Wiv.* chastity is asserted without preaching and the game of sex is treated as "amusing, judicious, and humane."

Parker, Patricia. "Interpreting through Wordplay: *The Merry Wives of Windsor.*" In *Teaching with Shakespeare: Critics in the Classroom,* edited by Bruce McIver and Ruth Stevenson, pp. 166–204. Newark: University of Delaware Press; London: Associated University Presses, 1994. (The essay is a pedagogic reworking of Parker's earlier article titled "*The Merry Wives of Windsor* and Shakespearean Translation," *Modern Language Quarterly* 52 [1991]: 225–61.)

Contrary to those who find the Latin grammar scene (4.1) expendable, Parker contends that the episode is "implicated in a larger discursive network" having to do with the literal sense of "translation" as "a transporting or carrying away." Her focus on wordplay reveals the intersection between the carrying away of words from their "proper" meaning and the carrying away of property, whether through commercial exchange or through theft—the latter constituting *Wiv.*'s major type of conveyance. The essay includes separate sections on pages and porters (who carry things from here to there and back), the cozening Germans who appear out of nowhere in 4.3 to steal the Host's horses, the translating of plots, and a series of translations implicating women as "secondary and accessory, . . . conveyed and cozening." Moving beyond the wordplay that shapes the dramatic action of *Wiv.* to scenes involving transfer and conveyance in other canonical texts, Parker concludes that "translation . . . is everywhere in Shakespeare."

Pittenger, Elizabeth. "Dispatch Quickly: The Mechanical Reproduction of Pages." *Shakespeare Quarterly* 42 (1991): 389–408.
    Pittenger uses the phrase "mechanical reproduction" to describe the mechanism through which textual, sexual, and social hierarchies are reproduced. The scene depicting the wives' reading of Falstaff's letters (2.1) illustrates perfectly the relationships between sexual and textual economies as represented in *Wiv.* Like Falstaff's duplicate copies of the same letter to Mistress Ford and Mistress Page (see especially lines 69–79), the play itself as a literary text exists in multiple transmissions: the Quarto version and the Folio *Wiv.*, nearly twice as long. The "misreproduction of meaning" and the mechanical repetitions found in the Latin language lesson (4.1) serve to demonstrate how resistances to the ideal of pure or unmediated transmission can be read as gendered, sexual, social, and nationalistic. On the basis of her analysis of 2.1 and 4.1, Pittenger suggests extending the idea of "mechanical reproduction" to four cultural domains: (1) the training and pedagogical practices through which the young male subject is formed and reproduced; (2) the patriarchal economy of the play through which heirs are generated as copies; (3) the principle of desire through which (in Freudian terms) impulses and fantasies are constantly "reprinted afresh" in "new editions," with only the names changing (e.g., Falstaff's reduction of the Windsor wives into "virtually

interchangeable units"); and (4) the material world of print through which texts are reproduced by the machinery of the printing press and by the manual labor of "mechanical" operators (compositors, pressmen, proofreaders). "In this play about a family of Pages and about the circulation of pages—both letters and boys," it is appropriate that the emphasis on material pages should assume "thematic and reflexive density."

Roberts, Jeanne Addison. *Shakespeare's English Comedy: "The Merry Wives of Windsor" in Context*. Lincoln: University of Nebraska Press, 1979.

In her reevaluation of *Wiv.*, Roberts concludes that it is "not aberrant, trivial, essentially Italianate, nor predominantly farcical." The first four chapters address the play's textual history, date of composition, sources, and generic classification. In chapter 5, a detailed critical reception of the "Windsor" Falstaff, Roberts argues that the character is "essentially the same man" as the Falstaff in the *H4* plays; in fact, she advocates reading *Wiv.* in conjunction with those plays, since the incapacitating and scapegoating of Falstaff in the final scene foreshadow his political rejection by Hal at the end of *2H4*. The play's support of social values and institutions, its hopeful outlook on life, and its respect for the logic of cause-and-effect relations firmly establish it as comedy rather than farce. Falstaff may be "festively rejected" in the ritual masque of Act 5, but his ultimate social inclusion in an atmosphere of reconciliation and harmony suggests that *Wiv.* is ultimately a "comedy of forgiveness." Fixing the play's date of composition in 1597, Roberts describes *Wiv.* "as an experimental and transitional drama, growing out of the histories and early comedies (especially those written between 1594 and 1597) and leading into the new freedom and complexity of the later plays."

Vickers, Brian. *The Artistry of Shakespeare's Prose*. London: Methuen, 1968. [See esp. pp. 141–56.]

In the chapter titled "The World of Falstaff," Vickers devotes the third section to Shakespeare's "virtuoso control of styles" in *Wiv.* Mistress Page and Mistress Ford are distinguished from other characters by virtue of their superior wit and use of imagery; the minor characters achieve a striking degree of individuation through particular verbal idiosyncrasies; and in the character of Ford, for the first time (excepting a few of Shylock's speeches) prose is used for a character and situation of some seriousness (Ford being comic but not a clown). Vickers pays special attention to the imagery and the rambling, disjointed syntax in Ford's soliloquy in 2.2.294–321; the use of prose to express such an "intense and realistically developed emotional state" is the play's major achievement. Among the individuating verbal "tics" singled out for discussion are Shallow's constant repetitions, Mistress Quickly's malapropisms, Nym's fondness for catchphrases (especially the word "humor"), and the Host's favorite word "bully" and his excessively clipped phrases.

Wall, Wendy. "Needles and Birches: Pedagogy, Domesticity, and the Advent of English Comedy," and "Why Does Puck Sweep? Shakespearean Fairies and the Politics of Cleaning." In her *Staging Domesticity: Household Work and English Identity in Early Modern Drama*, pp. 59–93 (esp. 90–93) and 94–126 (esp. 112–26). Cambridge: Cambridge University Press, 2002. (The first chapter originally appeared as " 'Household stuff': The Sexual Politics of Domesticity and the Advent of English Comedy," *ELH* 65 [1998]: 1–45; the second as "Why Does Puck Sweep? Fairylore, Merry Wives, and Social Struggle," *Shakespeare Quarterly* 52 [2001]: 67–106.)

Wall examines the staging of domesticity in *Wiv.* to illustrate her thesis that representations of household practices in the early modern period "helped to forge crucial conceptions of national identity." In the first chapter, where the focus is on vernacular nationalism, she claims that the Latin language lesson (4.1) embraids Englishness into the play's domestic themes. The linguistic pitting of Mistress Quickly's bawdy female puns and malapropisms against an academy "thoroughly infected by foreign (mis)speakers" vividly exposes the limits of a humanist pedagogy for a middle-class citizenry. Emerging from the "discursive connections among Latin, academia, and domesticity," as they relate to gender, speech, sexuality, and community, is a vision of nationhood based on the " 'everyday' language of the home."

In the second chapter, where the emphasis shifts to the class politics of popular myth, Wall suggests that the domestic components of fairylore underpin the "middling" ideology of Windsor's citizenry. Unlike the fairies of *MND,* who protect the procreation and status of the aristocracy, the fairies of *Wiv.* "dabble with those further down the food chain: they seek to safeguard the property and authority of citizens from encroachment by the upper classes." Because the play revolves around commerce, industry, and work, the fairies' concern for "full-scale cleansing" functions as the culmination of the drama, thereby demonstrating the fusion of popular folklore with the desires of a wealthy village citizenry, especially with the middle-class ideal of housewifery. In contrast to Erickson and Helgerson, who read 5.5 as privileging aristocratic interests, Wall argues that the final scene—"campy, stylized, and clearly over the top"—parodies courtly values. The collaboration of "demystified" fairies and triumphant housewives foregrounds the play's concern with the "governing power of everydayness" to provide a conception of England not "defined within the province of the court."

Werstine, Paul. "A Century of 'Bad' Shakespeare Quartos." *Shakespeare Quarterly* 50 (1999): 310–33, esp. pp. 310–17, 330.

   Werstine disputes "the power of memorial reconstruction to provide a full account of the origin[s]" of the so-called bad quartos of *Wiv.* (1602), *Ham.* (1603), *H5* (1600), and *Rom.* (1597). *Wiv.* is central to his argument because twentieth-century textual scholars have extended the hypothesis across these four texts by "constructing questionable analogies" between Q *Wiv.* and the others and, "then, by substituting murkily quantitative statistical analyses for the sharply defined qualitative differences" noted by W. W. Greg in his seminal work on Q *Wiv.* Werstine's examination of corresponding passages between Q and F *Wiv.* exposes problems with Greg's assertion that the Q text was composed from memory by the actor playing the part of the Host. While Q *Wiv.* evinces "occasional sudden improvements" that coincide with the Host's entrances, there are numerous instances where Q and F do not match even though the Host is present, and times where they show remarkable correlation despite his being absent. Werstine does not deny "the theory's partial explanatory power within" Q *Wiv.*, but finds no evidence to "characterize the origin of Q as a whole as memorial."

Shakespeare's Language

Abbott, E. A. *A Shakespearian Grammar.* New York: Haskell House, 1972.

This compact reference book, first published in 1870, helps with many difficulties in Shakespeare's language. It systematically accounts for a host of differences between Shakespeare's usage and sentence structure and our own.

Blake, Norman. *Shakespeare's Language: An Introduction.* New York: St. Martin's Press, 1983.
This general introduction to Elizabethan English discusses various aspects of the language of Shakespeare and his contemporaries, offering possible meanings for hundreds of ambiguous constructions.

Dobson, E. J. *English Pronunciation, 1500–1700.* 2 vols. Oxford: Clarendon Press, 1968.
This long and technical work includes chapters on spelling (and its reformation), phonetics, stressed vowels, and consonants in early modern English.

Houston, John. *Shakespearean Sentences: A Study in Style and Syntax.* Baton Rouge: Louisiana State University Press, 1988.
Houston studies Shakespeare's stylistic choices, considering matters such as sentence length and the relative positions of subject, verb, and direct object. Examining plays throughout the canon in a roughly chronological, developmental order, he analyzes how sentence structure is used in setting tone, in characterization, and for other dramatic purposes.

Onions, C. T. *A Shakespeare Glossary.* Oxford: Clarendon Press, 1986.
This revised edition updates Onions's standard, selective glossary of words and phrases in Shakespeare's plays that are now obsolete, archaic, or obscure.

Robinson, Randal. *Unlocking Shakespeare's Language: Help for the Teacher and Student.* Urbana, Ill.: National Council of Teachers of English and the ERIC Clearinghouse on Reading and Communication Skills, 1989.

Specifically designed for the high-school and undergraduate college teacher and student, Robinson's book addresses the problems that most often hinder present-day readers of Shakespeare. Through work with his own students, Robinson found that many readers today are particularly puzzled by such stylistic devices as subject-verb inversion, interrupted structures, and compression. He shows how our own colloquial language contains comparable structures, and thus helps students recognize such structures when they find them in Shakespeare's plays. This book supplies worksheets—with examples from major plays—to illuminate and remedy such problems as unusual sequences of words and the separation of related parts of sentences.

Williams, Gordon. *A Dictionary of Sexual Language and Imagery in Shakespearean and Stuart Literature.* 3 vols. London: Athlone Press, 1994.

Williams provides a comprehensive list of the words to which Shakespeare, his contemporaries, and later Stuart writers gave sexual meanings. He supports his identification of these meanings by extensive quotations.

Shakespeare's Life

Baldwin, T. W. *William Shakspere's Petty School.* Urbana: University of Illinois Press, 1943.

Baldwin here investigates the theory and practice of the petty school, the first level of education in Elizabethan England. He focuses on that educational system primarily as it is reflected in Shakespeare's art.

Baldwin, T. W. *William Shakspere's Small Latine and Lesse Greeke*. 2 vols. Urbana: University of Illinois Press, 1944.
Baldwin attacks the view that Shakespeare was an uneducated genius—a view that had been dominant among Shakespeareans since the eighteenth century. Instead, Baldwin shows, the educational system of Shakespeare's time would have given the playwright a strong background in the classics, and there is much in the plays that shows how Shakespeare benefited from such an education.

Beier, A. L., and Roger Finlay, eds. *London 1500–1700: The Making of the Metropolis*. New York: Longman, 1986.
Focusing on the economic and social history of early modern London, these collected essays probe aspects of metropolitan life, including "Population and Disease," "Commerce and Manufacture," and "Society and Change."

Bentley, G. E. *Shakespeare's Life: A Biographical Handbook*. New Haven: Yale University Press, 1961.
This "just-the-facts" account presents the surviving documents of Shakespeare's life against an Elizabethan background.

Chambers, E. K. *William Shakespeare: A Study of Facts and Problems*. 2 vols. Oxford: Clarendon Press, 1930.
Analyzing in great detail the scant historical data, Chambers's complex, scholarly study considers the nature of the texts in which Shakespeare's work is preserved.

Cressy, David. *Education in Tudor and Stuart England.* London: Edward Arnold, 1975.

This volume collects sixteenth-, seventeenth-, and early-eighteenth-century documents detailing aspects of formal education in England, such as the curriculum, the control and organization of education, and the education of women.

De Grazia, Margreta. *Shakespeare Verbatim: The Reproduction of Authenticity and the 1790 Apparatus.* Oxford: Clarendon Press, 1991.

De Grazia traces and discusses the development of such editorial criteria as authenticity, historical periodization, factual biography, chronological development, and close reading, locating as the point of origin Edmond Malone's 1790 edition of Shakespeare's works. There are interesting chapters on the First Folio and on the "legendary" versus the "documented" Shakespeare.

Dutton, Richard. *William Shakespeare: A Literary Life.* New York: St. Martin's Press, 1989.

Not a biography in the traditional sense, Dutton's very readable work nevertheless "follows the contours of Shakespeare's life" as he examines Shakespeare's career as playwright and poet, with consideration of his patrons, theatrical associations, and audience.

Fraser, Russell. *Young Shakespeare.* New York: Columbia University Press, 1988.

Fraser focuses on Shakespeare's first thirty years, paying attention simultaneously to his life and art.

Schoenbaum, S. *William Shakespeare: A Compact Documentary Life.* New York: Oxford University Press, 1977.

This standard biography economically presents the essential documents from Shakespeare's time in an accessible narrative account of the playwright's life.

Shakespeare's Theater

Bentley, G. E. *The Profession of Player in Shakespeare's Time, 1590–1642*. Princeton: Princeton University Press, 1984.
Bentley readably sets forth a wealth of evidence about performance in Shakespeare's time, with special attention to the relations between player and company, and the business of casting, managing, and touring.

Berry, Herbert. *Shakespeare's Playhouses*. New York: AMS Press, 1987.
Berry's six essays collected here discuss (with illustrations) varying aspects of the four playhouses in which Shakespeare had a financial stake: the Theatre in Shoreditch, the Blackfriars, and the first and second Globe.

Cook, Ann Jennalie. *The Privileged Playgoers of Shakespeare's London*. Princeton: Princeton University Press, 1981.
Cook's work argues, on the basis of sociological, economic, and documentary evidence, that Shakespeare's audience—and the audience for English Renaissance drama generally—consisted mainly of the "privileged."

Greg, W. W. *Dramatic Documents from the Elizabethan Playhouses*. 2 vols. Oxford: Clarendon Press, 1931.
Greg itemizes and briefly describes many of the play

manuscripts that survive from the period 1590 to around 1660, including, among other things, players' parts. His second volume offers facsimiles of selected manuscripts.

Gurr, Andrew. *Playgoing in Shakespeare's London.* 2nd ed. Cambridge: Cambridge University Press, 1996.
Gurr charts how the theatrical enterprise developed from its modest beginnings in the late 1560s to become a thriving institution in the 1600s. He argues that there were important changes over the period 1567–1644 in the playhouses, the audience, and the plays.

Harbage, Alfred. *Shakespeare's Audience.* New York: Columbia University Press, 1941.
Harbage investigates the fragmentary surviving evidence to interpret the size, composition, and behavior of Shakespeare's audience.

Hattaway, Michael. *Elizabethan Popular Theatre: Plays in Performance.* London: Routledge and Kegan Paul, 1982.
Beginning with a study of the popular drama of the late Elizabethan age—a description of the stages, performance conditions, and acting of the period—this volume concludes with an analysis of five well-known plays of the 1590s, one of them (*Titus Andronicus*) by Shakespeare.

Shapiro, Michael. *Children of the Revels: The Boy Companies of Shakespeare's Time and Their Plays.* New York: Columbia University Press, 1977.
Shapiro chronicles the history of the amateur and quasi-professional child companies that flourished in London at the end of Elizabeth's reign and the beginning of James's.

The Publication of Shakespeare's Plays

Blayney, Peter W. M. *The First Folio of Shakespeare.* Hanover, Md.: Folger, 1991.

Blayney's accessible account of the printing and later life of the First Folio—an amply illustrated catalog to a 1991 Folger Shakespeare Library exhibition—analyzes the mechanical production of the First Folio, describing how the Folio was made, by whom and for whom, how much it cost, and its ups and downs (or, rather, downs and ups) since its printing in 1623.

Hinman, Charlton. *The Norton Facsimile: The First Folio of Shakespeare.* 2nd ed. New York: W. W. Norton, 1996.

This facsimile presents a photographic reproduction of an "ideal" copy of the First Folio of Shakespeare; Hinman attempts to represent each page in its most fully corrected state. The second edition includes an important new introduction by Peter W. M. Blayney.

Hinman, Charlton. *The Printing and Proof-Reading of the First Folio of Shakespeare.* 2 vols. Oxford: Clarendon Press, 1963.

In the most arduous study of a single book ever undertaken, Hinman attempts to reconstruct how the Shakespeare First Folio of 1623 was set into type and run off the press, sheet by sheet. He also provides almost all the known variations in readings from copy to copy.

The Publication of Shakespeare Plays

Blayney, Peter W. M. *The First Folio of Shakespeare.* Washington, D.C.: Folger, 1991.

Ingeniously accessible account of the printing and publication of the First Folio—an ample illustrated catalog to accompany Folger Shakespeare Library's 1991 exhibition.

Hinman, Charlton. *The Norton Facsimile: The First Folio of Shakespeare.* 2nd ed. New York: W. W. Norton, 1996.

Hinman, Charlton. *The Norton Facsimile: The First Folio of Shakespeare.* 2nd ed. New York: W. W. Norton, 1968.

Key to
Famous Lines and Phrases

. . . I am almost out at heels.   [*Falstaff*—1.3.29]

. . . here will be an old abusing of God's patience and
the King's English.   [*Mistress Quickly*—1.4.5–6]

Why then, the world's mine oyster, which I with sword
will open.   [*Pistol*—2.2.2–3]

. . . this is the short and the long of it.
          [*Mistress Quickly*—2.2.59–60]

Setting the attraction of my good parts aside, I have
no other charms.   [*Falstaff*—2.2.105–6]

A woman would run through fire and water for such a
kind heart.   [*Mistress Quickly*—3.4.105–6]

As good luck would have it . . .   [*Falstaff*—3.5.85]

. . . a man of my kidney.   [*Falstaff*—3.5.116–17]

3 1901 05471 5398